Mary Land's
LOUISIANA
COOKERY

Illustrated by Morris Henry Hobbs

A reprint of the original by
The Cookbook Collectors Library

Steamboat Round the Bend

Table of Contents

Photo Credits: Leonard V. Huber, New Orleans, La.; Louisiana State Library; H. Armstrong Roberts.

Introduction

As Harnett Kane has stated in *Louisiana Hayride*, "Modern Louisiana is divided, as was the mother country, into three parts: the South, the North, and The City—New Orleans." Each section differs drastically in blood and bread. The North is predominantly Anglo-Saxon, with Teutonic inclinations toward simplicity and a more conservative way of life; the South, after sixty-four years of French domination and existence under ten flags, lives with a Gallic grace of heart and *joie de vivre*, and through the years has improvised both a table fare and a patois composed of French, Italian, Spanish, American, African, and Indian.

Because of this potpourri of nationalities, there is no way that one may write an academic history of Louisiana cuisine. We might just call it *tout à fait* for it is now comprised of the salutary ingredients of the Red Necks, the spirited esculents of the Acadians, the lush piquancy of the Creoles, and the subtle nuance of Red Bone flavors.

The *culinaire* fragments of this collection form a composite of both urban and provincial foods, partly foraged from friends along the banquette, byroad, and bayou; some are my own concoctions; others were passed down to me along with my grandmother's iron skillet. You may find some of my measurements indefinite for that is "our way"; my proportions elastic for need of not knowing "how many" . . . and I hope you will find a challenge to your own creative ability.

Although these recipes are basically stout provisions cooked up with a lusty flair and smacking of salt air and hickory smoke, a smidgen of more refined cookery has seeped in. I prefer my wilderness food "à la nude" and *sans* sauces because of the goodness of its natural flavor, but for the sake of those who must have their victuals "all fancied up" I have included some of the South's more frilly fare.

It is my belief that a skilled hand is not required in Creole cookery—that even a debutante of the kitchenette can prepare any food by applying the fundamentals of this cuisine. These simple rules may be applied individually or in combinations, depending on one's imagination and daring. In creating any improvisations of native foods it is always best to mate fowl, fish, and game with the fruits of the fields and woods that are currently in harvest, for all these edibles complement each other.

In Louisiana there is a tradition that when a girl marries she receives, as part of her dowry, the ancestral iron skillet. She is considered a social failure unless she develops a *haut ton* and applies it to her cookery. And in Louisiana today gastronomes may travel to the North, to the South, or to the City and find *un vrai régal* on the native tables.

MARY LAND

New Orleans, Louisiana

I
A Few Fundamentals

The French Market - Sunday Morning

A Few Fundamentals

There are five requisite elements in Louisiana cookery: the iron pot, the *roux*, stock, herbs, and alcoholic liquids. The component parts of the *cuisine Louisianaise* are the mystic cachet that has changed gourmands into gourmets.

THE IRON POT

The iron pot is essential because it retains the heat and does not burn its contents, especially the *roux*. Every type of dish is cooked on a "slow" fire. Time is meaningless, for Louisiana cooks know that *qui va doucement va surement* (going slowly is the secret of cookery). A large wooden spoon is used for the stirring and simmering that has gone on for almost three centuries.

THE ROUX

"First you make a *roux*" . . . in preparing almost any kind of dish. A *roux* is a sort of gravy that is the basis of innumerable "potables" including gumbos, stews, vegetables, and courses of fish, shellfish, game, and fowl. To make a *roux*, melt one tablespoon of shortening or butter (never old grease) in the iron skillet, then slowly sprinkle in a tablespoon of flour. Brown very slowly until the flour and fat are a dark brown. Gradually add hot water or hot stock and stir constantly. Add the other desired ingredients, spices, and herbs.

STOCK

From the time of the first *bousillage* cabin, a stock pot has had a prominent place on the Louisiana stove. Game meat and bones, fowl flesh and bones, whole fish and the fish heads (the flavor and oils are in the head), crawfish and their shells, shrimp and their shells, crabs and the scrapings from the shells, and oyster juice are all boiled for use as stock. Vegetables and other items are added to the stock for soups and stews. Small amounts of stock are used in making gravies for the roasting pan, in basting, and in almost all cooking. And remember, "ma chére, the mo' slow the stock is cook the mo' bet' it is."

HERBS

Present herbal knowledge is a heritage from the first settlers of the Louisiana Territory. Rations brought to the New World by the French conquerors were soon exhausted, but alliances with the Biloxis, Choctaw, and other Indians were made by those resourceful Lemoyne brothers—Pierre, the Sieur d'Iberville, and Jean Baptiste, the Sieur de Bienville. From association with the Indians the Frenchmen learned the culinary use of native game, fish, and fowl, as well as of herbs, roots, shrubs, fruit, berries, and trees. After Biloxi (Louisiana's first capital) was founded and New Orleans was established, the pioneers reached into the outlying *cyprières* (cypress groves) for land grants and a life that would be less tempestuous. Plantation homes were built and slaves were added to the ménage. The slave cooks learned more and more of Indian herb lore and to it added their own African seasoning magic.

Each home then had its herbary planted between the smokehouse and the "big house," for Louisianians took their seasoning seriously. Year by year new herbs have been added from India and Europe, but in spite of this continental greenery, the folk of Louisiana have clung to the first native herbs their forebears learned and loved.

In the use of herbs as seasoning a light touch is essential since overseasoned food is often ruined by a generosity that cannot be absorbed. Spices and herbs should leave only a hint of their existence—a suggestion of unknown savor to tantalize the palate.

If your seasoning is "sto' bo't," buy often in small packages so that it is always fresh; or if you are a herbalist with your own garden you will want to dry your herbs in a dry room on racks or in a slow oven and pack them in black jars for storage in a dark place.

Bear in mind that dried herbs are twice as strong as fresh ones. Let them steep a few minutes in hot stock or water before adding to the pot. Salad seasoning herbs should be steeped in olive oil before being tossed into the dressing or bowl. If you are preparing an uncooked dish, herbs and spices may be used more freely.

A *bouquet garni* (cheesecloth sack of herbs) may be used in all types of oven and pot cooking. Make up a few sacks at a time of each desired combination and keep in a jar for future use. The *bouquet garni* should steep awhile in the pot before removal. The beginner in herb cookery may use one-third of a teaspoon of herbs to one pint of liquid.

Angelica	Use leaves candied, or raw or cooked like celery.
Anise	Use plant boiled, or use raw in salad.
Anise Seed	Use in breads, applesauce, stews, soups, hot tea, cakes, and in preparation of some alcoholic beverages.
Artichoke (burr)	Use head boiled as a vegetable or pickled, and the heart as a salad.
Balm	Use leaves in soups, vinegar, drinks, and eggs.
Basil (sweet)	Use leaves in pickles, cheese dishes, tomato dishes, fish sauces, turtle soup, spaghetti, potatoes, fowl, game, cream cheese, and with mushrooms.
Bennet	Use leaves in soups, stews, and game.
Borage	Use leaves in drinks, pickling, salads, stews, and soups.

Burnet	Use leaves for delicate flavoring.
Caraway Seed	Use in breads, sauerkraut, apples, cheese dishes, tomatoes, beets, stews, soups, fried potatoes, and slaw; on *canapés;* and with livers, asparagus, and creamed onions.
Catnip	Use leaves in tea, stews, and soup.
Celery	Use boiled as a vegetable with game, fowl, and fish, or in salads, soups, and stews.
Celery Seed	Use as stalks are used.
Chard	Use leaf stalks in stews and game.
Chervil	Use leaves in eggs, fish, salads, butters, and fowl.
Chicory or Endive	Use leaves in salads or as a boiled vegetable.
Chives	Use in salads, soups, mashed potatoes, eggs, dressings, cheese dishes; with game, fish, and fowl.
Coriander	Use dried leaves in soups, stews, and sauces. Green leaves may be used for same, but they have a slightly bitter flavor.
Coriander Seed	Use in pickles, sauces, game, dressings, pastry, and breads.
Corn Salad	Use green leaves for salad, or cook as boiled vegetable.
Cumin	Use seeds in same manner as orégano.
Dandelion	Use leaves for salads; boil or fry in butter for use as a vegetable.
Dill	Use flowers, stems, and seed in pickles, salads, soups, and stews; with potato, vegetable, and cheese dishes; and in macaroni, sauerkraut and fish, cream cheese, sour cream, and cucumbers; also on *canapés.*
Escarole	Use leaves in salads and, boiled, in soups and stews.
Fennel	Use dried seeds on cookies, in breads, fish, and sauces. Boil inner stalks for use as a vegetable or use raw for salads.
Garden Cress (pepper grass)	Use boiled as a vegetable or for salads.

Garlic	Use pods for game, fish, or fowl, and in soups, stews, and sauces. Rub on uncooked meat. A soupçon of garlic is found in nearly all Louisiana food.
Geranium	Use leaves in cakes and other dishes requiring delicate flavoring.
Horse-radish	Use root fresh or dried in sauces, gravies, and game.
Kale	Use leaves as pot herb.
Lavender	Use leaves for delicate flavor in cakes, salads, and sauces.
Leek	Use leaf stalk as pot herb or in salads, meats, fowl, fish, and dried beans. Boil in several waters to curb flavor.
Lovage	Use leaf stem in salads and soups, or boiled, as a vegetable.
Marjoram	Use leaves as a companion for thyme and bay leaves in almost every type food except sweets. Rub on uncooked meats; use in game dressings and in tomato dishes.
Mint	Use fresh leaves in drinks, sauces, gravies, pickles, fruit salads, and cooked fruits; rub on uncooked game.
Mustard	Use leaves as pot herb or seeds raw in salads and sauces.
Nasturtium	Use leaves for delicate flavor in cakes and salads.
Orégano	Use leaves in Italian and Spanish dishes; with game, tomatoes, and Mexican food. (Never with eggs.) Put into stuffings and potatoes. Use sprinkled over uncooked fish.
Parsley	Use leaves in game, fish, fowl, salads, dressings, soups, stews, and squash. Makes a nice garnish.
Parsnip	Use boiled as a vegetable, or cooked with game.
Poppy Seed	Use in breads and with meals, noodles, vegetables, and sweet potatoes.
Purslane	Use leaves as pot herb or in salads.
Rhubarb	Use stalk as boiled vegetable or as dessert.

Romaine	Use leaves in salads; boil or fry in butter for use as vegetable.
Rosemary	Use sprigs in fowl, game, sauces, string beans, and stews.
Saffron	Use dried flower petals in fish, soups, rice, and stews. The powder is used in the same manner.
Sage	Use leaves in dressings, stews, soups, stuffings, goose, game, dried beans, onions, and cream cheese.
Salflower	Use dried petals in same ways as saffron.
Savory	Use leaves in eggs, fish, fowl, Irish potatoes, dressings, dried beans, squash, eggplant, stews, and stuffings.
Scallions or Shallots	Use leaf stalks in salads, soups, stews, game, fish, and fowl; also as a pot herb.
Skirrit	Use roots raw in salads or cook as pot herb.
Sorrel	Use leaves in salads, stews, and soups.
Spinach	Use leaves raw in salad or cooked as a pot herb. Put into sauces and stews.
Tarragon	Use leaves in pickles, salad dressings, sauces, tomatoes, fish, and fowl; good in all sea foods.
Thyme	Use leaves with bay leaves and rosemary in every kind of food except desserts. Use in chowders and with shellfish. Good in peas, carrots, onions, and stews.
Turmeric	Use powder in pickling.
Verbena (lemon)	Use leaves for delicate flavor in cakes.
Water Cress	Use leaves in butters, sauces, salads, game, fish, fowl, dressings, and salad dressings.

Aunt Mandy, of Westerfield Plantation, has her own ideas about seasoning. She claims that there are two "bossy" seasonings—green pepper and garlic, and she says green pepper is more "bossy" than garlic.

PICKLING HERBS

Balm, basil, borage, chive, dill, horse-radish.

SEED HERBS

Anise, caraway, celery, cumin, coriander, dill, mustard, poppy, sesame.

FRAGRANT HERBS

Burnet, geranium, lavender, lemon verbena, nasturtium, violet.

SWEET HERBS

Balm, basil, marjoram, mint, rosemary, savory, thyme.

SHARP-SEASONING HERBS

Cayenne and other pepper, chili, curry, dill, horse-radish, mustard, sage, tarragon.

"FINES HERBES"

Combinations of basil, chive, parsley, savory, tarragon, and other herbs are usually known as *fines herbes*.

FLOWERS

Marigold petals are used to garnish entrées and salads, nasturtium leaves and flowers, orange blossoms, and roses.

FUNGI
Mushrooms

Fresh mushrooms must be picked outdoors with extreme caution. The advice of an expert should be sought as many varieties of these fungi are poisonous.

Mushrooms, mushroom caps, and imported "cepes" are available in cans. Dried mushrooms may be obtained at stores and Italian markets.

Truffles

Natives of Louisiana claim that clusters of this fungus fruit grow wild near Cane River in Louisiana. Imported truffles may be bought in cans.

The old regime of Creole cooks considered truffles and mushrooms essential ingredients in sauces, soups, entrées and dishes of meat, fowl or fish. These fungus plants were also used as garnishes.

SUGAR AND SPICE

Allspice	Use whole with fresh berries, fish, meat, or sauces; powdered, with cooked fruits, desserts, sweet vegetables, game, and fowl.
Cinnamon	Use sticks in drinks, and the powder in sweet dishes, game, fowl, stews, and soups.
Cloves	Use whole in cooking crabs, shrimp, game, fowl, fish, fruits, and soups. Use powder in sweet vegetables, desserts, fruits, and for rubbing on game before cooking.
Curry	Use powder in game, fowl, fish, soups, stews, marinades, and with eggs and dressings; in shellfish and rice dishes, in sour cream dressings, and in mayonnaise.
Ginger	Use root in marinades and sauces. Use powder in desserts, sauces, vegetables, fruits, breads, game, fowl, crabs, and shrimp, and in candied ginger for sauces.
Mace	Use powder in fish sauces, sweet dishes, fruits, and cakes.
Nutmeg	Use whole in drinks or stews. Use powder in sweet dishes. Sprinkle it over drinks and desserts and in vegetables, game, stews, and soups.
Pepper	
Black	Use in game, fowl, fish, vegetables, salads, dressings, sauces, stews, and soups.
Cayenne	Use to give a higher lift to dishes. Hotter than black or white.
Chili	Use whole for pickling; in Spanish and Mexican foods; and in game, fowl, and sauces.
Pimiento	A mild pepper used whole or minced in soups,

	stews, vegetables, sauces, salads, game, fowl, and fish.
Tabasco	A "hot-hot" used to pep up tomato juice, vegetables, game, fish, fowl, sauces, stews, soups, and even in milk.
White	Use in fish and fowl, salads, and soups.

Sugar

Brown	Use in sweet dishes, in rum and other drinks, and in desserts.
White	Use in sweet dishes and to absorb pepper in overseasoned dishes.

WILD POT AND SALAD HERBS AND TUBERS

American Lotus	Parch and boil seeds. Bake tubers. Boil young leaves.
Arrowhead	Boil roots with meats or boil as vegetable.
Artichoke (Jerusalem)	Use as cultivated variety is used. Scrape and boil.
Bulrush	Boil and bake roots.
Cattail	Roast root.
Chicory	Use same as garden chicory.
Chufa	Boil or roast tubers. Use in milk drink.
Corn Salad	Also known as "field salet." Use as you would garden corn salad.
Butterfly Weed	Boil shoots and eat as asparagus is eaten.
Button Snake Root	This root was eaten as well as used as a good luck charm. Boil.
Dandelion	Use as garden variety is used.
Early Blue Violet	This is the wild okra, and is used for stews and soups. Good with fennel.
Evening Primrose	Stew roots, and either boil young shoots or eat them raw.
Garden Cress	Use leaves as garden pepper grass is used.
Ginger	Use for seasoning as ginger root is used. It was considered a heart stimulant by the Indians.
Groundnut	Roast or boil root. Roast beans.

Leeks	Use after boiling in several waters. Grind and use to dress uncooked fish, fowl, or meat.
Man-of-the-Earth (Indian Potato)	Roast roots.
Mamou (Coral Bean)	The root was once used to season, and to ward off colds. Boil or bake.
Marsh Marigold (Cowslip)	Pickle flower buds and boil leaves.
May Apple (Mandrake)	The fruit was used by the Indians in seasonings. The leaves and roots are poisonous.
Milkweed	Eat young spring shoots raw or boil. The young seeds may be cooked.
Mint	Use as garden mint is used.
Mushrooms	Pick only the nonpoisonous kind. Use as cultivated mushrooms are used.
Mustard	Use as garden mustard is used.
Onion	Use as shallots, scallions, and other onions are used. Grind wild onions and use sprinkled over fish to be broiled.
Passionflower	Gather the fruit (maypop) in summer or fall. Use in jelly.
Pepper (chili)	The chili pepper grows wild in Cameron Parish. Use as other peppers.
Pokeweed	Boil young shoots in two waters with teaspoon of vinegar. Eat young leaves raw for "poke salet." Berries and roots are poisonous.
Prickly Pear	The fruit of this desert plant is eaten raw.
Spring Beauty	Eat bulbs raw or boiled.
Thistle	Cut stalk and strip sides. Cut lengthwise and soak in vinegar thirty minutes. Eat raw with salt and pepper or boil.
Water Cress (Scurvy Grass)	Found near streams and used as cultivated cress is used.
Wild Rice	Soak overnight and boil.
Yucca	Boil flower buds. Roast ripe fruit. Peel and roast stalk.

TREES AND SHRUBS

Apple	Eat fruit raw and cook it in any way.
Basswood	Eat the buds fried or pickled.
Bay (red)	Gather the leaves in early summer. Dry and use for seasoning; pour cake batter over dried leaves; use leaves to smoke barbecue. Use the limbs as skewers.
Crabapple	Use for jellies.
Cypress	The ashes from this burned wood are used in making lye hominy.
Cherry (black)	Use the fruit for making wines, jellies, and preserves.
Chinquapin	Eat the nuts or use in cooking.
Citrus fruit (Grapefruit, Kumquat, Lemon, Lime, Loquat, Mandarin or Tangerine, Mock Orange or Chadee, Orange, Satsuma)	Citrus fruits are used for making preserves, wines, and sauces; of the mock orange only the peel is usable.
Fig	Use in jellies or preserves or eat uncooked.
Grenadine (wild pomegranate)	Use in syrups and sauces.
Hickory	Eat the nuts or use them in cooking.
Jujube (guava species)	Use for preserves and jellies.
Live Oak	The Indians gathered the acorns of this tree in the fall and parched and boiled them for bread meal.
Magnolia	Use the seed to rub a salad bowl.
May Haw and Other Hawthorn	Use the fruit for jellies and jams.

Mesquite	The Indians pounded the seeds and ate them.
Papaw	Eat fruit when dark brown and ripened.
Pear	Eat the fruit uncooked or make into jellies and preserves.
Pecan	Eat nuts or use in foods.
Persimmon	Use in wines and for seasoning; use in alcoholic beverages.
Plum (sloe and other)	Eat ripe fruit or use in cakes or to make beer or jellies.
Pomegranate	Use the seeds for syrups or sauces or eat them uncooked.
Red Bud	The buds may be pickled or fried. The flowers may be used in salads.
Sabal Palmetto (Cabbage Palm)	Cut a palm that is under five feet. (This kills the palm.) Remove the outer layer of the palm and peel down to the terminal bud. Cut the bud in thin slices. To use in a salad soak in ice water several hours and serve with salad dressing. To cook, boil the slices with salt pork.
Sassafras	Dry the leaves and pound with the end of a black gum tree limb. Dry in the oven or the sun. This greenish powder is known as filé, and was first made by the Choctaw Indians on Bayou Lacombe. The Creoles first called it filé flour. The root is boiled to make a medicinal tea.
Yaupon	The Indians gathered the leaves of this tree in the spring to make a tea that had medicinal qualities.
Walnut	Use the nuts in food or eat them raw or toasted.

BERRIES

Blackberries	Use for wines, jellies, and preserves.
Blueberries	Use for wines, jellies, and pies.

Elderberries   Use the berries for wines and jellies, the flowers for wines and in cake or waffle batter. (The bark is poisonous.)

Huckleberries   Use for wines and jellies.

Loganberries   Use for pies, wines, and jellies.

Mulberries   These may be used, but are not as good as the other berries.

Serviceberries   Use the berries fresh, or pounded and dried for jellies and wines.

Spicebush   Use the dried berries and leaves.

Strawberries (Snakeberries)   Use fresh with cake; in wines, jams, and jellies; and as a dessert.

Winterberries   Use for wines, jams, and jellies. The leaves may be used for making a tea.

All berries may be used to stuff wild game, fish, or fowl; in gravies and in biscuits and cakes.

NATIVE GRAPES

In 1830 there were eighty-eight species of grapes enumerated in this country; today the list has grown to eight hundred.

The native grapes of the South are too numerous to mention. Of the thirty species of native wild grapes grown in the United States the summer grape (*Vitis aestivalis Michx*), the summer fox grape or muscadine (*Vitis rotundifolia*), the post-oak grape (*Vitis lincecomii Buckl*), and the bird grape (*Vitis munsoniana*) are best known to Southerners. Other species of bunch grapes grow in the South, as well as those of a different botanical group. Since the earliest times in Louisiana the wild grapes have been used for jellies, jams, and wines, and the Indians taught the pioneers other uses for grapes—the vines were used to tie stuffed fowl and game, jellies were poured over the leaves, and the leaves were stuffed with a dressing and cooked in the oven.

All the wild grapes have provided valuable root-stocks and have played a vital part in the culture of grapes in America and in Europe.

SUSTENANCE

IN THE SPIRIT

Louisiana's colonial pioneers used a tafia or sugar rum in their food. Time has added whiskies, brandies, wines, and other alcoholic solutions to the iron pot. In Louisiana the best of friends will part in an argument over the question of cooking alcoholic liquids *in* food versus adding them *after* the heat is cut off. To a member of the "steeping sect" there is more bouquet in this second way and perhaps more alcohol, too. Anyway, soup may be laced with wine, entrées steeped in wines or other spirits, salads anointed with wine, desserts seduced by liqueurs, and brandy mixed, but not burned, in coffee.

A few offerings with spirit include:

Hors d'oeuvres	Sherry and Dubonnet, bitters, white wines.
Oysters	Absinthe, white wines.
Soups	
(bean and turtle)	Sherry.
(cream)	Sherry and claret.
(miscellaneous)	Claret and Burgundy.
Shellfish	White wines, especially vermouth.
Fish	White wines, especially vermouth, orange wine.
Fowl	
(dark)	Burgundy, port, and other red wines, rum, and brandy.
Game	
(dark)	Sherry and red wines, brandy, and rum.
(white)	Dry white wines and citrus liqueurs.
Eggs	Brandy and rum.
Vegetables	Sweet white wines and rum.
(sweet)	
Salads	White and red wines mixed with paprika as a dressing.
Desserts	Brandy, rum, and white and red wines.
Melons	Beer, ale, and also champagne.

Fruits	Cider, applejack, sweet brandies, and tawny port.
Cheese	Red wines, especially port.

GUIDE TO COOKING VEGETABLES

Vegetable	Time	Temperature
Anise	10 to 30 minutes	medium
Artichokes (Globe)	20 to 40 minutes	medium
Artichokes (Jerusalem)	20 to 40 minutes	medium
Asparagus	5 to 20 minutes	medium
Beans (dried)	20 to 60 minutes	medium
Beans (Lima)	20 to 40 minutes	medium
Beans (snap)	15 to 60 minutes	medium
Beets	30 to 60 minutes	medium
Broccoli	10 to 40 minutes	medium
Brussels Sprouts	10 to 50 minutes	medium
Cabbage (Chinese)	5 to 30 minutes	medium
Cabbage (red and white)	10 to 30 minutes	medium
Carrots	5 to 40 minutes	medium (or hot to fry)
Cauliflour	10 to 40 minutes	medium (or hot to fry)
Celery	10 to 20 minutes	medium
Chard (Swiss)	10 to 30 minutes	medium
Collards	30 to 60 minutes	slow
Corn (sweet)	10 to 60 minutes	slow (or hot to fry)
Cucumber	5 to 15 minutes	medium (or hot to fry)
Cushaw	20 to 40 minutes	medium or slow
Eggplant	20 to 40 minutes	medium or slow
Greens (Beet, Carrot tops, Chicory, Dandelion, Endive, Mustard, Lettuce, Parsley tops, Turnip, Watercress, and Others)	15 to 60 minutes	medium or slow

Vegetable	Time	Temperature
Kale	20 to 40 minutes	medium or slow
Kohlrabi	10 to 40 minutes	medium or slow
Leek	10 to 30 minutes	medium
Mirliton	20 to 50 minutes	medium
Mushrooms (dried or fresh)	10 to 40 minutes	medium (or hot to fry)
Okra	10 to 30 minutes	medium
Onions	20 to 40 minutes	medium
Parsnips	20 to 40 minutes	medium or slow
Peas (chick)	40 to 60 minutes	medium
Peas (dried)	40 to 60 minutes	medium
Peas (green)	10 to 40 minutes	medium
Peppers (hot and sweet)	5 to 30 minutes	medium (or hot to fry)
Potatoes (white)	20 to 40 minutes	slow (or hot to fry)
Potatoes (new)	10 to 30 minutes	medium
Potatoes (sweet)	20 to 50 minutes	medium (or hot to fry)
Pumpkin	20 to 50 minutes	medium or slow
Rhubarb	20 to 40 minutes	medium
Rutabaga	20 to 30 minutes	medium or slow
Salsify	20 to 40 minutes	medium
Scallions	10 to 40 minutes	medium (or hot to fry)
Shallots	5 to 30 minutes	medium (or hot to fry)
Skirret	20 to 40 minutes	medium
Spinach	10 to 30 minutes	medium (or hot to fry)
Squash	20 to 40 minutes	medium
Tomato	5 to 30 minutes	medium (or hot to fry)
Turnip	20 to 60 minutes	medium or slow

Nutritionists have enlightened the public on the importance of cooking vegetables with as little water as possible. The pressure cooker and double boiler method of vegetable cookery retain the maximum amount of vegetable juices, rich in minerals and vitamins.

Salt toughens vegetables and should be used to season after the vegetable is cooked.

GUIDE TO BREAD COOKERY

Type of Dough	Time	Temperature	Mixing	Baking
Biscuits Muffins Popovers	10 to 30 minutes.	moderate to hot oven.	Use cold liquid for dough. Blend fast, using hands as little as possible.	Preheat oven. Grease pan.
Yeast Breads	10 to 50 minutes.	moderate to hot oven.	Use cold liquid for dough. Blend fast. Let dough rise before baking.	Preheat oven. Grease pan.
Corn Bread	20 to 60 minutes.	moderate to hot oven.	Blend well. Use room temperature, or warm liquid.	Preheat oven or griddle. Grease pan or griddle.
Skillet Breads	20 to 60 minutes.	moderate to slow oven.	Blend well. Use room temperature liquid.	Preheat skillet. Grease skillet.

GUIDE TO DESSERT COOKERY
Cakes

Time	Temperature	Mixing	Baking
30 minutes to several hours	moderate or slow	Eggs must be fresh and well beaten. Liquid must be cold. Blend or work fast.	Preheat the oven.

Cookies

Time	Temperature	Mixing	Baking
8 to 40 minutes	hot	Blend fast. Use cold liquid.	Preheat the oven.

Pies (Baked)

10 to 60 minutes	moderate to hot	Blend crust fast, using ice cold fluid.	Preheat the oven.

Pies and Small Pastries (Fried)

5 to 30 minutes	hot	Blend well.	Have pie or pastry cold when ready to fry.

Custards and Puddings (Boiled and Baked)

20 to 60 minutes	moderate to slow	Blend well. Stir boiled custard constantly.	Preheat the oven. Cook in baking vessel inside of larger vessel holding water, or without extra vessel.

A slow oven is between 250° and 350°; a moderate oven, 350° to 450°; a hot oven, 450° to 550°. Electric heat is fastest; gas and liquid fuel heat, somewhat slower; and wood stove heat, slowest of all.

GUIDE FOR COOKING FISH
(Well done)

Amount To Buy Per Person	*Weight*	*Temperature*	*Cooking Time Per Pound*
1 pound	1 pound (whole)	moderate	15 minutes
½ pound	1 pound (Skinned, Scaled, and Cleaned)	moderate	15 minutes
½ pound	1 pound (Fillets, or Steaks)	moderate	15 minutes

The above table for fish cookery applies to all fish except the very large salt-water species. Jack crevallé, and other large fish must be cooked twice as long as the given cooking time for fish per pound.

The best method to use in testing fish to see if it is done is to use a toothpick. There is more danger of overcooking fish than of undercooking it. All fish should be simmered gently; never boiled hard.

GUIDE FOR SHELLFISH COOKERY
Shrimp (Boiled)

2 pounds	1 pound (in shells)	medium	15 minutes
1 pound	1 pound (peeled) (headless)	medium	15 minutes

Shrimp (Fried)

1 pound	1 pound (peeled) (headless)	hot	5 to 10 minutes

Amount To Buy Per Person	Weight	Temperature	Cooking Time Per Pound
Shrimp (Broiled)			
1 pound	1 pound (peeled) (headless)	moderate	10 to 30 minutes
Hard Crabs (Boiled)			
6 crabs	1 pound	medium	15 to 20 minutes
Soft Crabs and Busters (Fried and Broiled)			
2 to 6 crabs	1 pound (cleaned)	medium and hot	Frying—10 minutes Broiling—15 to 30 minutes
Crawfish (Stewed or Boiled)			
2 pounds	1 pound (peeled)	medium	15 to 60 minutes

GUIDE TO COOKING GAME

Amount of Game to Use Per Person	Weight	Temperature	Cooking Time Per Pound
Small Game			
1½ pounds	1 pound (before skinning and dressing)	moderate	30 minutes
1 pound	1 pound (skinned and dressed)	moderate	30 minutes
Large Game			
2 pounds	1 pound (before skinning and dressing)	moderate	30 minutes to 1 hour
1 pound	1 pound (after dressing)	moderate	30 minutes to 1 hour

In cooking game that you know is old use twice the time given for cooking time per hour. Do not use salt until meat or game has finished cooking.

GUIDE FOR COOKING MEAT

Amount of Meat to Buy Per Person	*Weight*	*Temperature*	*Cooking Time Per Pound*
Roasts and Other Large Cuts			
1½ pounds	1 pound	moderate	30 minutes to 1 hour
Steaks and Chops			
1 pound	1 pound	moderate	30 minutes
Liver			
½ pound	1 pound	hot (to fry) moderate (to roast)	30 minutes

Do not season meat with salt until it has finished cooking. Garlic, cut into the meat, may be used to tenderize.

GUIDE TO COOKING FOWL

Amount of Fowl to Use Per Person	*Weight*	*Temperature*	*Cooking Time Per Pound*
Turkey—Wild or Domestic			
1½ pounds	1 pound (before dressing)	moderate	30 minutes
1 pound	1 pound (dressed)	moderate hot (to fry)	30 minutes
Chicken			
1½ pounds	1 pound (before dressing)	moderate hot (to fry)	30 minutes

Amount of Fowl to Use Per Person	Weight	Temperature	Cooking Time Per Pound
Duck—Wild or Domestic			
1½ pounds	1 pound (before dressing)	moderate	30 minutes
1 pound	1 pound (dressed)	moderate	30 minutes
Pheasant			
1½ pounds	1 pound (before dressing)	moderate	30 minutes to 1 hour
Woodcock, Snipe, and Medium Size Birds			
1 bird	1 pound (dressed)	moderate hot (to fry)	30 minutes
Rails, Gallinules, and Coots			
½ to 1 bird	1 pound (dressed)	moderate hot (to fry)	30 minutes
Any Small Birds			
1 to 2 birds	½ pound (dressed)	moderate hot (to fry)	15 minutes

II
Bucolic Bits

Stairway at Evergreen (1840) - near Edgard

Bucolic Bits

These "little savories" should be served only as whets for one's appetite. Make them tasty and eye-appealing, but serve only a few.

CAVIAR PADDLEFISH (SPOONBILL CATFISH)

Remove roe from fish. The eggs may be salted and dried or fried in butter (see p. 229). Serve on brown toast with a slice of lime and minced shallot or onion. Stir caviar with wooden spoon and serve on china or glass plates.

SHERRIED SHRIMP

Mince twelve cleaned and boiled shrimp and mix with one-fourth cup of minced parsley, two minced hard-boiled eggs, two teaspoons melted butter, salt, pepper, and one-fourth cup of cream. Simmer a few minutes and add one-half cup of sherry. Serve on hot croutons.

SHRIMP CREOLE CANAPE

Mince six cleaned and boiled shrimp and two hard-cooked eggs; mix with one-fourth cup of Creole mustard, three teaspoons of lime juice, or mix with water cress butter. Serve cold on rye bread.

SHRIMP WHETS

Mash ten cleaned and boiled shrimp, while hot. Add a dash of Trappey's Torrido sauce, three tablespoons of minced chives, salt, pepper, and a dash of cayenne. Add a little cream and serve hot on toast.

COLD SHRIMP PASTE

Purée ten cleaned and boiled shrimp in food chopper. Add one-fourth cup of white wine, salt, pepper, and a dash of paprika. Blend well and spread on narrow slices of whole wheat bread. Roll and keep in refrigerator until ready to serve.

CRAWFISH TREE

Boil crawfish fifteen minutes. Use a large epergne and place crisp celery stalks in each vase. Place small lettuce leaves or water cress around celery and put whole crawfish all over epergne tree. Guests may peel their own crawfish.

SEA HAG CANAPE

Marinate ten cleaned and boiled shrimp for several hours in one cup of wine vinegar, two teaspoons of dry mustard, and one-fourth cup of olive oil. Cut up with one-fourth cup of minced celery and a dash of Red Devil sauce. Serve on crackers.

CRAWFISH CANAPE

Mix boiled crawfish tails with minced pickled onions. Serve on crackers.

CRAB CANAPE À LA GORENFLO

Mash up the fat from boiled crabs. Add one package of cream cheese and two teaspoons of olive spread, salt, white pepper, and a dash of Tabasco. Blend and stuff celery with the mixture. Serve with cold, boiled crabs and beer.

SPICED CRAB CANAPE

Sauté two cups of boiled crab meat in butter five minutes. Add one-fourth cup of pecan meats, one teaspoon of mace, one-half teaspoon of powdered nutmeg, and a dash of powdered cloves. Add one cup of cream and simmer a few minutes. Add one-half cup of sherry and serve hot on toast.

COLD CRAB CANAPE

Mix boiled meat of six crabs with four sweet dill pickles, juice of one lime, and enough mayonnaise to moisten. Serve on crackers.

FISH BALLS

Mix cooked, minced fish with mashed potatoes, salt, and pepper. Roll into tiny balls. Fry in butter five minutes and serve on toothpicks. Serve dill pickles on side.

RISSOLE

Stir together one pound of cooked minced fish, celery salt, minced chives, salt, and pepper. Add a bit of cream to moisten. Make thin French pancakes. Place fish mixture in cakes and fold over. Fry these stuffed cakes a few minutes in butter.

HOT OYSTERS DIABLE

Warm one dozen oyster shells and rub with garlic. Have oysters hot. Mix two teaspoons of chili sauce, one teaspoon of lemon juice, one dash of Tabasco, salt, and pepper to taste. Heat very hot. Place sauce in chafing dish. Place oysters in shells around dish. Let guests dunk oysters in hot sauce.

ENFANTS DE LA MER

Peel and clean two pounds of tiny river or marine shrimp. Soak in cream with salt and white pepper for fifteen minutes. Drain and sprinkle with paprika. Dredge in pancake flour. Fry in deep fat. Drain and place on colored cocktail toothpicks.

SHRIMP PUFFS

Boil two pounds of shrimp. Peel and grind shrimp meat with one-half cup of shallots. To this mixture add four cups of flour, one teaspoon of salt, dash of black pepper, dash of cayenne, two beaten eggs, one-half teaspoon of Worcestershire sauce, and two cups of milk. Blend and drop by the teaspoon into hot deep fat. Fry five minutes or until brown.

OYSTER FRITTERS

Mince one pint of oysters. Sift together two cups of flour and four teaspoons of baking powder. Add one cup of oyster juice to the dry ingredients. Add one teaspoon of Worcestershire sauce, one-fourth teaspoon of salt, one-fourth teaspoon of white pepper, three tablespoons of cream, and three beaten eggs. Blend, and add the oysters. Drop from small spoon into hot deep fat. Fry five minutes or until brown, and drain. Serve hot-hot with cold beer or ale.

BAYOU BOUCHEES

Mince two parts boiled, peeled crawfish with one part hard-cooked eggs and a bit of mayonnaise. Spread leaves of water cress on party rye bread and spread the crawfish mixture on the cress, leaving a fringe of cress all around.

OYSTER FLAKES

Break up into small pieces hardtack or oyster bread (see p. 244). Spread twelve minced oysters, one teaspoon of lemon juice, and one teaspoon of Worcestershire sauce on each crust. Serve with beer or ale.

HOT OYSTER COCKTAIL

Use four dozen oysters, one cup of chili sauce, one cup of cat-sup, one-half cup of chopped celery, two tablespoons of Worces-tershire sauce, one tablespoon of Tabasco sauce, one-half stick of butter, and one teaspoon of lemon juice. Place all ingredients in a saucepan. Heat and add the celery and the oysters. Let sauce and oysters heat, but do not bring to a boil. (Serves eight.)

PARTY EDAM CHEESE

Slice off top and scoop out the inside of cheese. Save part of the cheese wrapped in wax paper. Mix the other part with tawny port wine and dashes of powdered spices and toasted minced nuts. Fill edam cheese and keep cool, but do not chill.

HORSE-RADISH CHEESE

Blend one package of cream cheese with one cup of sour cream and one-fourth cup fresh horse-radish. Serve on crackers.

ZANGY ZIPS OF GAME

Blend one package of cream cheese with three teaspoons of horse-radish and a dash of Tabasco. Spread on slices of cold game.

ST. LOUIS SOUSE

Blend one package of cream cheese with one large minced onion and a dash of Tabasco, salt, and lots of black pepper. Add enough cream to thin. Use as a dunk for crackers or fritos.

CUCUMBER CREAM

Blend one package of cream cheese with one-fourth cup of sour cream. Add one and one-half cups of minced cucumber, four teaspoons of minced chives, juice of one lime, salt, pepper, and paprika. Dunk triangles of toast in this mix.

ITALIAN CHEESE DIPS

Blend one package of cream cheese with one cup of minced black Italian olives or one-fourth cup of minced chives. Add small dash of Tabasco, salt, and pepper. Add one-fourth cup of cream and use as dunk for hunks of Italian bread.

ROSE GERANIUM CANAPE

Mix one package cream cheese with six minced geranium leaves and one-fourth cup of May haw jelly. Serve as a dip for brown bread toast.

CHEDDAR DIP

Melt one pound of Cheddar cheese in a chafing dish with paprika and a pinch of salt. Add one cup of white wine or sherry and dunk hot crackers into chafing dish.

APPLE CHEESE

Scoop out a large apple. Mix one-half pound of grated Cheddar or American cheese with a dash of celery salt and paprika. Moisten with one cup of red wine and stuff into apple. Serve on nut bread.

JUMBO PECAN BALL

Place one pound of Roquefort cheese and one-half pound of cream cheese in electric mixer. Add juice of one onion, a dash of Tabasco, and a teaspoon of Worcestershire sauce. Roll into big ball and chill in refrigerator overnight. Roll in minced pecan meats until ball is covered. Cut and serve on crackers.

CHEESE DOODLES

Cut squares of American cheese and place on toothpicks with hunks of boiled shrimp or pieces of cooked game.

CHEESE CHERRIES

Grate sharp cheese, add a pinch of salt, and shape into balls. Roll in paprika. Place clove at one end and make stem with dried leaves of any small vine.

CHEESE DIP

Soften one-half pound of Cheddar cheese and two packages of cream cheese. Blend and add a dash of Tabasco, salt, and paprika. Add enough cold beer to soften. Dunk potato chips or crackers into the mix.

BOURBON BALLS

Roll out one box of vanilla wafers. Add small amount of melted butter and minced pecan meats. Moisten with bourbon whisky. Shape into balls and roll in powdered sugar.

PECAN BALLS

Blend one package of pimiento cream cheese with one-fourth cup of Cheddar cheese, salt, and paprika. Moisten with sherry wine and shape into balls. Roll balls in grated Cheddar cheese and place a pecan half at each end of ball. Chill.

PEPPER PECANS

Sauté one pound of pecan halves in butter. Add two teaspoons of Worcestershire sauce, a few dashes of Tabasco sauce, salt, and white pepper. Roast twenty minutes in slow oven. Serve hot.

GAME ROLLS

Mix two cups of cake flour and two teaspoons of baking powder with one teaspoon of salt. Sift. Work in two tablespoons of shortening and add one-half cup of milk. Knead and roll. Cut in strips and top with strips of fowl or game. Roll and hold in place with toothpicks. Bake in hot oven for fifteen minutes.

PETIT SQUARES

Sift together two and one-half teaspoons of baking powder, one-half teaspoon of salt, and two cups of flour. Mix in one and one-half tablespoons of lard. Add one-fourth cup of canned milk. Knead and roll. Cut into squares. Place chopped game or fowl in center, fold, and pinch edges. Dot with butter and bake ten minutes in hot oven.

GAME RAREBIT

Make a *roux* with two tablespoons of butter and one tablespoon of flour. Brown and add one and one-half cups of cream or canned milk. Stir well and add one cup of grated American cheese. Stir until melted. Add salt, black pepper, and paprika. Add pieces of cooked game and simmer a few minutes. Serve on hot, toasted French bread.

PÂTÉ CANARD

Boil duck livers, mince and sauté in butter with minced shallots or chives. Add dash of Tabasco and few dots of cream. Serve on rye toast.

DUCK SIPPETS

Boil duck livers fifteen minutes. Mince, and sauté five minutes in parsley butter. Mince pieces of cooked duck and add to livers. Serve on hot sippets. (See p. 252.)

FOREST PÂTÉ

Mince one cup of game. Next mix two cups of flour, two tablespoons of baking powder, one-fourth teaspoon of salt, and one cup of sweet milk. Add one beaten egg and two teaspoons of melted butter. Add one cup of game and drop on greased pan. Bake thirty minutes.

DUCK TIMBALES

Sauté diced pieces of cooked duck (or goose) with minced celery in butter. Add two minced hard-boiled eggs and one cup of cream, salt, and pepper. Place in small pastry shells or pour over tiny hot biscuits.

DUCK CHUTNEY

Mince cold duck (or goose) and minced chutney. Moisten with bit of cream. Make thin French pancakes. Place mixture in cakes and fold over. Fry these stuffed cakes a few minutes in butter.

SLICED TURKEY MELON

Cut slices of honeydew melon. Place slices of turkey breast on each melon slice. Top with minced pistachio nuts.

OLIVIER MODICUM

Roll strips of turkey around big green olives on toothpicks. Serve hot or cold.

PICKLED PECKS

Place hunks of cold game and slices of sweet pickle together on toothpick.

MINT CANAPE

Mince leftover wild fowl and fresh mint leaves. Add bit of homemade mayonnaise. Serve on hot crackers with a soupçon of nutmeg on top.

EGGS GULF STREAM

Boil six eggs, and cut in half. Mix yolks with cut-up cooked fish or boiled shrimp or crawfish, minced dill pickles, one teaspoon of Creole mustard, and two teaspoons of lime juice. Stuff the emptied whites.

EGGS MARDI GRAS

Scoop out uncooked eggplant. Mash yolks of two dozen hard-boiled eggs with minced sweet pickles, salt, and pepper. Add small amount of salad dressing. Fill eggplant and top with grated cheese and minced chives. Serve with hot crackers.

SALOON EGGS

Pickled eggs still have a prominent place in New Orleans bars. To prepare them, boil fresh eggs for a half hour, peel, and while still hot place in a crock of hot vinegar with grated spiced beets, spices, and salt. When the liquid and eggs cool, place in a glass container.

CREOLE TOMATO CROÛTES

Peel six tomatoes, mince, and drain well. Mix with one bunch of minced water cress, one teaspoon of horse-radish, two teaspoons of olive oil, and one teaspoon of vinegar. Serve on rye toast.

CELERY GUACAMOLE

Mix one ripe avocado and one-fourth cup of shallots in an electric mixer. Add salt, pepper, paprika, and a dash of Tabasco. Stuff one-inch pieces of celery with mixture, sprinkling paprika over each piece.

HOT ASPARAGUS CANAPES

Trim the crusts from twelve slices of bread and cut slices of cooked game or fowl to fit. Dip each of twelve green asparagus spears in mayonnaise. Place the spears at one end of the bread covered with game or fowl and roll up. Fasten with toothpicks and toast under the broiler. Serve hot.

CHUTNEY CRACKERS

Mix minced chutney with a little powdered ginger. Mix with soft butter and chill. Serve cold on crackers.

CHIVE POP CORN

Keep corn in a tightly covered jar. Heat iron skillet and put corn in skillet. Cover skillet and shake over a slow fire until corn is all popped. Melt butter and add salt and either two teaspoons of garlic salt or one pod of minced garlic and one cup of minced chives. Pour over hot corn.

BEER BALLS

Marinate melon balls in beer or ale for several hours. Pour fresh beer over balls and serve on melon half.

PISTACHIO BISCUITS

Sauté pistachio nuts in butter and toast in oven. Add a dash of dark rum and place inside of tiny hot biscuits. (See p. 247.)

III
Potage

Acadian Weaver of the Teche Country

Potage

The French *joie de vivre* was responsible for the pot, kept on the back of the stove, into which green herbs and stock were put. This savory *potage* always came in handy at times when an overdrawn budget might limit the menu. A *soupe-en-famille* was made with *bouilli*, game, fowl, fish, and the contents of the herb pot served as an entire meal with rice and a salad. These big soups are still served as a meal today under such names as gumbo, bisque, stew, or *pot-au-feu*. Soups are simmered from twenty minutes until four hours, depending on the basic ingredients. One quart of soup serves about four.

POT-AU-FEU

Stew any small game in an iron pot until almost done. Then add one bunch of carrots, one-half bunch of turnips, three onions, and four potatoes. Add one quart of stock, one can of mushrooms, and one cup of parsley. Beer or ale may be added to the pot before serving. Bits of salted fowl or *oiseau confit* (pickled fowl) also are often used as a soup seasoning. (Serves four.)

GUMBO

Gumbo is a pungent mixture, inherited from Africa and the West Indies. Any shellfish, fish, game, or fowl may be used as a base. It should be served in a large bowl, about half full, with boiled rice piled high on one side. Over this is sprinkled black-green filé powder. But first make a *roux*. Sauté four large, minced onions in one stick of butter. Add two tablespoons of flour and brown slowly until it turns a very dark brown. Then add two quarts of hot stock. Add one pod of minced garlic, one cup of minced green peppers, one-half cup of minced celery, three bay leaves, four teaspoons of thyme, salt, pepper, and any other desired seasoning. Stir and simmer two hours. Peel one pound of raw shrimp and place in pot. Simmer shrimp about twenty minutes. Add two cups of cooked crab meat and simmer a few minutes. Toss in one dozen oysters and simmer until oysters curl. Serve hot. Any game or fowl may be used in place of shellfish. The gumbo may be served from a tureen. (Serves four.)

DUCK HUNTERS CAMP GUMBO

Make a *roux* and add one pint of hot water. Add five cups of duck gizzards, salt, pepper, and a dash of Tabasco. Slowly add another pint of hot water and cook for forty minutes or until gizzards are done. Then add duck livers, two bay leaves, a pinch of rosemary, and celery salt. Add more hot water and simmer thirty minutes until livers are done. Serve in a bowl with boiled rice and filé. Serve with hot French bread and red wine. (Serves four to six.)

POULE D'EAU GUMBO

Marinate *poule d'eau* in venison marinade (see p. 76) overnight. Dry and fry for five minutes in butter or until brown. Add two large minced onions and slowly add two quarts of hot water. Simmer on a low fire for one hour or until tender. Just before serving add two tablespoons of filé. Serve with rice. *Poule d'eau* must be skinned and the fat removed before cooking. (Serves four.)

GUMBO ZHÈBES (DES HERBES)

Select four pounds of any one or a combination of seven greens (mustard, spinach, turnip tops, beet tops, collards, lettuce, and cabbage).

Boil the greens up to three hours with either a ham hock or a piece of salt bacon. Remove from the fire, drain, and save the pot liquor. Brown one tablespoon of flour in two tablespoons of lard and make a *roux* with onions. Fry the meat. Chop greens together with parsley, green and red peppers, salt, and pepper. Next add the greens to the *roux*, meat, and pot liquor, and simmer for two hours. Serve with boiled rice. This gumbo may be cooked with any game. (This soup is served on Holy Thursday for good luck.) (One quart of soup serves four.)

CREOLE GUMBO FOR LARGE GATHERINGS

Fry ten smoked sausages, minced, in a large skillet. Remove from pan and drain. Add one cup of cooking oil. Gradually add 100 gallons of hot water. Fry ten pounds of ham, chopped, and add to water and oil with 105 pounds of raw, peeled shrimp; fifty-two minced onions; ten pods of garlic, minced; seventeen minced bell peppers; one bottle of soy sauce; ten stalks of minced celery; one cup of flour; three bottles of Red Devil sauce; and 115 pounds of crab meat. Cook for two or three hours. Add four gallons of raw oysters and cook just until the edges curl. When ready to serve, sprinkle the contents of one bottle of filé over the individual servings. Serve with boiled rice. (Serves 150.)

CRAWFISH SOUP A LA VIOSCA

Wash six quarts of live crawfish in running water, removing the dead ones and the trash. (Do not leave in water as they will drown.) Season six quarts of water with salt to taste and bring to a vigorous boil. Dump in live crawfish and parboil ten minutes. Drain and discard the water and allow the crawfish to cool. Pick the crawfish and remove the black strings from the tails. Remove the fat body (not the stomach) from the head with a small spoon and add this to the meat. Chop two onions and one clove of garlic fine. Heat one tablespoon of lard or cooking oil and add one tablespoon of flour, and the onions, and garlic. Fry until mixture is a light brown. Add two tablespoons of canned tomatoes and cook over a slow fire for five minutes. Add three quarts of water, and one sprig of thyme, one of parsley, two bay leaves, and four sprigs of celery. Add salt and pepper to taste and boil fifteen minutes. Add the crawfish meat and fat and cook on a slow fire for one hour. When the soup is served add filé powder if desired and place a teaspoon of minced, hard-cooked eggs and a slice of lemon on each plate of soup. (Serves eight or more.)

CRAB BISQUE

Boil one dozen or more crabs in seasoned water for twenty minutes or until done. Make a *roux* of one tablespoon of flour and one tablespoon of cooking oil. When *roux* is brown add one large can of strained tomatoes and four quarts of hot water. Add two bay leaves, one sprig of thyme, one-half teaspoon of fennel, salt, pepper, and a dash of Tabasco sauce. Peel and clean crabs. Add the scrapings from the boiled crab shells and one cup of crab fat (removed from the boiled crabs). Simmer an hour. Pick the meat from the crabs and add to the other ingredients. Simmer the crabs in the liquid for five minutes. Sprinkle minced parsley and minced hard-cooked eggs over each serving. Garnish with a slice of lemon. A dash of sherry may be added when ready to eat. (Serves eight.)

BISQUE OF SHRIMP

Fry small pieces of salt pork for five minutes. Drain and put aside. Sauté one cup of minced shallots in butter for five minutes. Add twelve peeled new potatoes and one quart of hot water. Add a *bouquet garni* and cook about twenty minutes or until potatoes are done. Add one pound of peeled raw shrimp and cook fifteen minutes. Remove *bouquet garni* and add four cups of cream. Simmer ten minutes, add salt pork, and lace with white wine. Serve with boiled rice. (Serves four.)

ST. LANDRY BISQUE

Wash and boil six quarts of live crawfish in cold water for fifteen minutes with *bouquet garni*. Make a dressing of three cups of bread crumbs, one cup of minced onions, one cup of minced parsley, and four quarts of cut-up crawfish tails. Put aside. Pound the remainder of tails and place these in a *roux*. Add one cup of minced shallots, one cup of minced celery, pinch of thyme, three bay leaves, six cloves, one teaspoon of nutmeg, salt, pepper, and one quart of beef stock. Simmer ten minutes and strain. Stuff heads of crawfish with dressing, roll in flour, and fry ten minutes in butter. Drop into strained soup. Serve with boiled rice. (Serves two.)

QUICK BISQUE

Pound one pound of cooked crawfish tails and sauté for five minutes in butter with minced parsley and minced shallots. Add one can of bouillon and one can of tomato soup. Simmer twenty minutes. (Serves two.)

BREAUX BRIDGE BISQUE

Prepare crawfish as in "St. Landry Bisque." Peel tails and scrape heads with tails into dish. Mince tails in dish with minced shallots, minced celery stalks and tops, and minced parsley. Sauté in butter for five minutes. Add fine bread crumbs and beaten egg yolk. Stuff heads. Roll in flour, fry in butter and place in oven to keep warm. Make a *roux* and add minced shallots, celery, parsley, powdered thyme, lemon juice, cayenne, salt, pepper, powdered cloves, and three bay leaves. Add two quarts of hot water or stock. Simmer about an hour. Drop in the warm heads and add one cup of sherry wine. (Serves four to six.)

SOUPE AUX CRABS TALLY-HO

Cook one dozen fat crabs in three quarts of gently boiling (never hard boiling) water seasoned with spices, salt, and pepper. Pick out crab meat and put aside. Put four tablespoons of cooking oil in a frying pan, heat, and brown two tablespoons of flour slowly. When brown, add one medium-size onion, one clove of garlic, two tablespoons of celery, one tablespoon of lemon, and two tablespoons of parsley, all chopped fine, and cook for ten minutes. Next put in one can of tomato paste and let fry until it leaves the pan dry when stirred with a spoon. Add picked crab meat and let come to a boil. Add one box of vermicelli and boil ten minutes longer. Season with bay leaves and thyme. (Serves eight.)

BOUILLABAISSE AND COURT BOUILLON

The secret of bouillabaisse and other chowders is in the blending of fish, herbs, wine, and water. They are at their best when cooked shortly after the fish or shellfish are caught.

GULF BOUILLABAISSE

Use one each of redfish, red snapper, blackfish, and sheepshead. Remove heads and boil fifteen minutes per pound in enough water to make one quart of stock. Add a *bouquet garni* of thyme, bay leaves, chervil, and onions. Strain stock after it boils down to a pint and put aside. Rub sliced fish with salt, pepper, powdered dill, minced thyme, and olive oil. Next, cook a dozen cleaned, hard crabs, four pounds of unpeeled shrimp, and six pounds of unpeeled crawfish tails in the fish-head stock and let simmer a few minutes with one pint of white wine. Next, fry sliced fish in olive oil for twenty minutes, turning only once. Remove fish from iron skillet and pour into the skillet six fresh, cut tomatoes, one pod of garlic, one-half bunch of shallots, and the stock (after removing shellfish) and simmer for five minutes. Next, mix one-half teaspoon of saffron with a little stock and spread over each fish slice. Serve fish and shellfish on a platter and the soup in a tureen with chunks of French bread that have been rubbed with garlic and fried until golden brown. (Serves four to six.)

GOLDEN MEADOW BOUILLABAISSE

Prepare three quarts stock as in "Gulf Bouillabaisse." Do not use shellfish. Fry for a few minutes, six whole, cleaned mullet in olive oil with six sliced tomatoes, two shallots, red and green peppers, and one pod of garlic. Add stock and one quart of water to fish. Simmer on a charcoal outdoor burner for three hours. Serve with rice. (Serves four to six.)

COURT BOUILLON POISSON ROUGE

Make a *roux* by stirring one tablespoon of flour into two tablespoons of fresh lard. Brown slowly and add twelve mashed allspice, three sprigs each of thyme, parsley, and marjoram, one pod of garlic, one-half bunch of shallots, and six tomatoes cut fine. Add two quarts of water and boil with salt and cayenne pepper for five minutes. Add sliced redfish and the juice of one lemon and simmer thirty minutes or until the fish is done. Serve with mashed potatoes. (Serves four to six.)

BAYOU COURT BOUILLON

Use slices of any large fish. Dip in pancake flour and fry in olive oil about twenty minutes. Put aside. Next mix one quart of chicken soup stock, one pod of garlic, one cup of chopped parsley, one cup of chopped shallots, two sprigs of thyme, two bay leaves, one sprig of marjoram, and one dash of red pepper. Simmer ten minutes and add one cup of dry white wine. Pour over fried fish and serve with garlic bread. (Serves four.)

A SOUP FOR LENT

Boil several cleaned fish heads (the eyes removed) in four quarts of water with salt, pepper, two bay leaves, one sprig of thyme, one teaspoon of rosemary, one teaspoon of fennel, one-half cup of minced celery, and one cup of minced shallots. Simmer for two hours. Strain and serve with minced hard-boiled eggs and minced parsley. (Serves eight.)

VELOUTÉ DE POISSON

Boil any large gulf fish in a cheesecloth bag in two quarts of water, seasoned with a *bouquet garni*, salt and pepper, and lemon for thirty minutes. Strain stock and save. Flake fish as fine as possible. Sauté flakes in butter. Add minced chives and a pinch of basil. Add one cup of cream and fish stock. Simmer long enough to have a velvet-smooth soup. (Serves six.)

SOUPE DU JOUR

Boil two pounds of meat or fowl in four quarts of water for one hour. Add six peeled and sliced carrots, six slices of yellow pumpkin, three sliced peeled turnips, and one-fourth cabbage head. Season with pinch of thyme, two bay leaves, salt, white rice, and gumbo filé. (Serves eight.)

SOUTH LOUISIANA CHOWDER

Simmer four whole or sliced fish in four quarts of water for forty minutes with a *bouquet garni* until tender. Remove bones and flake the fish. Save the stock. Sauté one cup of minced shallots, one cup of celery, one-half cup of parsley, and one bell pepper in olive oil for five minutes in an iron skillet. Add stock and one-half pound of thinly sliced potatoes to skillet. Simmer for twenty minutes until potatoes are tender. Add fish and one cup of hot milk; let simmer a few minutes. (Serves eight.)

NORTH LOUISIANA CHOWDER

Fry several slices of salt bacon in an iron skillet for ten minutes. Drop in slices of bass or any large fresh-water fish and sauté a minute or so. Place alternate layers of bacon, fish, sliced onion, sliced potatoes, and crackers in a casserole. Season with salt and black pepper. Pour in enough hot water to cover contents of casserole. Cook in oven for fifteen minutes until water is cooked out and potatoes are tender. Cover casserole contents with cream and cook for forty minutes or until fish is done. Serve with corn pone. (Serves two.)

LAGOON CHOWDER

Sauté one pound of peeled, cooked shrimp and four cups of cooked, picked crab meat in butter five minutes. Add one-fourth cup of minced parsley, celery salt, cayenne, salt, and white pepper. Pound one box of crackers and add to shellfish. Add one-half stick of butter and one quart of cream. Simmer a half hour. Serve with boiled rice. (Serves four.)

BRENNAN'S POTAGE DE LA MER

Chop four small onions and sauté in butter for five minutes. Let brown. Add four teaspoons of flour and cook for five minutes. Gradually add a half-gallon of rich stock, one can of strained tomatoes, one-half pound of okra, and salt, pepper, and cayenne. Make a *bouquet garni* of thyme, bay leaves, and parsley and cook in the potage. Add twenty-four large, peeled, cleaned shrimp, and six cleaned hard crabs. Simmer for two hours on a slow fire. Add twenty-four oysters and let simmer until the edges curl. Serve with boiled rice. A bit of filé may be added when ready to serve. (Serves eight.)

ROOSEVELT HOTEL TURTLE SOUP

Dice one pound of fresh turtle meat and braise in sherry wine. Add four quarts of meat stock and simmer for two hours. Season with the desired herbs and salt and pepper. Add minced hard-cooked eggs and chopped parsley to each serving. (Serves four.)

TURTLE SOUP

Cut one pound of turtle meat into small pieces. Boil meat with spices one hour or until meat is tender. Drain and make a *roux*. Add meat to *roux* with six peeled tomatoes, four minced peppers, and one cup of minced shallots. Add one quart of stock and simmer one hour. Add any desired herbs. Lace with sherry. Top with minced hard-cooked eggs. (Serves two.)

OYSTER SOUP NEW ORLEANS

Mince one green spring onion and one sprig of celery. Smother in butter, adding one teaspoon of flour and one dozen minced oysters and simmer two minutes. Add one pint of hot water or hot chicken broth. Simmer slowly ten minutes. Add a pinch of chopped parsley. Season with salt and pepper to taste. (Serves two.)

OYSTER STEW I

Heat one quart of milk in one pan with salt and pepper. In another pan heat one quart of oysters and juice. Combine oysters and milk. Add one cup of minced shallots and minced celery. Heat until oysters curl. Serve with crackers. (Serves four.)

OYSTER STEW II

Mix two teaspoons of flour with one-half cup of warm milk in a double boiler. Add three teaspoons of butter and slowly add eight cups of cream, four tablespoons of grated white onion, a dash of nutmeg, salt, and white pepper. Simmer ten minutes, stirring constantly. Add three cups of minced oysters and one cup of oyster juice. Simmer about ten minutes. Serve topped with whipped cream and nutmeg. (Serves four.)

TURKEY SOUP

Simmer turkey bones with one quart of water, two bay leaves, one cup of minced celery, dash of white pepper, salt, and paprika. Simmer for thirty minutes. Lace with sherry wine. (Serves four.)

POTAGE OF SMALL GAME

Disjoint any small game and stew in three quarts of water with a *bouquet garni*, and a dash of powdered allspice, celery salt, salt, and pepper. Cook for about one hour or until meat falls from bones; remove bones and cut meat in small pieces. Sprinkle soup with minced parsley. (One pint of soup serves two.)

ENGLISH VENISON SOUP

Mix cut-up, uncooked venison with one cup of diced turnips, one-half cup of minced parsley, one cup of minced onion, and two cups of celery. Braise in butter for twenty minutes. Add six quarts of beef stock, three bay leaves, one sprig of thyme, one can of tomato paste, salt, pepper, and three teaspoons of sugar. Cook slowly for two hours. Strain and serve with corn bread. (Serves twelve.)

DOVE BROTH

Simmer disjointed pieces of dove for thirty minutes or until tender. Add a dash of salt, white pepper, and one-half bottle of ale. Sprinkle with Parmesan cheese and serve hot. (One quart of soup serves four.)

BRIER PATCH SOUP

Pick and wash any type of wild berries, though blueberries are best. Simmer the berries in water for thirty minutes or until tender. Add a *bouquet garni* of spices if desired. Strain and add the juice of one lime and a bit of butter. Serve hot with orange rice. (See p. 207.)

POT LIKKER

Strain one quart juice from any greens. Add chopped hard-boiled eggs and serve as soup with corn pone. (Serves four.)

RED BEAN CAJUN SOUP

Soak one pack of red beans in cold water overnight. Drain and place in pot with one cup of minced shallots, one cup of minced peppers, one teaspoon of salt, two quarts of water, six teaspoons of Worcestershire sauce, and a ham hock or piece of game or fowl. Simmer for two hours or until beans are tender. Mash the beans and strain. Lace with sherry. (Serves four.)

SOUP OF OKRA

Simmer one quart of water and one pound of beef or game for one hour, making a good stock. Add three pounds of fresh, minced okra, ten peeled, chopped tomatoes, a dash of celery salt, garlic salt, salt, and white pepper. Simmer about one hour. Serve with boiled rice. (Serves four.)

SPANISH CORN SOUP

Sauté grated corn cut from six ears with two cups of minced green peppers and two cups of minced shallots. Add one quart of fowl stock, four teaspoons of chili powder, one can of minced pimiento, salt, and pepper. Simmer about one hour. Add cream if desired. (Serves two.)

ASPARAGUS TIP SOUP

Wash twenty-four asparagus tips, cut in pieces, and put tips aside. Simmer stalks for ten minutes with two quarts of fowl stock, one cup of minced celery stalks and tops, a dash of salt, a pinch of white pepper, and a pinch of basil and other herbs. When asparagus is done strain soup stock. Cook tips in a little seasoned water for five minutes. Sprinkle tips on soup when placed in soup plate. (Serves eight.)

ONION SOUP

Slice ten large red onions. Sauté in butter. Add one quart of beef or game stock and simmer fifteen minutes. Add one teaspoon of blackstrap molasses, one-fourth teaspoon of salt, and one teaspoon of white pepper. Simmer for ten minutes. Sprinkle pieces of toasted French bread with Parmesan cheese and drop in soup when ready to serve. (Serves two.)

VICHYSSOISE

Chop up one bunch of celery, one-half bunch of anise, one cup of celery tops, and one cup of chives. Boil with twelve peeled new potatoes twenty to twenty-five minutes. Add one quart of cream and simmer for five minutes. Strain and serve chilled with fresh minced chives. (Serves four.)

GOURMET'S VICHYSSOISE

Mince twelve celery hearts and simmer in one pint of water with a little minced dill and one cup of leeks. Peel twelve potato marbles and drop in. Let simmer thirty minutes or until potatoes are tender. When ready to serve, place in cream soup bowls and float sour cream over the top. Sprinkle with minced parsley. (Serves two.)

PURÉE DES NOIX

Pound one pound of pecans or walnuts. Sauté in butter five minutes and add one pint of fowl stock, and a dash of celery salt, cayenne, and salt. Simmer thirty minutes. Top with whipped cream. (Serves two.)

CARROT CONSOMME

Grind two bunches of carrots; mix with one pound of minced almonds, and sauté in butter. Add six cups of fowl stock and simmer thirty minutes. Add one cup of cream and simmer fifteen minutes. Sprinkle with minced parsley. If a cold soup is desired, do not sauté the carrots and almonds. (Serves two.)

TOMATO JUICE SOUP

Heat one teaspoon of olive oil and sauté one cup of minced green peppers, one-half cup of minced celery, and one cup of minced cucumbers for five minutes. Add one large can of tomato juice, a dash of Tabasco, one teaspoon of lemon juice, a pinch of salt and cayenne, and a pinch of basil. Simmer ten minutes or longer. When ready to serve, sprinkle with minced parsley. Serve with slices of bread brushed with melted butter and Parmesan cheese and toasted. Serve hot. (Serves two.)

ORANGE SOUP

Simmer segments from six fresh oranges with three cups of fresh orange juice for ten minutes. Add three teaspoons of grated orange peel, one-half teaspoon of cinnamon, and one-half teaspoon of ginger. Simmer a few minutes longer. Run through a sieve and add one or two cups of chilled orange wine. Serve cold with segment of orange afloat. (Serves two.)

This soup may be made with any fruit or berries.

SOUPE AUX MARRONS

Boil one-half pound of chestnuts for twenty minutes and remove shells. Soak nuts in butter a few minutes and bake in oven for twenty minutes. Slice toasted nuts and mix with six cups of fowl stock, a pinch of celery salt, a pinch of cayenne, a pinch of mace, and salt. Simmer a half hour and serve hot. (Serves two.)

CUCUMBER SOUP I

Simmer for ten minutes or until tender six peeled and sliced cucumbers with one-half cup of minced shallots. Add six cups of chicken stock and cook ten minutes. Lace with white wine. (Serves two.)

CUCUMBER SOUP II

Simmer for ten minutes or until tender six peeled and sliced cucumbers. Add one can of milk or four cups of cream and one cup of minced pecans. Simmer about ten minutes. (Serves two.)

BROTH OF WATER CRESS

Sauté one bunch of water cress in butter a few minutes. Add four cups of cream, a dash each of paprika, salt, and white pepper. Simmer for three minutes. Lace with white wine. (Serves two.)

SHALLOT PORRIDGE

Sauté one bunch of minced shallots in butter for five minutes. Add one quart of hot water and twelve small, peeled new potatoes, and a pinch of salt, and white pepper. Simmer for thirty minutes or until potatoes are done. Add one-half cup of whipped cream. (Serves four.)

LEEK FORCÉ

Boil twelve leeks in water for ten minutes. Drain and boil in fresh water for ten minutes. Add six cups of beef or game stock, and a dash of salt, garlic salt, and white pepper. Simmer for ten minutes, strain and serve. Sprinkle with Parmesan cheese. (Serves two.)

CRÈME DE LAITUE SOUPE

Grind one head of lettuce with one-half cup of shallots. Sauté lettuce and shallots in butter a few minutes. Add three cups of fowl stock, a pinch of celery salt, a pinch of cayenne, and salt. Simmer five or ten minutes and serve hot. Sprinkle with celery seed. (Serves two.)

SAGO SOUP

Soak two ounces of sago in water for one hour. Wash and boil in plain water for thirty minutes or until clear. Add two cups of sugar, a pinch of nutmeg, and a pinch of salt. Add one bottle of white wine and serve cold. Float a few fresh berries on top or a thin slice of apple sprinkled with nutmeg. (Serves four.)

MINESTRONE SOUP

Soak one cup of navy or other type dried beans overnight in cold water. Wash and place in a kettle with one quart of cold water, a dash of salt, pepper, three bay leaves, a pinch of thyme, a pinch of rosemary, and a bit of garlic. Boil for one hour or until beans are tender. Remove beans and strain stock. Sauté for five minutes three tablespoons of minced parsley with two tablespoons of minced shallots and one cup of fresh, peeled tomatoes. Add the bean stock and one cup of minced cabbage. Simmer cabbage for twenty minutes. Add beans and simmer a few minutes more. Strain soup through a sieve, mashing beans well. Add one cup of boiled spaghetti and simmer for an additional ten minutes. Serve hot. Sprinkle with Parmesan cheese when ready to serve. (Serves four.)

TURNIP SOUP

Pare twelve turnips and cut into small pieces. Place in a pot with one quart of fowl stock or hot water and simmer over a slow fire until the turnips are tender, about twenty minutes. Season with a little butter, celery salt, white pepper, and salt. Sprinkle with minced celery tops. (Serves four.)

CANTALOUPE SOUP

Cut up the inside of one melon. Add one quart of fowl stock and a *bouquet garni* of spices. Cook ten minutes or until the melon is tender. Serve with slices of uncooked melon. (Serves four.)

VIOLET SOUP

Make a soup out of some fowl bones and pieces of fowl and two quarts of water. When this has cooked several hours, strain and add a dozen or so early blue violets (wild okra). Simmer this for an hour. Serve with boiled rice. (Serves four to six.)

CHEESE SOUP

Scrape and peel one bunch of carrots. Cut in small pieces and simmer in two quarts of fowl stock, salt, white pepper, and two bay leaves. When the carrots are done, after about ten minutes, remove and mash. Remove the bay leaves. Place the carrots back in the stock and add a tiny bit of saffron and one cup of grated Cheddar cheese. Heat until the cheese is melted. Serve hot. (Serves eight.)

IV
Salads

The Moss-Gatherers

Salads

Salad-making is a true mirror of one's personality, for it either reflects imagination and charm or it reveals a drab and listless character. Louisiana cooks know that the salad, more than the entrée or any other course, can set the tone of a meal, and salad-making in this state is performed with a combination of flair and ritual.

Ingredients are chosen for color and texture, and water cress, lettuce, *escarole*, and romaine may be the salad-bowl companions of raw cauliflower or boiled ground artichoke. In the spring, the salad sorcerer's hand is touched with a special magic, for then he may roam the fields and woods gathering wild greens to mix with the tender sprouts from his own garden and producing results both exotic and exciting.

So important a place does salad-making assume in the South that in many dining rooms—private and restaurant—a special side table is used for mixing the salad. Salad ingredients are always carefully washed, dried in a clean cloth, and chilled before using, of course. They should be mixed in a large wooden bowl, with a wooden fork and spoon, after the bowl has first been rubbed with salt and a pod of garlic (or, for sweet salads, magnolia seeds or nasturtium or geranium leaves). A *chapon* or piece of dry bread should be placed in the bottom of the bowl during the mixing; it is removed before serving.

After the salad has been served the bowl should be wiped with a damp cloth but never washed with soap and water in order to be sure that only desirable flavors are blended into future salads.

A CHAPON

Use a large piece of stale bread or zwieback. Rub with garlic or sprinkle with garlic salt. Leave in bottom of bowl and toss salad. Remove after greens are mixed.

BLENDING OF GREENS

In making a leafy salad always break material with your hands. Pour the dressing in very slowly, tossing salad as dressing is poured. Be sure that all the greens have been completely dried so they will absorb all the dressing.

BAYOU LAFOURCHE
CREOLE LETTUCE

Use the unheaded, garden variety of lettuce. Mix one large package of cream cheese with one cup of minced shallots or chives and a dash of Tabasco, white pepper, and salt. Fill each crisp leaf of lettuce with mixture. The leaves of a headed lettuce may be stuffed, left headed, and sliced at the table. (Serves four to six.)

CAESAR SALAD

Mix five pounds of broken-up greens with one cup of radishes, four anchovies, one cup of minced shallots, one cup of minced celery, and one cup of minced peppers. Stir French dressing into greens. Pour one beaten egg over salad bowl. Toss again and top with Parmesan cheese. Croutons fried in butter may be added. (Serves ten.)

CRACKLIN' SALAD

Make one cup of cracklings and keep crisp in warm oven. (See recipe for "Cracklin' Bread," p. 248.) Mix with one bunch of water cress and one head of garden lettuce. Serve with French dressing or mayonnaise. (Serves six.)

FRENCH TWIST SALAD

Break up one large head of lettuce. Mix with French dressing. Just before serving add one cup of twisted pieces of the crust of a French bread loaf. (Serves four.)

KOHLRABI

Peel one pound of kohlrabi and slice. Let stand in ice water and salt several hours. Mix with one pound of kale and one pound of endive or romaine. Dress with French dressing. (Serves six.)

RABBIT FOOD (OR MIXED GREENS)

Mix any wild, edible, leaf herbs with any garden greens. Mix with French dressing, and cover bowl with sliced radishes or minced spring onions.

ROOSEVELT CHAPEAU SALAD

Blend two pounds of washed and well-drained garden greens with bits of tomato, minced radishes, and minced shallots. Sauté tiny croutons in butter with one pod of minced garlic. Add to salad when ready to serve and dress with French dressing. (Serves eight.)

CABBAGE PALM SALAD

Cut a Sabal palmetto or cabbage palm that is under six feet (this also kills the palm), and remove outer layer. Peel down to terminal bud. Cut strips of bud and soak in ice water. Serve with French dressing. (Serves four to eight.)

WILD CHICORY SALAD

Pick one pound of wild chicory leaves. Mix with one pound of dandelion leaves and minced wild onions. Dress with French dressing. (Serves four.)

FIELD SALET

Wash and tear two pounds of corn salad with two pounds of tender leaves of pokeweed. Dress with French dressing and hard-cooked eggs. (Serves six.)

POKE SALET

Pick tender, young pokeweed leaves. Serve with hard-boiled eggs and French dressing. The root and berries of this plant are poisonous.

SCURVY GRASS SALAD

Pick scurvy grass (cress) and wash. Mince grass and add to one bunch of water cress or a head of lettuce. Dress.

THISTLE SALAD

Cut thistles in early spring when they are about three to six inches tall. Remove flower leaves and peel stalk. Slice lengthwise and soak in wine vinegar for thirty minutes. Chill and serve with a dressing of salt, pepper, and olive oil.

WILD WALDORF SALAD

Use one pound of "eatin' apples" and any wild nuts. Peel and cut up the apples. Squeeze the juice of one lemon over them. Add the nut meats and mayonnaise dressing. (Serves four.)

ANISE IN OIL

Wash and slice anise very thin. Soak in ice water for a half hour. Place on lettuce and dress with Spanish olive oil mixed with a little celery salt and anchovy paste.

JERUSALEM ARTICHOKES

The French were introduced to these tubers by the Indians. Leave the artichokes in the ground during the winter, dig up in spring. Peel two pounds of artichokes and boil in salted water for thirty minutes or until tender. Marinate in olive oil and vinegar overnight then wipe dry. Serve on any salad green with minced chives and dressing. (Serves six.)

AVOCADO

Cut an avocado in half and remove seed. Mix salt, white pepper, and lime juice. Pour into each half. (Serves two.)

GUACAMOLE

Peel four avocados and slice in small pieces. Mince one cup of onions or shallots and blend in an electric mixer. Add a dash of paprika, cayenne, salt, and black pepper, and enough vinegar and olive oil to moisten. Blend well and chill. Serve on a lettuce leaf. (Serves four.)

AVOCADO VINAIGRETTE

Mix one pound of boiled, peeled shrimp with one cup of minced celery hearts and one tablespoon of capers. Dress with a French dressing mixed with dry mustard and a little Creole mustard. Serve in avocado halves. (Serves four.)

SPICED BEETS

Cook one bunch of beets in water and spices for forty minutes or until tender. Peel. Marinate in vinegar and spices in refrigerator. Slice and serve on lettuce with French dressing. (Serves four.)

SOY SALAD

Mince one pound of Chinese cabbage, one can of water chestnuts, and one can of bean sprouts. Mix three tablespoons of soy sauce with one cup of mayonnaise and dress salad. (Serves eight.)

PEASANT SLAW

Cut one red or green cabbage. Wash and leave in ice water for half an hour. Drain well and mix with one cup of minced shallots or chives and "Sweet Boiled Salad Dressing" (p. 234). Just before serving toss in one cup of very crisp bacon pieces. (Serves ten.)

SALADE RUE RUSTIQUE

Peel one bunch of carrots and cut in long, narrow slivers. Place in ice water for one hour. Drain and dry. Slice two cucumbers very thin and marinate in vinegar and oil. Drain the cucumbers and mix with the carrots. Serve on water cress with a French dressing. (Serves four.)

CAULIFLOWER EN PYRAMIDE

Grind one raw cauliflower with six shallots and marinate mixture in oil and vinegar for several hours. Drain and mix with one cup of minced ripe olives. Serve in mounds with French dressing. (Serves six.)

CHARD AUX FINES HERBES

Boil ten stalks of chard for twenty minutes or until tender. Chill and serve with French dressing mixed with *fines herbes.* Serve on lettuce. (Serves six.)

CUCUMBERS CLAIBORNE

Peel six young cucumbers. Slice and marinate in oil and vinegar for a half hour. Drain and mix with nasturtium leaves. Serve with French dressing. (Serves six.)

CUCUMBER JELL

Dissolve one envelope of gelatin in one-half cup of cold water. Mix one cup of shredded pineapple, one cup of sliced cucumbers, one teaspoon of onion juice, one cup of peeled, seedless grapes, one teaspoon of salt, and one-half cup of sugar. Blend with gelatin and pour into molds. Chill. (Serves four to six.)

LEEK SALADE SOIGNÉE

Boil three pounds of wild or garden leeks in several salted waters for twenty minutes. Drain. Chill and serve on lettuce with French dressing. The leeks may be marinated in olive oil while chilling. (Serves six.)

LETTUCE BOURRÉ

Wash lettuce and keep headed. Scoop out part of inside with grapefruit knife. Mix part scooped out with raw grated carrots, raisins, minced chives, and French dressing. Pack filling into lettuce head and chill. Slice when ready to serve. (Serves four to six.)

OKRA SALAD

Boil two pounds of young okra in salted water for twenty minutes or until tender. Chill and sprinkle with minced shallots. Serve on lettuce with French dressing. (Serves four.)

GREEN PEA SALAD

Drain a large can of large green peas and marinate them overnight in French dressing and garlic. Drain and mix with one broken-up head of lettuce and a little minced celery. Dress with French dressing. (Serves six.)

PEPPER SALAD

Cut the top off of a large green pepper, and remove seeds. Mix one large package of cream cheese with three teaspoons of chopped onion, a pinch of salt, a dash of white pepper, and three teaspoons of minced pimiento. Stuff pepper shell and chill. When ready to serve, slice crosswise and serve on lettuce. (Serves six.)

CALCASIEU POTATO SALAD

Peel six pounds of new potatoes and boil gently thirty minutes or until tender. Marinate in oil and vinegar several hours. Serve with chives on lettuce with dressing. (Serves eight.)

HOT POTATO SALAD

Peel and boil two pounds of old potatoes, mash with a little olive oil, and season with salt and white pepper. Add a dash of Tabasco and prepared mustard. Mix with minced sweet pickles. Serve hot on water cress with a dot of mayonnaise. (Serves six.)

SALADA

Mince three pounds of raw spinach with four hard-cooked eggs and a little minced onion. Add one-fourth cup of chopped olives, one-half cup of pieces of salami, and one can of anchovies. Mix with French dressing. Chopped raw asparagus may be added. (Serves six.)

SALADE COMPOSÉE

Tear four pounds of any garden or wild salad herbs apart and wash. Dry and break into small pieces. Mix the herbs with one cup of slivers of radishes and one cup of minced raw cauliflower, six strips of green pepper, six slices of peeled carrots, six slices of unpeeled cucumber, and twelve onion rings. Season with salt and white pepper. Dress with French dressing. (Serves ten.)

RADISH MELANGE

Tear inner leaves of two pounds of fennel and mix with twelve sliced radishes and ten raw minced Brussels sprouts. Mix with French dressing. (Serves six.)

ROOTS IN ESCABECHE SAUCE

Boil two bunches of carrots and one bunch of turnips separately in seasoned water for thirty minutes or until done. Peel and slice. Slice three onions thin. Make a sauce of two cups of olive oil, one cup of vinegar, one pod of minced garlic, one-half cup of minced ripe olives, and one-half cup of minced pimiento. Simmer this sauce for five minutes. Put in onions, carrots, and turnips while it is hot. Let the mixture cool, and then leave in the refrigerator for several hours. (Serves eight.)

ACADIE WHIP

Mix two pounds of blackberries and one cup of walnuts. Marinate in white wine and nutmeg for one-half hour. Dry and place on water cress. (Serves four.)

PAT'S CHERRY SALAD

Boil together the juice from one large can of black cherries and enough water to make one and one-half cups of liquid. Dissolve one tablespoon of gelatin in a little cold water. Pour cherry liquid over gelatin and let cool. When almost cold, add one-half cup of sherry. Stuff canned cherries with one-half cup of pecans and add these to liquid. Pour into a mold and chill. Lemon juice may be substituted for the sherry. (Serves eight.)

CHRISTMAS SALAD

Grind one package of raw cranberries and two cups of shelled pecans. Add some brown sugar to dissolved cherry jello. Combine the ingredients. Pour into molds. Chill and serve with Creamed Mayonnaise or Renée Dressing. (Serves six.)

ORANGE SALAD

Cut segments of six Louisiana oranges. Marinate segments with slices of four ripe avocados in orange wine for fifteen minutes. Drain and serve in avocado shells. (Serves four.)

CHUTNEY PEARS

Simmer peeled fresh pears with candied ginger for ten minutes. Chill and serve on water cress. Top with "Creamed Mayonnaise" (see p. 235) and chutney.

PINEAPPLE AUX AMANDES

Marinate twelve fresh-cut pineapple spears in orange wine for thirty minutes. Drain and mix with almonds. Dress with "Renée Dressing" (see p. 236). (Serves four.)

EASTER SALAD

One is supposed to be a fool all year unless one eats an Easter egg at Easter. Make a salad of two pounds of broken-up lettuce or other greens and six Easter eggs peeled at the table and cut up in the greens. Add dressing and salt and pepper. (Serves six.)

BONITO SALAD

Clean and fillet the fish, but do not remove skin. Simmer gently with a *bouquet garni* and cut-up limes until tender. Cool in the liquid. Remove, skin, chill, and flake. Place in a bowl with minced dill pickles and minced celery, salt, white pepper, paprika, and celery salt. Toss and serve on lettuce. Top with mayonnaise. Cobia, mackerel, or any number of other salt-water fish may be made into salads in the same way. (A five-pound fish serves eight to ten.)

CRAB CUPS

Boil twelve crabs and remove meat and claw meat. Mix with two teaspoons of minced onion, a dash of cayenne, salt, pepper, and one-fourth cup of minced celery, two minced pimientoes, and chili powder. Mix with mayonnaise or French dressing. This salad may be served in pimiento cups. (Serves four.)

CRAB HOLLANDAISE

Place six boiled crabs around a large dish with a small dish of Hollandaise sauce (see p. 217) in center. Dig out the crab meat and dunk into the sauce. Mayonnaise may be used in place of hollandaise sauce. (Serves two.)

JELLIED CRAB

Peel and slice three cucumbers. Simmer in clear water until they are tender. Dissolve one package of gelatin in one cup of the strained cucumber water. Mix with three thinly sliced raw cucumbers, one cup of cooked crab meat, one teaspoon of onion juice, one teaspoon of celery salt, and salt and pepper to taste. Chill and serve on water cress. (Serves four.)

JELLIED CRAWFISH

Dissolve one package of gelatin in cold water. Add two cups of hot fish, fowl stock, or fowl bouillon. Add one cup of minced celery hearts, one-half cup of minced pimiento, one-fourth cup of minced sweet pickles, and two or three cups of boiled crawfish tails. Season with white pepper and salt. Pour into a large, round mold and chill. Place cold potato salad in center of mold when served. (Serves four.)

SALADE D'ÉCREVISSE

Boil and peel six pounds of crawfish tails. Place a quarter head of lettuce on a salad plate. Pour dressing of "Bayou Lafourche Boogalee Sauce" (see p. 223) over lettuce and top with crawfish tails. (Serves eight.)

SALADE LOUISIANE

Fry six frog legs, remove meat from bone, and cut up. Mix the meat with one cup of flaked, cooked fish and one pound of boiled crawfish. Dress with mayonnaise or "Renée Dressing" (see p. 236). Serve on water cress with crackers toasted with butter, celery salt, and paprika. (Serves eight.)

SHINE'S SHRIMP SALAD

Marinate three pounds of boiled, peeled, cleaned shrimp in French dressing with four teaspoons of dry mustard, lots of black pepper, a dash of Tabasco, and salt added to dressing. Remove from marinade and mix with one-half cup of fine-minced celery stalks and tops, two cut-up hard-boiled eggs, and a dash of paprika. Add some of the marinade and chill. Scoop out a hole in a fresh Creole cabbage and fill cabbage with salad. Spoon cut and place on lettuce leaves. (Serves six.)

SHRIMP NEPTUNE

Marinate one pound of boiled, peeled, cleaned shrimp in "Paprika Dressing" (see p. 236) for half hour. Place sauce and shrimp on shredded lettuce and serve. (Serves four.)

BRENNAN'S SHRIMP RÉMOULADE

Make a sauce of six tablespoons of olive oil, one-half teaspoon of pepper, one-fourth cup of minced celery hearts, one-half cup of chopped white onion, two tablespoons of vinegar, four teaspoons of Creole mustard, a little horse-radish, a little minced parsley, and salt and pepper to taste; chill several hours. Chill two pounds of boiled, cleaned, and peeled shrimp for several hours. Place the shrimp on shredded lettuce and top with the sauce. (Serves eight.)

ROOSEVELT HOTEL SHRIMP RÉMOULADE

Blend two beaten egg yolks, one-half pint of Creole mustard, one-fourth cup of vinegar, the juice of one lemon, and salt and pepper. Beat well. Slowly add one pint of Wesson oil, beating constantly as in making mayonnaise. When sauce has thickened, add one bunch of minced green onions and one-half stalk of minced celery. Soak four pounds of peeled, cleaned, boiled shrimp in sauce for about four hours. Serve on lettuce.

SHRIMP IN SOUR CREAM

Mix one pound of boiled, peeled, cleaned shrimp with one-half cup of minced onion and one cup of celery. Add "Creole Sour Cream Sauce" (see p. 224). Serve on lettuce. (Serves four.)

SHRIMPERS' SALAD BOWL

Mix two pounds of cold, boiled fish flakes with two pounds of boiled, peeled shrimp, and one cup of boiled meat of crabs. Mix with French dressing and one cup of cold boiled potatoes. Throw in any herbs handy. Eat on the deck of a boat. (It's a Gulf tradition to eat these fruits of the Gulf while the net is in the water.) (Serves six.)

TOMATO SHRIMP

Marinate one pound of boiled, peeled, cleaned shrimp in "Tomato Sauce" (see p. 225) for several hours. Serve in four peeled, scooped-out tomatoes. Top with dot of mayonnaise. (Serves four.)

GREEN TROUT SALAD

Clean, scale, and boil one largemouth black bass (known as "green trout") with a *bouquet garni* until tender. (Save stock for

other dishes.) Chill and flake in a bowl with one-half cup of
minced chives, one-fourth cup of minced green peppers, and one-
fourth cup of minced celery stalks and leaves. Add salt and white
pepper and a dash of cayenne. Toss with mayonnaise. Serve on
romaine. (Serves six to eight.)

SALADE BOCAGE

Simmer four cups of cooked game in sherry for ten minutes.
Drain and mix with one-fourth cup of minced celery, one-fourth
cup of minced bell pepper, salt, pepper, and a dash of Tabasco.
Mix with mayonnaise and top with minced parsley. Serve on
shredded lettuce. (Serves four.)

TURKEY SALAD

Cut up two cups of cold, cooked turkey, and mix with two
minced apples and one cup of shelled walnuts. Mix with mayonnaise. Serve on water cress. (Serves six.)

WATER FOWL SALAD

Cut up four cups of cooked duck or goose and mix with one
minced cucumber, one minced green pepper, dash of Tabasco, salt,
and pepper. Mix with mayonnaise. Serve on lettuce. (Serves six.)

Plantation life - an era of ease

V
À Poil et à Plume

A cotton field

À Poil et à Plume

(Hairy and Feathered)

Louisiana is a land of extremes in terrain over which wild life finds a healthy and varied habitat. High, wooded bluffs drop suddenly into marsh meadows, and cypress swamps may turn unexpectedly into hills of hardwood.

Along the coastal region the Choctaw and Chickasaw were the first known game gourmets. One of their favorite dishes was concocted by skewering chunks of turkey meat, venison, and bear meat and so impaling it over the fire that the bear fat would flavor the other meat.

The Choctaw and Chickasaw were not alone in valuing bear meat for its juices and flavor. In the early days of the province, the Louisiana black bear ranked with the buffalo or bison in numbers and importance, and bear oil was an article of trade. Today, the spread of agriculture and excessive hunting have crowded Louisiana's bear from his original haunts and forced him to seek the wooded jungles and swamp thickets.

More plentiful for the present-day hunter are the fleet-footed white-tailed or Virginia deer, which may be found from the state's northern boundary to the mouth of the Mississippi. Though occasionally disparaged by "furriners," the whitetails are large in both size and number. A recent estimate set the deer population of the state at between sixty and seventy thousand, and a twelve-point, three-hundred-pound buck was killed near Chacahoula Swamp in 1954. For those who have followed the song of the deerhound few sports can compare with the chase of this deer.

Magnolia, perfume of Louisiana, and its state flower

SOME DO'S AND DON'TS IN THE PREPARATION OF LARGE GAME

DO kill game quickly, for a struggle will impair the flavor of the meat.

DO bleed deer or other large game at once, for retention of blood after death toughens the meat. To bleed, sever artery at base of neck or just in front of breastbone.

DO place deer in dressing position. This varies with the section of the country: in some sections animals are hung by the head; in some by the rear legs; in others it is placed on the ground in a downhill position. In any case, legs should be spread far apart.

DO dress animal by making a cut from breastbone to tail; cut a circle around anus and genitals and remove them and large intestine. If animal is to be "woods dressed," remove liver, kidneys, heart, windpipe, and gullet, and saw through pelvic bone. If it is to be "hog dressed," remove only the intestines.

DO skin animal by making an incision over hock and back of legs. Remove feet, make an incision behind the tendon in rear of legs, and remove legs at knee. Split breastbone, then pull off skin toward head.

DO wipe interior clean and dry, but do not wash; allow air to circulate in the cavity.

DO hang for several days or weeks in freezing temperature. Chill as soon as possible.

DO use venison chart on p. 74 as a guide in butchering.

DO use a sharp knife and a meat saw for cutting.

DON'T attempt to butcher a large animal without the help of a butcher or other expert if you are inexperienced.

DO remove head and neck first, then divide animal by sawing down backbone. Cut rear shank and shoulder, follow by breast, ribs, flank, loin, rump, round, and rear shank.

DON'T remove fat until ready to cook.

DO use plenty of fat or oil in cooking any large game except bear.

DO rub well with salt, paprika, and black pepper.

DO use a marinade for all parts of large game except tender steaks.

DON'T remove the fat from venison if a more gamey taste is desired.

DO cook meat in wine to tenderize.

DO use garlic to reduce extreme gamey taste.

DON'T incise or pierce a cut of meat while it is cooking lest you lose valuable juices thereby.

DO start with boiling water if meat is to be boiled in order to preserve juices.

DO cook venison shortly after deer is killed; the meat starts to toughen after the first six hours.

DON'T use salt until after the meat is cooked; salt toughens meat if applied before cooking.

DO use sugar—either rubbed on the meat or cooked with it—as a tenderizer.

DON'T neglect to check state and federal game laws concerning the tagging, storing, and shipping of game. Be sure to tag carcass with hunter's name and address.

MARINADE FOR LARGE GAME

In a deep crock, mix one fifth bottle of good red wine, one pint of wine or tarragon vinegar, two hot peppers or peppercorns, four bay leaves, one teaspoon of salt, one teaspoon of sesame seed, four sticks of cinnamon, two cups of minced shallots, one teaspoon of dry mustard (optional), one teaspoon of thyme, one teaspoon of shaved ginger, one-half teaspoon of basil, one-fourth teaspoon of rosemary, one-fourth teaspoon of sage, one teaspoon of whole cloves, two whole nutmegs, one cup of minced celery stalks and tops, and one or more teaspoons of curry powder (optional).

After mixing these ingredients, add meat and allow to marinate for twelve to thirty-six hours. The marinade may also be used for basting after straining and heating.

To pickle game, cut the meat from the bone, rub with salt and red pepper, and steep in marinade overnight. Pour off liquid and put meat in jars. Keep for several days on ice.

BEAR

In preparing bear meat, hang the carcass for several days. Marinate the meat as you would venison or the meat of any older animal intended for roasts, stews, and ragouts. Only the meat of a young bear is tender enough for broiling, and during the mating season, the meat of the adult male is not good eating in any form. If proper food has been plentiful, bear meat is best at the end of the winter, and the yearlings are tastiest after they have fed on a diet of choice nuts and berries.

The recipes for bear may also be used for wild boar.

BEAR DOUCEMENT

Use a thick rib steak already marinated. Wipe dry and pound with powdered cinnamon, salt, and pepper. Dust with flour and sear in hot grease. Add venison or beef stock to cover, one-half stick of butter, one teaspoon of brown sugar, and one teaspoon of nutmeg. Simmer slowly for two hours in covered skillet. Turn often until done.

BEAR RIBS

The ribs may be stewed as are those of venison. First marinate overnight.

BEAR STEAKS

Marinate six steaks, cut about an inch thick, and then wipe dry. They should be well ripened. Pound salt, pepper, and dry mustard into meat, dust with flour, and sear on both sides. Add a small amount of stock of venison or bear. Cook for one hour or until done. If steak is tough, add more liquid and cook longer. Serve with hot potato salad and pickles. (Serves eight to ten.)

GERMAN BEAR

After marinating thick (two-inch) steaks, pound in ground ginger and salt. Sear meat in hot grease and add hot marinade liquid and a *bouquet garni*. Add one cup of minced shallots and simmer one hour per pound or until done. When done, add ginger snaps to gravy.

RAGOUT OF BEAR

Cut two pounds marinated meat into small pieces. Sprinkle with minced shallots, salt, pepper, and flour. Sear in hot grease. Then add stock of venison or beef, butter, Worcestershire sauce, a dash of Tabasco, and mushrooms. Simmer one hour to the pound or until done. (Serves six.)

ROAST OF BEAR

Age a roast several days. After marinating, wipe dry, and rub with powdered allspice, salt, and pepper. Dust with flour and sear for forty minutes in a hot oven. Cook for two hours or longer in slow oven, basting often with hot marinade and stock.

SMOKED BEAR

Make a box-shaped pit in ground. Build a hickory fire and let burn slowly. On top of pit place a tin box with holes on one side. Hang bear meat in tin box and smoke slowly for several hours.

DEER
CHOPS
(Saddle and Loin)

Some folk claim that chops are better than any other part of the deer. They do not have to be marinated. Cook thirty minutes to the pound.

CHOPS AU LAIT

Marinate chops in cream, salt, and pepper overnight. Wipe dry and rub with olive oil. Dust with flour and fry for thirty minutes or until done. Serve with cream gravy and boiled rice. (Serve one chop per person.)

CHOPS POINTE A LA HACHE

Rub chops with salt and pepper. Marinate in orange juice for thirty minutes. Wipe dry, rub with olive oil, and dust with flour. Fry in hot butter for thirty minutes or until done. Serve with orange marmalade and hominy. (Serve one chop per person.)

ROASTS
(Chuck, Saddle, Loin, Rump, and Shoulder)

ENGLISH CHUCK ROAST

Marinate. Wipe dry and rub with salt, pepper, and olive oil. Dust with flour. Sear in a very hot skillet and cook thirty minutes per pound in roasting pan in a slow oven. About thirty minutes before roast is done, add whole carrots, new potatoes, and onions. The roast must be basted constantly with hot marinade. Roast until vegetables and meat are done. Serve with mashed potatoes. Roasts may also be rubbed with olive oil, stuck with a pod or two of garlic, sprinkled with salt, pepper, and orégano, and roasted in a paper bag until done. (Place the bag in a roasting pan.)

ETHEL STEVENS' ROAST

Rub a five-pound roast with salt and pepper and insert one clove of garlic in center. Roast in oven at 130°, increasing to 170° by the time meat is done (about three hours). (Use meat thermometer.) Baste often with butter and white wine. (Serves ten.)

GARLIC BUTTER ROAST

Fry three minced pods of garlic in olive oil until brown. Rub thin roast with salt, pepper, and olive oil. Fry for forty minutes in garlic oil. When done, remove meat and add a small amount of hot water to garlic and oil to make gravy. Add a small amount of butter if desired.

LOIN ROAST IN CREAM

Marinate. Wipe dry and rub with salt, pepper, and salt pork. Dust with flour and sear roast in a hot oven. Cook in a slow oven until three quarters done, basting often with one part hot marinade and one part beef bouillon or stock from venison bones. Add one pint of fresh, heavy cream and one cup of minced shallots. Cook thirty minutes to the pound or until done. Make a gravy. Cut slivers of almonds, fry in butter, and crisp in oven. Sprinkle almonds in gravy. Serve with boiled rice.

ROAST À LA CHUKA CHAHA

Place a five-pound venison roast on a spit for two and one-half hours over a low hickory fire. While cooking, baste with a mixture of butter, Worcestershire sauce, lime juice, salt, and pepper. As the meat browns on the outside cut slices off and drop into a pan of barbecue sauce. Continue cutting the meat as it browns. This method gives you browned outside meat all the way through. (Serves ten.)

RUMP SALMI

Marinate a five-pound roast. Wipe dry and rub with salt, pepper, and chili powder. Rub with olive oil and dust with flour. Sear in a hot oven and cook in a slow oven for two and one-half hours, basting often with half marinade and half venison or beef stock to which have been added one pound of minced ripe olives and one cup of minced pimientos. Mushrooms or capers may be added if desired. (Serves ten.)

UNE PÂTE DE VENAISON
SHOULDER-ROAST

Marinate. Wipe dry and rub with salt, pepper, and cayenne. Rub well with olive oil, then dust with flour. Sear on top of stove in an iron skillet. Then brown, add hot marinade and half hot venison stock or bouillon stock, and simmer on top of stove thirty minutes. Place in oven and roast thirty minutes to the pound, basting often. Add twelve whole brandied peaches and cook until done. Add one cup of peach brandy and steep. Pour one cup of cognac over roast. Light the brandy and serve aflame.

VENISON À LA MYRTLE GROVE

Place a venison roast (about ten pounds) in a Dutch oven. Braise it in one inch of cooking oil. Gradually add one bottle of sauterne and cook for five hours. Several pods of garlic may be rubbed on meat to tenderize it. (Serves fifteen.)

VIANDE DE HAUT GOÛT

Marinate a ten-pound venison roast overnight in venison marinade. Wipe dry and sear in an iron skillet on top of the stove. When seared on each side place in a roasting pan with slices of Trappey's Dulcito peppers, and some slices of green peppers. Add one pod of minced garlic, one cup of minced shallots, one-half cup of Italian olive oil, and hot water or stock. Roast for five hours in a moderate oven until the meat is tender. (Serves fifteen.)

VENISON STEAKS

(Loin, Haunch, and Chuck)

ALE STEAK HASH

After four steaks are marinated, cut in large cubes and brown in butter. Add one-half cup of minced chives, one bay leaf, a pinch of thyme, and one or more bottles of ale. Simmer for one hour or until done. Season with salt and paprika. (Serves eight.)

BARBECUED VENISON

Marinate steaks and wipe dry. Rub with salt and pepper. Broil for forty-five minutes over open pit, basting often with sauce of lemon juice, Worcestershire, dash of Tabasco, and butter. Turn until done. Serve with chunks of hot French bread.

BEER STEAKS

Soak thin, tender steaks in beer overnight. Bake for forty minutes or more in ginger beer. Spread powdered ginger mixed with honey over top, and brown.

BLANQUETTE

Fry steaks for forty minutes. Add some stock and a *bouquet garni*. Simmer a few minutes. Add cooked green peas and sliced hard-cooked eggs.

CAJUN COLLOPS

Cut two pounds of venison steak into small cubes. Sear in oleo-margarine. Add one quart of game stock or hot water, two bay leaves, one sprig of thyme, a pinch of basil and rosemary, salt and pepper to taste, one-fourth cup of shallots, and one-half teaspoon of powdered allspice. Cook two hours over a slow fire. Add one teaspoon of Tabasco and one-fourth cup of minced celery leaves a half hour before the two-hour period is up. Pour the stock off the meat and strain. Make a *roux* and slowly add the hot, strained stock and one cup of cream. Sprinkle with paprika and serve this sauce over the cubed meat on slices of French-bread toast. (Serves six.)

CAJUN STEAK

"First you make a *roux*," then add two jars of wild grape jelly and let melt. Add one cup of good red wine and let steep. In another skillet, fry for thirty minutes steak that has been prepared by rubbing with salt, pepper, and flour. When done, pour *roux* into skillet with steak and add more wine if desired.

LAKE BISTINEAU CHUCK

Use a thin piece of chuck and marinate it. Rub with salt, pepper, and pork drippings. Dust with flour and sear on top of the stove. Roast in a slow oven thirty minutes to the pound, basting often with venison or beef stock. When half done, add one or more jars of wild May haw jelly and cook until done.

NESBITT'S FRIED STEAK

Use tender meat, which does not need to be marinated. Pound salt and pepper into steak rounds. Dust with flour and fry in butter thirty minutes or until done. Sautéed mushrooms may be served with it.

VENISON GRILLADES

Pound salt, pepper, and paprika into steaks. Dust with flour. Sear in hot grease and add one-half cup of lime or orange juice, three cups of venison or beef stock, one-quarter cup of Worcestershire sauce, one minced bell pepper, one cup of minced shallots, one cup of peeled Creole tomatoes, a pinch of rosemary and thyme, and two bay leaves. Simmer for one hour or until done. Serve with hot grits.

SOY VENISON

Cut two pounds venison steaks into cubes. Marinate the cubes overnight in a mixture of one-half cup of soy sauce, one minced pod of garlic, and three cups of good olive oil. Drain the cubed meat and broil for forty minutes on skewers with water chestnuts. (Serves four to six.)

TROPICAL VENISON

Fry steaks for twenty minutes or until tender in butter. Add one minced green pepper and six pineapple spears. Sauté for ten minutes. Add one cup of pineapple juice mixed with four teaspoons soy sauce, and steep.

WINE STEAK

Pound a thick steak, then pound salt and pepper into steak. Rub with bacon drippings. Sear until brown, then add a small amount of homemade red wine, cooking approximately sixty minutes. Keep adding wine slowly until steak is done.

DEER HEART

Marinate overnight. Wrap heart with slices of salt pork. Roast over coals or in the oven one hour or longer. (Serves approximately six.)

GLACÉ DE VIANDE

Marinate two pounds of cut-up venison overnight. Boil four pigs' feet and two veal knuckles until tender in water with four cut-up onions, one bunch of celery, four peppers, three bay leaves, and one-half cup of cloves. Cook until meat falls from bones. Strain. In an iron skillet boil the venison for one hour and add a small amount of water and a pinch of allspice and nutmeg. Cook until the meat is tender. Gradually add the strained stock and the juice of one lemon. Simmer until stock is cooked down. Pour into mold and chill. (Serves six.)

LIVER BORDELAISE

Slice the liver. Dust with flour. Brown in oil and add red wine, minced shallots, one pod of garlic, and butter. Stew for one hour or until done. The slices of liver may be marinated overnight before cooking. The liver may be eaten immediately after the deer is dressed. (Serves six to ten.)

PETE'S RAGOUT

Sear four slices of venison in grease. Add one cup of cut-up onions. When onions are brown, add one bottle of red wine and let simmer for one hour or until done. (Serves six.)

RAGOÛT DELICIEUX

Use two pounds of marinated meat cut in one-inch pieces. Sear in hot grease and add venison or beef stock. Simmer thirty minutes or until half done, then add one cup of raisins and one cup of minced pecan or walnut meats. Simmer an additional thirty minutes or until done and add one cup of sherry. Let steep and serve with mashed potatoes. (Serves four.)

STEW ARLATEX

Bear fat was considered by the Choctaw Indians the best flavor for venison. Today any fresh grease, butter, or oleo is used for this dry game. Use four pounds of marinated meat and cut in one-inch pieces. Sauté mushrooms, one cup of minced shallots, and one green pepper in butter. Add meat and brown. Add beef or venison stock and some of hot marinade. Simmer for two hours until almost done. Then add whole, peeled new potatoes, whole carrots, and shaved corn. Simmer an extra thirty minutes or until vegetables are done. (Serves eight.)

VENISONBURGERS

Have butcher grind two pounds of marinated meat. Add six ground shallots and mix with enough canned milk or cream to moisten. Add salt, pepper, a dash of Tabasco, and a pinch of marjoram and mace. Fry for thirty minutes in hot butter. Serve with raw onion and pepper relish, or with sour cream game sauce (see p. 224). (Serves four.)

AND A SAUSAGE A LA WOLD

Grind up meat of any fowl or game or both. Sauté the ground meat in butter with minced shallots. Add several cups of red wine and a *bouquet garni* of spices and herbs. Simmer until meat is done. Remove the herb bag and let simmer until thick. Add one cup or more of seasoned bread crumbs. Let mixture cool. Mold into patties and fry a few minutes in butter, or stuff into scalded, cleaned hog intestines. Broil.

SMALL GAME

Muskrat, rabbit, raccoon, squirrel—in fact, almost any small game you can think of—makes popular table fare for Louisiana diners, and all are eagerly hunted in their season. The muskrat, or marsh hare, used to be of value only for his pelt; but today his flesh is relished by epicures everywhere. In *mon pays* we like him "mo' bet' " when he's sautéed in a Creole sauce—but among the marsh folk muskrat potpie is a special favorite too.

"Ole Man Cottontail," like "M'sieu Muskrat," likes the reedy patches and watery plains, and he is hunted in every parish in the state. His flesh early made a popular dish among the German colonists who settled the *côte des allemands* on the Mississippi in the eighteenth century, and many a recipe for rabbit has been handed down in these families.

There are two kinds of raccoon in Louisiana—the dark coon of the timber tracts, and his cousin, the salt-water raccoon that abounds in the marshy areas. The latter subspecies has a more yellowish coat and is outlawed in some parishes. Clean in their dietary and personal habits, coons are known to the trappers of the lowlands as *shoui,* a Choctaw name. The French settlers called them *chat* and named Mississippi's Cat Island after its numerous raccoon denizens.

But probably the universal sport of the field in the state is the hunting of Louisiana's "bushy tail." Of the 16,183,171 acres of forest land in the state, almost 13,000,000 are the range of both the grey and the fox (or black) squirrel. The grey squirrel prefers the wooded tangles of the low inlands, and the fox squirrel abounds in the rolling hills and creek beds of the uplands. The greatest hazard for both species is the hurricanes that destroy their hollow-tree homes and ruin the forest mast on which they live.

Despite their extensive range and the fact that both species breed twice a year, these Louisiana squirrels are not easy to locate. They nap during the warm winter days and are difficult to see in the green winter woods. The canny hunter learns, however, to detect their gastronomic whimsies—sweet nuts, berries, or plums—and settles near the location of these delicacies.

SOME DO'S AND DON'TS IN THE PREPARATION OF SMALL GAME

DO fatten small game on milk and corn bread for three weeks before killing if possible.

DO kill quickly, dress, and bleed. To dress, make an incision from ribs to anus, remove intestines, and allow blood to drain. Remove head and wipe body cavity with a clean cloth. If dressed in the field, the animal may be left in its skin and wrapped in foil or paper for the trip home.

DO wear rubber gloves while cleaning game, for the animals may have tularemia.

DO skin by making a crosswise incision three inches long along the back; pull skin from hind legs toward head, then from incision toward tail.

DO leave small game in the refrigerator for several days or hang for at least forty-eight hours before cooking.

DO brush inside cavity with butter and lemon juice when ready to cook.

DO fry or broil young game, dusting it with a mixture of cinnamon and flour before browning.

DON'T try to cook older game by quick methods; parboil first, then pressure-cook or bake.

DO marinate older game in a mixture of olive oil and wine vinegar before cooking.

DO singe porcupine quills first, then scrape skin smooth.

DO remove kernels under front leg and along back of raccoons and opossums.

DO remove musk glands and string-like cords from legs of muskrat.

DON'T neglect to check state and federal laws concerning the tagging, storing, and shipping of game. Be sure to mark each wrapped package of game with species, number enclosed, and name and address of hunter.

BAKED SMALL GAME

Use any small game. Wash. Wipe with lemon cloth and rub inside with lemon and melted butter. Stuff cavity with pork sausage and sew up. Cook for one hour or longer in slow oven, basting often with lemon and currant jelly.

BURGOO

This is an old Southern dish. Sear disjointed small game in fresh lard or bear fat. Add some game stock or hot water and simmer with spices for several hours or until meat is almost done. Add cut-up pieces of pumpkin or cushaw (without the rind) and simmer another thirty minutes until the meat and vegetables are done. English burgoo was made outdoors in an iron pot using any game or fowl and several kinds of root vegetables. It was cooked at least ten hours over a slow fire. (One pound of meat serves two.)

PIT BARBECUE

Use any small game. Make a pit in ground. Burn hickory wood down to coals. Place wire grill over pit or make a frame of poles. Place animal on grill or frame. Baste often with barbecue sauce. Cook for one hour or until tender.

PRESSURE-COOKED SMALL GAME

If cooking tough game, wash and cut into serving pieces. Sear meat in hot grease with cooker top off. Then add one-half cup of water, salt, pepper, and one-half cup of chives. Close cooker and cook twenty minutes after pressure is up on cooker.

SMALL GAME A LA PROVENÇALE

Use any small game. Wash and quarter. Rub with pepper, salt, and butter. Fry chopped salt pork in skillet; add game, hot water or stock, one cup of chopped shallots, one-half cup of celery, and two bay leaves and cook for one hour, or until tender. Then remove extra juice and thicken with butter and flour. Add one cup of sherry and steep.

SMALL GAME PIE

Use any small game. Wash and quarter game and soak in lemon juice for several hours. Wipe dry and shake in paper bag of flour, salt, and pepper. Sear in hot grease, then simmer for one hour in hot water with *bouquet garni*. Add four carrots, two chopped onions, and six peeled new potatoes. Thicken with flour. Pour into a casserole that has been lined with pie crust. Top with crust and bake for twenty minutes in a hot oven.

SMALL GAME SAUTÉ BELLE

Wash and quarter rabbit or other small game. Sprinkle with salt, pepper, and flour. Fry in butter until brown, turning only once. Add minced shallots, cayenne pepper, and cream. Stir and simmer for one hour or until done. Sprinkle with nutmeg and serve with boiled rice. (Serves four.)

TENDERIZED SMALL GAME

The origin of this recipe is obscure, but it makes any common game an epicurean delight. Clean and disjoint the game, or cut the meat from the bone. Dust with salt and pepper. Rub with a pod of garlic. Rub well with vinegar or marinate in vinegar a few minutes. Place in a covered bowl in refrigerator for several days. Prepare any way desired. In Louisiana game is usually fried about thirty minutes. (Serves four.)

CHIPMUNK

A pity to eat this little bit of forest life, but such is done—and often! Dress the animal and remove kernels. Sprinkle with orange juice and rub with butter. Parboil ten minutes. Braise in hot grease. Add hot orange juice and minced raw ham. Simmer for twenty minutes. Add a little orange wine and let steep. (Serve two per person.)

MUSKRAT
FRIED MARSH HARE

Disjoint and parboil four dressed muskrat for twenty minutes. Drain and dry. Dip pieces of muskrat into a batter of egg yolks, one cup of cream, one cup of flour, and salt and pepper. Fry until crisp (about thirty minutes) in deep fat over slow fire. Make gravy by adding more cream and flour. Sprinkle with paprika. (Serves four.)

MUSKRAT CASSEROLE

Parboil six dressed muskrat in hot water for twenty minutes, with salt, and pepper. Add minced celery and shallots, salt, and cayenne pepper and continue boiling until meat falls from bones. Discard bones. Place one layer of meat and one layer of half-boiled new potatoes in a casserole with cream to cover. Top with slices of onion and bake for one hour. (Serves five or six.)

SHERRY MUSKRAT

Boil two dressed muskrat until meat falls free. Discard bones. Make a sauce by mixing the liquid left in pot and two hard-boiled eggs minced, one-half stick of butter, two tablespoons of flour, salt, pepper, and three teaspoons of dry mustard. Simmer a few minutes and add one cup of sherry. Add meat to sauce and steep. (Serves two.)

STEWED MUSKRAT

Fry slices of salt pork, then add dressed muskrat and a little hot water, salt, pepper, and bay leaf. Cook for forty minutes. When tender, pour off juice and brown meat in bacon drippings. (Serves one.)

OPOSSUM

A clear, cold night, baying of hounds, and flash of flambeaux form a picture dear to the Southerner's heart. Treeing possums has long been a nocturnal sport with country folk of the Deep South. Whether it be the large Virginia possum, the small Gulf possum, or the long-tailed Texas possum, both the hunt and its reward are exciting experiences. If the possum is taken alive, pen and feed him for two weeks on milk, bread, and persimmons.

CLAY-BAKED POSSUM

Prepare possum as for kitchen baking. Roll in a sheet of moist clay and cover with a bed of coals. Bake from one to four hours, depending on size and age of possum. Break away the clay and eat. (Serves six.)

IDLE ACRES PLANTATION POSSUM

Scald, dress, and pick hairs off possum. Do not skin. Wash well with hot lemon water. Place in a pressure cooker with a little water, salt, pepper, and hot red and green peppers. Cook fifteen minutes per pound. Drain and dust outside with black pepper. Pour some liquid over possum and roast until brown with peeled Louisiana yams. (Serves six.)

POSSUM ARKANSAS STYLE

Skin and dress possum. Wash inside and out with hot lemon water. Boil in hot water with salt, pepper, and sage for thirty minutes. Dust with flour and roast for one hour with paprika, strips of red and green peppers, salt pork strips, and hot water. Baste often until done. Cook sweet potatoes around possum if desired. (Serves six.)

POSSUM LOUISIANA STYLE

Dress and skin possum. Remove entrails, glands, head, and tail. Wash inside and out with hot water. Marinate overnight in large-game marinade (see p. 76) or soak in salt water. Rinse with hot water and wipe dry. Parboil one hour with salt, pepper, pepper-corns, and cut-up lemon. Remove fat. Stuff with herbs, butter, and bread crumbs. Sew up. Dust with flour and roast in oven for thirty minutes or until tender, basting often with beef stock. Serve with Louisiana yams. (Serves six.)

POSSUM DRESSING
À LA GOWANLOCH

Brown one large minced onion in lard, add chopped possum liver and cook for about forty minutes or until done. Add two cups of bread crumbs, one hard-cooked egg chopped fine, salt, and black and cayenne pepper. Add enough hot water to moisten. Use as possum stuffing.

RABBIT
CAJUN RABBIT

Skin and disjoint rabbit. Marinate overnight in enough red wine to cover, two pods of garlic, olive oil, spices, and a little thyme and bay leaf. Make a *roux* and in it fry rabbit pieces. Sim-mer for one hour or until tender on a slow fire with some of the strained marinade. (Serves four.)

COMPÈRE LAPIN

Dress, wash, and cut up rabbit. Sprinkle with salt and pepper and dust with flour. Brown in skillet in hot grease. Add one cup of minced shallots and two cups of sour cream and bake for one hour or more in oven in an iron pot. Add flour to cream gravy if desired. (Serves four.)

HASENPFEFFER

Dress a rabbit and cut into serving pieces. Marinate in large-game marinade (see p. 76) for thirty-six hours, turning often.

Sauté two cups of minced shallots with two cups of minced raw ham until ham is done. Remove from skillet. Dust rabbit with salt, pepper, and flour. Brown in skillet. Add strained, hot marinade to rabbit, ham, and onion. Simmer in a covered skillet for one hour or until done. Add one cup of red wine and steep if desired. (Serves six.)

KEBAB

Cut rabbit or other small game into chunks. Impale on skewers or tree branches. Baste with butter and lemon and broil for forty minutes over coals. Bay-tree skewers are best. (Serve one skewer to a person.)

MELISSA'S RABBIT AND TURNIPS

Dress and wash rabbit. Cut in quarters. Dredge in salt, pepper, and flour. Fry for forty minutes in deep fat, covered. Drain and serve with turnips and corn bread. (Serves four.)

MEXICAN RABBIT PIE

Dress, clean, and cut up one rabbit. Boil for thirty minutes with *bouquet garni* until done. Sauté one pod of minced garlic in hot grease with three cups of minced shallots. Add two cups of corn, two cups of peeled and cut tomatoes, one cup of minced black olives, one teaspoon of curry powder, three teaspoons of chili powder, salt, and pepper. Mix three cups of yellow corn meal with one egg yolk and one cup of chicken stock. Mix all ingredients together and bake in casserole for one hour. (Serves six.)

RABBIT CHOP SUEY

Dress, and clean two rabbits. Boil for one hour in water with a *bouquet garni*. Save stock. Cut up the meat and fry it in hot grease, adding one can of drained bean sprouts, one can of water chestnuts cut fine, one-half bunch of minced celery, and six chopped onions. Let simmer a few minutes and add one can of bean shoots. Next dissolve two tablespoons of cornstarch in three tablespoons of cold water and two tablespoons of soy sauce. Add this to mixture. Next add one tablespoon of Bead molasses and a little salt. Simmer a few minutes and add some stock. Serve in soup bowls with boiled rice and soy sauce. (Serves six or more.)

RABBIT IN A BLANKET

Boil rice. When done, stir in one-half cup of minced shallots, one cup of minced cooked rabbit, salt, and pepper. Steam head of cabbage for ten minutes. Remove leaves. Stuff each leaf with rice mixture. Place all stuffed and folded leaves in a casserole. Pour "Creole Sauce" (see p. 216) over it. Bake for twenty minutes. (Serves four.)

RACCOON

If possible, pen coon for a week or so and feed on milk, corn bread, and persimmons. When ready to cook, parboil for one hour. Roast for thirty minutes with yams. Remove outer fat.

BAKED COON

Marinate in vinegar and pepper overnight. Dry and rub with garlic. Roast for two hours, basting often with hot water and one clove of garlic, salt, and pepper. Bake fifteen minutes per pound. (Serves six.)

COON VIN ORDINAIRE

Dress and skin as in "Baked Coon." Soak overnight in a marinade made of enough "dago" red wine to cover, one cup of minced shallots, salt, and pepper. Dry. Strain marinade. Rub coon with garlic and then with olive oil. Pour marinade over coon and bake one hour or longer, basting often. Add peeled Louisiana yams when half done. (Serves six.)

DRUNK COON

Skin and dress raccoon. Rub with gin and bake for one hour or more, basting often with hot water, pepper, and salt. When done, pour in one-fourth cup of dry French vermouth and steep a few minutes. (Serves six.)

SPICED COON

Skin and dress as in baked coon. Parboil with salt, pepper, and peppercorns. Rub with cinnamon and allspice. Dust with flour and bake until done, basting often with stock containing whole apples and one teaspoon of brown sugar. Stuff with dressing of bread crumbs, pecan meats, and orange juice if desired. Roast for two hours. When done, sprinkle with brown sugar and brown. Sprinkle with minced pecans and serve with pineapple fried in butter. (Serves six.)

SQUIRREL
OUTDOOR STEW

Boil slowly in a big iron pot over coals, ten washed and butter-rubbed squirrels in a mixture of thirty peeled tomatoes, ten cans of corn, four pounds of sliced salt pork, five pounds of peeled potatoes, ten onions, and two pounds of butter beans. Cook one hour or until squirrels are tender. Use enough salt and pepper to season and some Worcestershire sauce. When done, thicken with flour and simmer a while longer. (Serves twenty or more.)

SQUIRREL BELLE CHASSE

Use four squirrels. Dress, clean, and cut in serving pieces. Rub with lemon and keep in refrigerator overnight. Wipe with damp cloth and rub with salt and pepper. Dust with flour and fry until brown (about forty minutes). Cover with cream and bake in oven for twenty minutes. (Serves five or six.)

SQUIRREL HEAD POTPIE

Boil ten squirrel heads until tender in just enough water to cover. Make pie crust and line casserole. Place a layer of heads and some juice. Dot with butter and sprinkle with salt and pepper. Make another layer of heads, juice, and more pie crust strips. Cook in oven for one-half hour. (Serves six.)

SQUIRREL RAVIOLI

To make a filling for this type of pasta, sauté one pod of garlic in a teaspoon of fresh bacon grease, and add one cup of minced, cooked squirrel meat and one cup of minced water cress.

To make pasta, mix one cup of flour with one teaspoon of salt. Place in a wooden bowl and make a hole in center of pasta. Place one beaten egg in hole and pour one teaspoon of butter over egg. Moisten this with warm water. Knead. Roll out on a floured board and cut into oval shapes. Stuff dough ovals with filling and fold. Pinch the edges with a fork. Drop gently into boiling salted water and simmer fifteen minutes. Place on a platter with the sauce given for "Meat Balls" (see p. 171). Serve with Parmesan cheese. (Serves four to six.)

SQUIRREL STEW

Dress forty squirrels. Place the squirrels in a big iron pot over coals. Place three bottles of cooking oil in the pot. Let the meat braise for ten minutes. Add one bushel of peeled tomatoes, one package of cornstarch, ten sliced onions, four pounds of cut-up game or pork, twelve dozen ears of corn (cut from the cob), ten green peppers sliced, one bunch of celery minced, four red peppers (with seeds removed), one cup of Worcestershire sauce, one-fourth cup of Tabasco sauce, salt, and pepper. Simmer several hours with two gallons of water. (Serves fifty or more.)

DES OIE ET CANARDS
(About Geese and Ducks)

Each year thousands of feathered tourists come to Louisiana to sojourn among the four million acres of the state's fifteen-hundred-dred mile strip of coastal marsh and tidal plateau. Among the visitors are the majority of all the blue geese in North America, as well as the Canada goose, Hutchin's goose, snow goose, lesser snow goose, lesser Canada goose, brant, and white-fronted goose. They make their pilgrimage southward each Fall in a nonstop flight of a few days during which they seem to be hurrying on to a family reunion among the grassy flats and shell deposits.

Great flocks of all kinds of ducks also make their seasonal journey to Louisiana, some drifting into the inland lakes, oak flats, and rice fields, and others soaring straight for the deltaic coast. Like the geese, they choose the route known as the Mississippi Flyway—a great aerial traffic artery—for their annual migrations, and among their numbers are the mallard (*canard français*), American pintail (*paille-en-queue*), gadwall (*canard gris*), blue-winged teal (*canard printanière*), green-winged teal (congo duck), cinnamon teal, shoveler (spoonbill), baldpate (*zinzin*), canvasback (*canard cheval*), black duck (*canard noir*), wood duck (*canard branchu*), mottled duck (*canard des isles*), red head (*violon*), greater and lesser scaups (*dos gris*), ringneck, fulverous tree duck, ruddy duck (gotdam), old squaw, bufflehead (*marionette*), American goldeneye (*canard Canadien*), merganser (*bec-scie*), and other species of pond and sea ducks. Almost all of them, with the exception of the merganser, are considered tasty eating; two of them— the wood duck and the mottled duck—are year-round residents, and the former is protected by stringent laws.

Most of the wintering ducks and geese remain in Louisiana for the entire season, but others relax, refuel, and wing on to spend the winter in Central and South America, returning to Louisiana for a while on their return trip northward. Folk on the bayou say that a band of blue geese lingers behind each season to estimate the next year's food supply before joining their web-toed brethren back up north. Fantastic, yes—but possibly true, as any hunter who has been outsmarted by a goose can tell you.

SOME DO'S AND DON'TS IN THE PREPARATION OF WILD FOWL

DO kill fowl at once to retain the full flavor.

DO draw at once and brush fowl cavity with vinegar if it has been shot through the intestines.

DO remove the craw of all fowl except ducks and geese (their gizzards do the grinding work on their food), and the intestines and oil sac in the tail.

DO remove the fat from coots to eliminate some of the wild taste;

wash them in water with a little soap, rinse well, and marinate in citrus juices overnight.

DO hang ducks and geese more than one day—the longer hung, the gamier the taste, and in Louisiana this *faisandé* is considered desirable.

DO remove tendons from the legs of fowl.

DO pluck fowl dry.

DO pluck fowl that is to be frozen before refrigerating and hang in moisture-proof paper bags in near-freezing temperatures.

DO leave feathers on fowl that is to be shipped on ice.

DO stuff fowl with apples and celery overnight, removing the stuffing before cooking.

DO rub fowl with lemon juice, herbs, and olive oil or butter.

DO fry or broil young fowl; stew, roast, fricassee, or pressure-cook old fowl.

DO use a wet dressing for old birds.

DO use cold water for fowl that is to be boiled or parboiled.

DO cook fowl with wine to tenderize and garlic to reduce the high flavor.

DON'T skin any fowl except coot.

DON'T scald fowl.

DON'T soak fowl in brine. If it is fishy in taste, cook with onion or garlic.

DON'T wash the cavity of fowl if you are still in camp, for contact with water will start deterioration.

DO investigate state and federal laws concerning the tagging, storing, and shipping of wild fowl. It is advisable to mark wrapped packages with the species of fowl, number enclosed, and name and address of the hunter.

HOW TO CARVE FOWL

Place cooked fowl on a platter, the feet pointing toward the carver. With left hand, stick carving fork in fowl breast and hold firmly. With carving knife in right hand, cut thigh joint and force leg away from body of fowl. Next cut wing joint, severing wing from body. Then, holding knife at an angle, slice breast, cut-

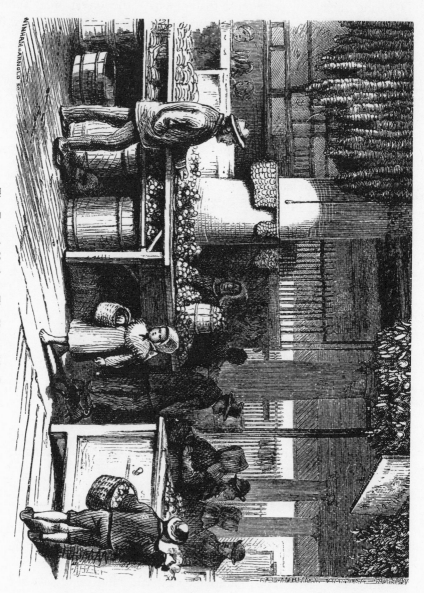

The French Market - The Vegetable Corner

ting in a downward motion from a position near the fork. In carving turkey or other large fowl the leg may also be sliced.

When one side of fowl has been carved, the other may be carved in the same manner.

BAKED DUCK

After duck is dressed rub inside and out with butter. Stuff with sauerkraut and sew up. Cook thirty minutes per pound or until done. Baste with beef or chicken stock. (Serves two.)

BAKED CANVASBACK

Dress duck. Rub with lemon, salt, pepper, and butter. Make a dressing of one cup of minced celery sautéed with one-half cup of minced shallots. Add two cups of wet bread (squeezed) and one cup of pecans. Stuff duck and baste often with butter and cooked-giblets stock. Bake thirty minutes per pound or until done. More stock may be added to baste. (Serves two.)

BAKED FRENCH DUCK

Stuff duck with turnips or with a dressing made of cooked wild rice, minced shallots, minced parsley, and boiled giblets. Use enough butter to soften dressing. Baste often with hot water or bouillon and bake from one to three hours, depending on age of the duck. (Serves two.)

BAKED MALLARD

After dressing duck, stuff with chicken livers which have been sautéed in butter mixed with minced green olives. Bake thirty minutes per pound or until done in a hot oven, basting often with a sauce of butter and stock. (Serves two.)

BRAISED PINTAIL DUCK

After a duck is dressed, brush inside and out with a sauce made of butter, lemon juice, salt, and pepper. Stuff fowl with raw turnips and sew up or close with skewers. Place on a rack in pan, cover, and roast with one-half cup of beef stock. Cook about forty minutes per pound. (Serves two.)

BROILED CANVASBACK

After dressing a young duck, split it and rub with salt and white pepper. Place bacon strips over bird and broil, basting often with a sauce of hot water, butter, and minced shallots. Broil for thirty minutes or until done. (Serves two.)

CONGO DUCK

The congo duck in Louisiana is actually the green-winged teal and was named for the (also small) Congo slaves. After picking and cleaning the duck, rub it with butter and place whole in pan. Make a sauce of chopped mint, butter, and a small amount of mint jelly. Roast thirty minutes per pound or until done. Baste often with this sauce. When done add one jigger of green crème de menthe to the sauce and steep the duck in the sauce for one hour. Garnish with mint and lemon. White wine must be served with teal. (Serves one.)

DUCK A LA NUDE

Clean and pick one duck. Rub with lemon and fresh bacon grease. Place over low coals on aluminum foil or under broiler for forty minutes basting with butter and lemon. (Serves two.)

DUCK ON THE COALS

Split one duck down the back after it is picked and cleaned. Place on coals and cook forty minutes or until done. Pour a sauce of melted butter and parsley over the duck when ready to serve. (Serves two.)

DUCK MANDARIN

Clean and dry-pick a duck. Rub with butter and soy sauce. Stuff with a dressing of cooked wild rice (see p. 206), minced celery, minced water chestnuts, and bean sprouts. Sew duck up and place

Louisiana mandarin segments around it in the roasting pan. Roast thirty minutes per pound or until done. Baste with orange wine to which has been added small pieces of candied ginger. Add orange wine and steep when done. (Serves two.)

MUD-BAKED DUCK

Mud-baking is a favorite way of cooking duck in the Mississippi Delta country. The duck must be drawn, but the feathers may be left on. Roll out a sheet of moistened clay and wrap the duck in it. Place in a bed of hickory coals and cover with the coals. Bake up to three hours, depending on the size and age of the bird. The skin peels off when the mud is removed, and the bird is then ready to eat. Any small bird or animal may be cooked in this manner. (Serves two.)

TEAL CHÉNIÈRE

Use a young duck. After picking and cleaning, split it and rub the inside with butter. Place in a pan and broil for twenty minutes, turning often until done. Pour brandy over duck and serve aflame on a silver platter. (Serves one.)

TEAL WITH CHERRIES

Clean and pluck a teal duck. Leave in refrigerator overnight after stuffing with apples and celery. Remove apples and celery and stuff with large black cherries that have been marinated in cherry wine. Bake thirty minutes per pound, basting with a sauce of butter and cherry wine. (Serves one.)

ROAST DUCK WITH BERRIES

After picking and cleaning one duck, rub with butter. Mix one jar of blackberry jelly with one stick of butter, and season with salt and pepper. Place in pan with duck. Stuff duck with wild blackberries and sew up. Roast for thirty minutes per pound or until done. Baste often with sauce. Add one cup of red wine to remaining sauce when done and let duck steep in this for one hour. (Serves two.)

SPAGHETTI WITH DUCK

Sauté one cup of minced shallots, one cup of minced green peppers, and one pod of garlic in butter. Remove garlic. Add twelve fresh, peeled tomatoes, a pinch or orégano, salt, cayenne, three cans of mushrooms, and two bay leaves. Simmer thirty minutes. Add slices of one cooked duck to this sauce and let them remain in sauce thirty minutes. Remove bay leaves. Boil one pound of Italian spaghetti in water for ten minutes, and rinse under cold, running water. Drain and place in bowl. Pour hot sauce over spaghetti and sprinkle with Parmesan cheese. (Serves six.)

TORTILLAS WITH DUCK SAUCE

Make tortillas by sifting one cup of corn starch, one-half teaspoon of salt, and three tablespoons of corn meal. Mix with one-half cup of milk. Add two beaten eggs and three tablespoons of melted butter. Bake cakes about twenty minutes on preheated griddle.

For the sauce, sauté in butter one minced onion and one pod of minced garlic. Add two cups of chopped cooked duck. Add three peeled, chopped tomatoes, three teaspoons of chili powder, one teaspoon of cumin seed, and a pinch of coriander. Simmer for ten minutes and serve on tortillas. This sauce may also be served with fried eggs. (Serves four.)

GOOSE
BREAST OF GOOSE

The cooked breast of a goose may be sliced, and served cold with a wine sauce or served with brandy poured over it and lighted before serving. Be sure to heat the brandy before pouring. (Serves six.)

GOOSE DES ALLEMANDS

Draw and pick one goose. Rub inside cavity with vinegar, salt, and pepper. Hang in a refrigerated place. Save the blood drippings. Mix blood with one cup of vinegar and place in the refrigerator. Disjoint the goose and rub with garlic and olive oil. Place in an iron skillet and braise. Slowly add meat stock, one cup of minced shallots, one cup of minced celery, a few bay leaves, chervil, and thyme. Cook goose thirty minutes per pound or until tender. Add vinegar-blood to meat stock and simmer about one hour. (The vinegar keeps the blood from congealing.) Remove goose and strain stock. Place stock back in skillet and add two cups of red wine, two teaspoons of flour, and a dash of paprika. Simmer ten minutes more and serve with goose and boiled rice. (Serves eight.)

MOLE OF GOOSE

Sauté the cooked breast of one goose in butter for ten minutes. Separately sauté minced green peppers, almonds, and ground cinnamon and cloves. Add several bars of chocolate and one-half cup of grapefruit rind. Add one cup of cream and pour mixture over slices of goose. Simmer a few minutes and sprinkle with sesame seeds when ready to serve. Serve with Spanish rice (see p. 206). (Serves six.)

ROAST BRANT

Pick and clean one goose and rub with butter. Stuff cavity with orange segments and wild nut meats. Sew up and place in pan. Make a sauce of orange juice, fried goose livers, one stick of butter, salt, white pepper, and a dash of cinnamon sugar. Roast goose for thirty minutes per pound or until tender. Baste often with sauce. (Serves six.)

ROAST GOOSE

After the goose is plucked dry and drawn, rub the cavity with lemon juice, white pepper, and salt. Stuff the fowl with peeled apples and leave in the refrigerator overnight. In the morning remove the apples and stuff with a dressing. Sew up, rub the fowl with fresh bacon grease, and tie the legs and wings to the body. Place a wet towel over the goose and baste often with stock or bouillon. Roast thirty minutes per pound or until tender, and serve with "Apricot Sauce" (see p. 217) or other fruit sauce. (Serves eight.)

Stuffing

Wash two cups of wild rice and soak overnight. Boil as in "Boiled Wild Rice" (see p. 206). Sauté minced shallots and mushrooms in butter. In another skillet fry chicken or fowl livers for twenty minutes or until tender. Mince livers and add to shallots and mushrooms. Add one-half cup of fowl broth and the wild rice. Mix and stuff the fowl. (Serves eight.)

WILD TURKEY

As a native of this country, the wild turkey is our truly American game bird and should rank first among the species *Gallus americana*. His natural intelligence, regal attire, and majestic posture have made him king of all feathered royalty and have earned him man's respect as well.

The wild turkey is one of Louisiana's few nonmigrant fowl, and small flocks of them may still be found feeding and roosting together in the upland ridges and river valleys of this part of the Deep South. In any gathering of hunters, "talking turkey" is a favorite pastime, and the questions of what "callers" to use, the best methods of hunting, the feed and habitat that best enhances wild turkey flavor for use on the Christmas table—all these are topics of endless conversation. But, whether he's bottomland- or bluff-fed, "Ole Longbeard"—hard to hit but good to eat—is elegant fare for gourmets.

In preparing a turkey for the indoor table, place in the refrigerator for twenty-four hours before stuffing and cooking. Rub fowl with butter and dredge lightly with flour. Sew up bird after stuffing, cover with a thin, wet towel, and roast for thirty minutes per pound, basting occasionally.

BOILED TURKEY

Back in the days when there were many old, tough toms roaming about the woods, they were boiled over the campfire, stuffed with celery, onions, herbs, and wild nut meats, then simmered an hour or more over a slow fire. This fowl stock was skimmed often. (Serves eight.)

FOWL À LA WESTERFIELD

If one really wants to "put on the dog" and is of the chosen few who have the means, he may enjoy a festive holiday fowl à la Westerfield:

Take one quail, dressed; one duck, dressed; one goose, dressed; one turkey, dressed. Sauté each fowl in butter. Stuff quail with pecans. Place quail in duck and stuff sliced peeled apples around it. Place duck in goose with orange segments around it. Place goose in turkey and stuff corn meal dressing around it. Bake in an uncovered roaster three hours or longer, basting often.

FOWL EN GELÉE

Boil the fowl for an hour or more with bay leaves, thyme, rosemary, and chopped lemon, shallots, celery stalks and tops, one clove of garlic, and cloves. Remove fowl when tender and cut up. Let stock boil down to one cup of liquid. Strain. Mix fowl, capers, minced pimiento, and stock with two envelopes of dissolved gelatin. Mold and chill. (Serves six.)

GRANDPÈRE TOMAS

If the turkey is on the senile side, cook by steaming. Place the disjointed bird in a casserole with powdered spices, butter, and apple juice. Place casserole in a turkey roaster and pour water in almost to top of casserole. Place top on roaster and steam for several hours. Any ancient fowl or small game should be tender and "good eatin'" after this process. Herbs may be substituted for spices. (Serves eight or more.)

TURKEY HARICOT

Sauté one cup of minced shallots in butter with twelve small half-cooked new potatoes for five minutes. Add a small amount of chicken bouillon, stock, or giblet stock and cook until potatoes are done. Add cut-up pieces of cooked turkey and four cut hard-cooked eggs. Simmer a few minutes. Add one-half cup of thick cream and simmer a few minutes more or until hash is thick enough.

Serve with hot grits and hot biscuits for a real Southern breakfast. (Serves eight.)

WILD TURKEY BREASTS

Soak breasts in cream overnight. Cut in pieces. Dry and dip in egg yolk and then in pancake mix. Fry in butter for twenty minutes or until tender. Serve with a sauce of bread crumbs, mushrooms, green peas, capers, and cream. Old birds may be parboiled until done then the breasts cut out to fry. (Serves six.)

TURKEY DRESSINGS

Dressing No. 1

Mix approximately four cups of bread crumbs, one stick of butter, three cups of chopped apples, two cups of chopped celery, one cup of raisins, pinch of marjoram, salt, pepper, and three cups of parboiled giblets.

Dressing No. 2

Mix one pan of corn bread, one-half loaf of bread crumbs, enough melted butter to moisten, three hard-cooked eggs cut fine, one cup of minced celery stalks and tops, and six minced sausages.

Dressing No. 3

Toast one loaf of sliced bread and break into small crumbs. Parboil three cups of giblets in measure for measure of water and orange wine. Mix bread crumbs with giblets and add three cups of pecans, minced and sautéed in butter. Add one teaspoon of melted butter and one-half teaspoon each of mace, cinnamon, and ground nutmeg. Mix with a small amount of sherry and stuff fowl.

Dressing No. 4 (à la Maman)

Sauté six smoked, minced sausages a few minutes. Remove and sauté in same skillet for five minutes one cup of minced shallots, one cup of minced green peppers, one cup of minced celery, and one pod of minced garlic. Add one can of minced mushrooms and one cup of minced walnuts or hickory nuts. Place sausage back in pan and add four hard-cooked, minced eggs and one-fourth cup of minced celery tops. Boil giblets in pan of bouillon stock until done. Mix giblets and other ingredients with corn bread crumbs and two cups of white bread crumbs. Moisten with giblet stock. Stuff bird, leaving enough dressing to cook a separate panful.

Dressing No. 5

Sauté one can of mushrooms with four cups of minced almonds and five pieces of crisp bacon in butter for a few minutes. Mix with four cups of cooked wild rice and enough white wine to moisten. Let cool and stuff bird.

Dressing No. 6

Mix one loaf of French-bread crumbs and salt and pepper with two cans of potted meat, one can of minced lobster, one large can of mushrooms. Sauté in butter. Stuff fowl and baste with one pound of melted butter and one quart of white wine.

CAMPFIRE TURKEY

The glow of a campfire adds magic to the flavor of wild turkey. Here is the method as practiced back in the North Louisiana hills. Use a young bird and stuff with any dressing. Sew up. Rub with bacon drippings. Dust with flour and hang on a crane before a reflector fire or over a steady hickory fire. Mix hot water with bacon drippings and place in a pan under fowl. Baste and turn often. Boil giblets in dripping pan and add flour for gravy.

BOBWHITE OR QUAIL

Our French-speaking cousins call the bobwhite *perdreau* and *oiseau*, but to most Louisianians this game little fellow is just plain *bird*. According to ornithologists, the bobwhite is indigenous to North America, and acquired its name from New Englanders who thought that this bird resembled the European species they had known. Virginians called the same bird partridge after his counterpart in the Old World. One may hunt bird practically all over the state, even though he is an upland fowl—in the maritime borderlands and swamps, as well as in the arable districts and in the longleaf pine stands. A Western subspecies of quail also has been introduced into Louisiana and is known locally as the Texas bobwhite. This imported species is a fast ground-runner and is shorter in stature than the Louisiana bird.

CAILLES AUX RAISINS

(As prepared and served at Owen Brennan's French and Creole Vieux Carré Restaurant in New Orleans.)

Pick, clean, and dress six quail without removing the heads. Rub the inside cavity with salt and pepper, then place five or six peeled grapes in the opening of each bird. Truss, placing the legs alongside the breasts and securing the heads over the left thighs. Use a fine needle and thread for this operation. Next rub the outside of each bird with salt and pepper. Spread a little butter over the surface. Wrap each bird in a grape leaf and tie with thin slices of salt pork. Roast the birds in a hot oven for fifteen to eighteen minutes, using about two tablespoons of melted butter for basting. Roast older birds for a longer time. Discarding the trussing ties, arrange the birds, heads out, on a heated platter to keep them warm. Next remove all fat from the pan and add one-half cup of dry white wine, reducing it over a moderate flame to one-fourth cup of liquid, meanwhile scraping the pan thoroughly. Add two-thirds cup of rich veal stock and bring to a boil. Next add about three dozen peeled grapes, heated but not boiled. After tasting the sauce for seasoning, pour over the birds distributing the grapes evenly among the birds. A large bunch of white grapes in the center of the dish makes an effective garnish. Serve the birds hot. (Serves six.)

COUPLE DE PERDRIX

Dress two birds and rub with lemon-butter (see p. 223). Grill thirty minutes with a sauce of one stick of butter, one-fourth cup of lime juice, and one cup of raisins. Serve on toast with sauce. (Serves two.)

DUTCH OVEN QUAIL

This is either an inside or an outside dish. If outside, cook over coals. Melt one stick of butter in a pot with one can of mushrooms or wild nut meats, in which put cleaned, picked birds. Brown well in open Dutch oven over fire; then place top on Dutch oven and cook for forty minutes over slow fire on low coals, adding more butter if needed. When done, add one cup of white wine and let stay near fire until ready to eat. (Serve one quail per person.)

ETHEL'S BOBWHITE

Rub two birds with salt and pepper. Dredge with flour. Brown lightly in fat, then cover and add a small amount of boiling water. Allow birds to steam thirty minutes or until done. (Serves two.)

GOLDEN YAM QUAIL

Dress four quail and stuff with cooked giblets and minced shallots. Partially bake four large yams. Remove the potatoes from oven and make a hole in center. Place quail in yams, and stuff pecan meats around them. Stick several pieces of butter around birds and close yams. Bake slowly for about forty minutes or until done. (Serves four.)

KISATCHIE QUAIL

After four birds are picked and cleaned, soak overnight in refrigerator in equal parts of milk and cream. Dry and shake in a bag with salt, pepper, and flour. Fry in butter in a deep skillet about twenty minutes or until done. Remove birds from skillet and make a cream gravy by browning one-fourth cup of flour and then slowly adding warm cream. (Serves four.)

MEXICAN QUAIL EXOTIC

Soak two disjointed quail overnight in cream, salt, and pepper. Dry and brown evenly in olive oil. Sprinkle with salt, pepper, and grated nutmeg. Place in a casserole with sliced mushrooms and some of the mushroom juice. Bake thirty-five minutes in a moderate oven. Serve hot with rice and guava jelly. (Serves two.)

QUAIL TICKFAW

After four birds are cleaned and picked, rub with melted butter, salt, and pepper. Tie wings and legs to body. Broil under slow fire for about thirty minutes, basting often with salted butter, one tablespoon of flour, and one teaspoon of Worcestershire sauce. (Serves four.)

QUAIL PONTALBA

After birds are picked and cleaned, split down back. Shake in paper bag containing pancake flour, salt, and pepper. Fry for twenty minutes in butter in a deep skillet. Remove quail from skillet and make a sauce of two cups of orange wine, one cup of orange segments, one cup of nut meats, and three tablespoons of grated orange peel. Bring to a boil and place birds in sauce to steep for thirty minutes. (Serve one bird per person.)

QUAIL WITH EGGPLANT

Peel ten eggplants and cut in cubes. Place them in a small amount of clear water and simmer for thirty minutes or until tender. Sauté four minced onions with four pods of garlic. Add one minced bell pepper. Sauté until tender but not brown. In a Dutch oven place six quail (either whole or cut in halves) with one cup of cooking oil. Add three ounces of sauterne and sauté. Then add the contents of the skillet and the well-drained eggplant. Cook over a slow fire for about forty-five minutes or until the quail are done. Add two ounces of sauterne and let steep for an hour. (Serves six.)

Squirrels, ducks, or other game and fowl also may be cooked by this recipe.

ROAST QUAIL

Clean and pick, but never skin, birds. Sear them ten minutes in a skillet with butter and then impale on a green stick wrapped with bacon. Roast thirty minutes per pound over coals. Turn often until done. (Serve one quail per person.)

YELLOW RICE AND BIRDS

Rub disjointed birds with lime, salt, and pepper. Fry twenty minutes in butter. When done add one cup of sliced apples, one cup of sliced pineapple, one-half cup of raisins, and two cups of red wine. Let steep and serve with Spanish rice (see p. 206). (Serve one quail per person.)

COOTS, GALLINULES, AND RAILS

Generally known as "marsh" or "mud hens," these marsh-loving birds are Louisiana's most unsought and unsung fowl. For the most part, they are retiring and do their traveling about by night, and, because of these characteristics, are scorned by out-of-state hunters as poor shooting. Only the Florida and purple gallinules—the fancy dans of the shoreland colonies—are exceptions to this generally retiring attitude; they are fond of making daylight treks along the highway to show off their flashy plumage.

Despite the shyness of the coot or *poule d'eau*, and of the clapper, king, Virginia, yellow, and small sora rails, all the bayou folk know that they are tasty eating when properly prepared, and they greatly relish them.

BAKED POULE D'EAU

Skin two coots and remove all fat to destroy the strong taste. Dress them and then brush inside and out with lemon juice, salt, and pepper. Let stand in refrigerator overnight. Wipe with damp cloth and split in halves. Parboil with pinch of soda. Shake in paper bag with flour, salt, and pepper. Sear for five minutes in hot butter. Bake thirty minutes per pound in oven, basting with a butter sauce. Serve with wild rice; or serve only the breasts fried in butter and then simmered in white wine. (Serves two.)

COOT BREASTS AU LAIT

Skin two coots and remove fat. Parboil in water for thirty minutes with a *bouquet garni* of herbs. Remove the breasts and place in a casserole. Cover with cream; season with salt, white pepper, and paprika. Cook for twenty minutes in a casserole. Top with strips of pimientos. (Serves two.)

COOTS IN SOY SAUCE

Prepare and parboil two coots as above. Remove breasts and marinate them in a mixture of four teaspoons of soy sauce, one-fourth cup of lime juice, a dash of salt, and several slivers of ginger root. Let soak for several hours. Drain and broil for thirty minutes, basting with marinade and melted butter. Add slices of water chestnuts when almost done. Garnish with slices of celery hearts. (Serves two.)

CURRIED COOT BREASTS

Skin two coots and remove their fat. Parboil for thirty minutes in clear water with a *bouquet garni* of spices until tender. Cut breasts and prepare curry as in "Curried Crabs" (see p. 143), substituting coot breasts for crab meat. (Serves two.)

MUD HEN CASSEROLE

Prepare one coot as above. Place in a casserole with chopped celery, shallots, mushrooms, and hot chicken bouillon and cook forty minutes or longer. When tender add one-half cup of sherry and let steep. (Serves two.)

GALLINULE À LA BOGUE FALAYA

Dress and skin one bird. Brush with lemon juice, salt, and pepper and let stand in the refrigerator overnight. Wipe with a damp cloth. Brush with butter and let simmer for forty minutes or until done in a mixture of one teaspoon of paprika, one cup of minced shallots, one quart of stock, one pod of garlic, one-half cup of minced celery stalks and tops, and black pepper. (Serves one or two.)

RAIL GRAND CHENIER

Dress two rails. Brush with lemon juice and let stay in refrigerator overnight. Wipe with damp cloth. Brush with butter, salt, and pepper. Broil thirty minutes under the broiler, basting with a sauce of lemon, butter, and melted guava jelly. Serve with whole guavas and boiled rice; or grill with bacon and lemon. (Serves two.)

DOVES

Dove to most Louisianians is the Eastern mourning dove or turtle dove that loves and lingers in the corn and cane fields, but the Western mourning dove, the Eastern white-winged dove, and the Eastern ground dove also thrive in Louisiana. The ground dove has a fiery disposition, although small in size. In Louisiana it is considered bad luck to kill this bird. The pigeon or rock dove is also sometimes found wild in Louisiana.

Doves prepared in any way should be brushed first with melted butter outside and then inside with lemon or lime juice.

BAKED DOVES

After two birds are picked and cleaned, brush with melted butter, salt, and pepper. Stuff with a dressing made of a pinch of cinnamon, a pinch of coriander, a teaspoon of chutney, one cup of bread crumbs, and one-half cup of walnut meats. Sew bird up and place in a pan with one cup of water and two cups of orange juice. Bake for twenty-five minutes or until done. Add one cup of orange wine and segments of oranges. Let steep for thirty minutes. (Serves two.)

DOVE CHANTECLAIR

After dressing four birds, marinate overnight in enough red wine to cover. Sauté one cup of minced shallots and two cans of minced mushrooms for ten minutes in butter in an iron skillet. Add birds and enough chicken stock to cover. Add *bouquet garni* and simmer slowly for twenty minutes with cover on skillet until half done. Remove spice bag. Add tiny new potatoes and simmer for twenty minutes or until potatoes are cooked. When fowl is done, add one cup of red wine and steep. (Serves four.)

DOVES IN CHAMPAGNE

Dress six birds and rub with butter, salt, and white pepper. Place them in a Dutch oven with one fifth bottle of champagne. Cook for forty minutes or until done. Remove the birds. Pour the sauce into a double boiler and add four cups of cream. Stir. Cook five minutes. Add the beaten yolks of three eggs to sauce. Cut the fires off under boiler and blend in eggs. Keep boiler on the warm stove. Pour the warm sauce over the birds that have been kept hot. Sprinkle with minced, toasted macaroons. (Serves six.)

DOVES SAUVAGE

After two doves are cleaned and picked, truss by tying wings and legs to body. Wrap bacon slices around bird. Place in a pan and roast for thirty minutes, basting often with a sauce of hot water, lemon, and butter. Serve on toast with gravy drippings. (Serves two.)

DOVE SAUCE PIQUANT

After four birds are dressed, shake in a paper bag with flour, salt, and pepper. Fry in butter for twenty minutes. In another skillet sauté for ten minutes one cup of minced shallots, four peeled Creole tomatoes, two slices of green pepper, one hot red pepper, one-half pod of garlic, two bay leaves, a pinch of rosemary, and a sprig of thyme. Add three cups of chicken stock and simmer one hour. Then add one cup of sherry and place birds in sauce to steep thirty minutes. Serve with rice. (Serves four.)

DOVES SAUTÉ FLORENTINE

Dress and broil three birds for thirty minutes. Make a sauce of one cup of ground spinach and one-fourth cup of parsley, one cup of bread crumbs, two beaten eggs, and cream to moisten. Simmer this sauce twenty minutes. Serve over the broiled doves on toast. (Serves three.)

DOVE VIN BLANC

Dress four birds and fry twenty minutes in olive oil. Sprinkle with flour and add enough beef bouillon to cover. Add one teaspoon of whole cloves, two cinnamon sticks, two nutmegs, paprika, salt, and white pepper. Simmer for ten minutes. Add one can of mushrooms and one cup of minced shallots that have been sautéed in butter. Add one cup of minced ripe olives and one cup of white wine. Let steep thirty minutes. Reheat and serve with Spanish rice. (Serves four.)

POULET AU POT

Cut two cleaned doves in halves. Braise in a skillet. Add some fowl stock and simmer for forty-five minutes with several whole nutmegs, two cinnamon sticks, and four slices of lime. Two ruta-bagas sliced very thin may be added. When done, drop small dumplings into the pot and cook for ten minutes. (Serves two.)

SPICED DOVES

Dress two birds and rub with mint. Place in foil with thick cream, mint, salt, white pepper, powdered cinnamon, nutmeg, and all-spice. Close foil, wrap, and cook for forty minutes on coals or in an oven. (Serves two.)

BROILED ORTOLAN

The ortolan—actually the bobolink or reed bird—is mentioned in the earliest histories of Louisiana and apparently was a favorite of the early settlers. A toothsome bit of eating, it should be prepared by placing it under the broiler for twenty-five minutes, basting often with a sauce made of one cup of lime juice, two teaspoons of Worcestershire sauce, two dashes of Tabasco sauce, and one stick of butter. Serve on toasted trenchers of French bread, pouring the sauce over the bread.

PHEASANT

This fowl is not a native of Louisiana, but is raised on large plantations and hunted here. It should be hung longer than other fowl.

GAMMON'S PHEASANT

After bird is picked and cleaned, and the oil sac at base of the tail removed, rub with salt and white pepper. Marinate in sherry for several hours. Fry six pork sausages and put aside. Sauté in butter for five minutes one cup of minced shallots, one-half cup of minced celery stalks and tops, and one-half cup of minced green peppers. Then add one cup of mushrooms and one cup of walnut meats to skillet. Add sausages to pan and mix well with three cups of cooked rice. Stuff bird and sew up. Place giblets in roasting pan. Roast thirty minutes per pound. Baste often and add a small amount of flour for gravy. (Serves four.)

PHEASANT À LA TROJAN

Disjoint one pheasant. Season with salt and pepper, dust with flour, and brown on both sides. Put in a stew pot with one jigger of sherry. Cover and steam two minutes in just enough brown gravy to cover pheasant. To one can of mushrooms add sixteen whole, pitted green olives and one small onion, finely minced. Let mixture stew until pheasant is tender (about one hour). Season with salt, a dash of Worcestershire, and sherry to taste. (Serves four.)

PHEASANT FRICASSÉE

Skin a young bird. (A pheasant is skinned only when it is to be fried.) After the bird is dressed cut it in several pieces and rub with salt, pepper, and butter. Place in an iron skillet and fry five minutes. Then add one can of chicken consommé, one-half cup of butter, four tablespoons of lime or orange juice, one teaspoon of Creole mustard, one cup of chopped truffles, and a dash of nutmeg. Simmer one hour or until done. Serve with rice cakes and currant jelly. (Serves two to four.)

PHEASANT WITH SHERRY

After bird is picked and cleaned, and the oil sac at base of tail removed, rub with salt and white pepper and butter it inside and out. Stuff with any turkey dressing and bake in hot oven thirty minutes per pound or until done. Baste often. When done pour two cups of sherry over fowl and let steep in liquid for an hour. Make the dressing a little more moist than usual since pheasant is very dry. (Serves four.)

BRACE OF STARLINGS

Pick and clean two starlings. Rub with melted sesame butter, salt, and pepper. Either broil or roast for twenty minutes, basting with a mixture of lemon juice, Worcestershire sauce, and butter. Serve the brace on toast. (Serves one.)

WILSON'S SNIPE

The marsh meadows and grassy flats are the favored haunts of the snipe of the delta parishes. He is an elusive fowl, taking long siestas by day and later partaking of a progressive nocturnal dinner among the sloughs and flats. Truthful hunters declare that this snipe makes hard hunting through the saw-grass bogs and that, even when spotted, his sudden spiral flight leaves the gunner gasping for breath and cursing his empty bag. But in spite of his erratic antics in the air and the hardships of hunting him through 'gator holes and bulrush, he is often sought, since all *batture* dwellers know that grilled snipe, wild rice, and red wine make a real feast. The Indians called this bird "cache-cache" because of his hide-and-seek ways.

BARBECUED SNIPE

Dress four birds. Brush inside cavity as well as outside with lemon juice and melted butter. Broil for twenty minutes, basting with a mixture of lemon juice, Worcestershire sauce, and butter. (Serves four.)

BÉCASSINE PAPRIKA

Dress four birds. Shake in a bag of flour, salt, and pepper. Fry for ten minutes. Remove from pan and make a gravy of three parts sour cream and one part chicken bouillon. Add paprika, salt, and enough flour to thicken. Place birds back in pan and simmer for twenty minutes or until tender. If desired, add one cup of white wine and steep. Serve with boiled rice. (Serves four.)

BROILED SNIPE

Dress two birds and brush with butter, salt, and pepper. Place on a broiler and baste with a mixture of two teaspoons of Worcestershire sauce, one-fourth cup of lemon, and one stick of butter. Broil for thirty minutes. Pour brandy over birds and serve aflame on a pewter platter. (Serves two.)

WOODCOCK SAINT TAMMANY

Dress bird and brush with melted butter, salt, and pepper. Place in a casserole with a small amount of chicken bouillon and strawberries. Roast thirty minutes. (Serves one.)

FOWL COCONUT

Punch the eyes of a large coconut. Drain and save the milk. Saw the coconut in half. Blend together two cups of boiled rice, one-fourth cup of shredded coconut, one teaspoon of curry powder, one teaspoon of nutmeg, two teaspoons of butter or oleo. Moisten with coconut milk. Add one cup of minced, cooked fowl and place all the ingredients in the coconut halves. Cook in a vessel placed in hot water in the oven or on top of the stove. Cook until the coconut meat is tender (about forty minutes). Serve hot. (Serves two.)

VI

Foods of the Gulf
and Inland Waters

Market-Garden on the Coast

The New Orleans Market - Soldiers exchanging rations for fruit and other food

Foods of the Gulf and Inland Waters

Louisiana is a liquid land of creeks, bayous, ponds, coastal and oxbow lakes, lagoons, canals, bays, streams, and rivers: the Sabine, the Ouachita, the Calcasieu, the Red, the Pearl, and—of course—the Mississippi. The great Father of Waters flows between Louisiana and Mississippi for half the length of Louisiana, then passes entirely into this state, bringing with it rich topsoil deposits that create a fertilizing action for the development of marine life.

The wide-spreading mouth of the Mississippi with its delta lies wholly within the state, forming a mass of estuaries. These arms of the sea reach upward into Louisiana's wilderness of sea marsh, and here during the Fall months is found one of the greatest concentrations of tarpons in United States waters. Louisiana has one tidal cycle instead of two, and at certain times the saline waters of the Gulf invade the inland bays and streams, causing them to become brackish and bringing an influx of different species of fish and marine life that offers uncertain and exciting conditions to the angler.

The Gulf of Mexico—Louisiana's southern boundary—is the meeting place and home of some of America's finest game fish. One hundred and forty miles south of Grand Isle the sea is over two thousand feet deep, and from these depths the ocean floor rises to form the coastal shelf lying just off the Louisiana mainland. Cruising along the rim of this continental highway are the migrant game fish which, in their search for smaller aquatic delicacies, make the Louisiana coast one of the finest game-fishing areas to be found anywhere.

From placid bayou to shimmering Gulf, the waters of Louisiana are a seemingly limitless and delightful source of good eating for the people of the state and provide the inspired ingredients for many of the tasty dishes given here.

SOME DO'S AND DON'TS IN THE PREPARATION OF FISH

DO kill fish immediately after catching, for fear causes endocrine gland secretions to enter the blood stream and harm the flavor of the fish.

DO draw at once and freeze if possible.

DON'T leave a catch dangling over the side of the boat for hours.

DO scale sun fish and other panfish. Remove front fins, head, and viscera by cutting fish from back of head to vent. Anal and dorsal fins may be removed after cooking.

DO make panfish fillets by holding fish with back straight up, cutting skin on each side from head to tail, and peeling it off; then cut meat as close to backbone as possible from head to tail.

DO clean larger fish on a spread-out newspaper, using a sharp knife. In a forward movement, cut fish from just below gill to backbone; then from backbone toward tail, cutting through rib bones but not through fish itself. Next, cut almost to tip of tail and spread halves open. If fish is to be skinned, hold by tail and cut fillet loose. Head and remains may then be disposed of in rolled-up newspaper.

DO clean fish on off-shore fishing trips by making a slit and removing entrails, or by removing head, tail, fins, and entrails.

DO skin fish caught in stagnant waters to avoid "mossy" taste.

DO marinate in lemon juice to improve flavor and partially cook fish.

DO rub with dill, olive oil, and a dash of vermouth for flavor.

DO cook fish with head on if possible, for flavor and oils are in the head. If it is cut off, save and boil for stock.

DON'T allow water to boil hard when cooking fish; simmer gently.

SALT AND BRACKISH WATER FISH

The waters of the Gulf and those of the coastal marshes that form Louisiana's southern boundary are crowded with a variety of fish that literally makes the area an angler's paradise. Here the eager fisherman may drop his line for porgy, silversides, spadefish, rabbit fish, striped mullet, croaker, sea catfish, gaff-topsail catfish, silver sea trout, spotted weakfish, spot, sandfish (or sand perch), ladyfish, blue runner, sheepshead, silver perch, fluke (or summer flounder), pigfish, tripletail, red snapper, gulf king whiting (or southern kingfish), striped bass, pompano, channel bass, bluefish, bonito, little tuna (or false albacore), cobia (or lemon fish), dolphin, cre-vallé, grunt, black drum, Spanish mackerel, an occasional painted mackerel, king mackerel, wahoo, black jewfish and other grouper, tarpon, ray, sailfish, shark, barracuda, and other species known and unknown. And, as exciting as their variety in number are the endless and fascinating ways of preparing this marine bounty—a few of which are given here as suggestions to the inventive cook.

CROAKERS

Scale and clean. Dip in cream and then in salt, pepper, and meal. Fry fifteen minutes in deep fat. Serve with fried grits. (Serve two per person.)

PUFFER (RABBIT FISH)

Remove head, skin, and clean. Dip in cream, then in rolled cornflakes. Fry for fifteen minutes in deep fat. (Serve one or two to a person.)

SILVER PERCH

Scale and clean. Dip in egg and then in salt, pepper, and corn meal. Fry for ten minutes in deep fat. (Serve one or two to a person.)

SILVER SEA TROUT

Clean and scale. Fry as you do puffer and serve with a sauce of sautéed minced shallots, minced green peppers, toast crumbs, and white wine. (Serve one or two per person.)

SILVERSIDES

Scale and clean. Dip in salt, pepper, and corn meal. Fry ten minutes in deep fat. (Serve several fish per person.)

SPADEFISH

Prepare and cook as recipe for "Sunfish au Bob Scearce," (see p. 139) or broil with a butter-caper sauce. (Serve three to a person.)

STRIPED BASS

Scale and clean one bass. Soak in white wine for fifteen minutes. Dip in pancake flour and fry in butter until half done. Place in deep skillet with hot water to cover. Add two teaspoons of wine vinegar, a pinch of mace, and a pinch each of allspice and cinnamon. Simmer thirty minutes more. (This fish may also be skinned.) (Serves one.)

BLUE RUNNER

Skin, split down middle, and cook under broiler fifteen minutes to the pound, basting with butter and lemon. (Serves one or two.)

BONITO ESCABECHE

Fry four fillets in butter twenty to thirty minutes. Simmer wine vinegar and water with a *bouquet garni*, a pinch of mace and dill, one-half cup of cut-up onions, salt, and pepper. Marinate fillets in the strained vinegar sauce for an hour. Drain and serve cold with sliced hard-boiled eggs and dill pickles. (Serves two.)

FLOUNDER

Flounders may be fried, boiled, broiled, or baked. To broil, score and dust with curry powder, then cook fifteen minutes per pound with a butter sauce. (Serves one.)

LADYFISH

Scale, clean, and bone four fish. Place in a shallow pan in oven and cover with a sauce of one-fourth cup of minced parsley, one pod of garlic, one-half cup of shallots, one teaspoon of Worcestershire sauce, one-half stick of butter, and a pinch of mace. Cook in oven for thirty minutes. (Serves four.)

BILOXI BACON

Mullet is the staple fish of Coast people. (They claim to live off the mullet in the summer and the Yankee in the winter.) This fish is prepared in many different ways — smoked, broiled, boiled, fried, and cooked fifteen minutes per pound. (Serve one or two fish per person.)

BOILED MULLET BOUQUET GARNI

Place scaled, cleaned fish in cheesecloth bag with spices. Boil in a shallow pan until tender. (Test with a toothpick.) Let steep in pan after fire is cut off. Serve cold with a sauce of mayonnaise (see p. 235) and capers. (Serve one or two fish per person.)

WHITING (GROUND MULLET)

Clean and scale. Then rub with olive oil, dust with salt, white pepper, mace, and allspice, and dip in beaten eggs and pancake flour. Fry fifteen minutes per pound in deep fat. Sauté minced almonds in butter, adding minced pieces of candied ginger. Spread mixture over fish. (Serve one or two fish per person.)

SMOKED MULLET

Marinate fish in lemon juice, olive oil, and Worcestershire sauce. Place on a wire rack over pit. Make a fire of hickory and burn down to coals. Cook fifteen minutes per pound. When fish are half done, place bay leaves, sassafras roots, and thyme under them and smoke until done. Baste often with a sauce made of butter and dry mustard. (Serve two fish per person.)

SHEEPSHEAD

Rub cleaned fish with olive oil and butter. Sauté minced shallots, minced celery, minced green peppers, and pimiento in butter. Add bread crumbs and stuff fish. Bake fifteen minutes per pound, basting often with tomato juice. (Serves two or more.)

SOLE AU VERMOUTH

Clean and wipe dry. Rub with olive oil. Turn dark side up and score with knife. Dust with salt and pepper. Marinate for five minutes in lemon juice, dry mustard, a dash of Tabasco, and melted butter. Broil fifteen minutes per pound in hot oven and baste with marinade to which a dash of vermouth has been added. (Serves one.)

FILLET OF GULF TROUT AND SOFT-SHELLED CRABS SAUTÉ AMANDINE

Cut fillets of four weakfish and prepare six soft-shelled crabs for cooking. Dredge the fillets and cleaned crabs in pancake flour or in a batter. Fry separately in deep fat about twenty minutes each or until done. Arrange on a platter with the fillets in the center and the crabs around them. Garnish with slices of lemon and parsley sprigs. Melt butter and mix with slivers of almonds that have been blanched and toasted in the oven. Pour the almond-butter sauce over the fish or serve in a separate bowl. (Serves four to six.)

WALTER'S FRIED TROUT

Clean and fillet. Rub with olive oil. Dip in beaten egg yolks and rolled corn flakes. Fry in butter for twenty minutes.

SPOTTED WEAKFISH

Skin, clean, and wipe dry. Rub with lemon and olive oil. Cut in fillets and fry for twenty minutes in butter. Place fish on silver platter, and pour one cup of rum over it. Serve lighted. (One fish serves one or two.)

ALBACORE SUPREME

Clean and fillet. Dust with flour, white pepper, and salt. Fry in hot peanut or olive oil twenty minutes. Add enough fowl stock to cover. Simmer thirty minutes per pound with one teaspoon of mace, two teaspoons of allspice, and one-half teaspoon of ground ginger. Pecans may be ground up and sprinkled over fish when served. (This tuna-like fish may be skinned.)

VIOLETTE HOLDER'S BARBECUED FISH

Dress and clean several small fish (weakfish, bass, or other fish). Brush with butter and lemon juice, and sprinkle inside and out with salt and pepper. Wrap each fish in waxed paper, then in cleaned corn husks, aluminum foil, or cabbage leaves. Tie with a string and place on the grill of a barbecue pit. Cook fifteen minutes to the pound, or until the corn husks are charred and the fish is tender. (If foil is used, cut down on amount of lemon juice for the foil retains all the original seasoning.) (Serve two fish per person.)

BLACK JEWFISH

A small fish is best. Cut into steaks and soak in lemon. Rub with olive oil, then soak in sherry for thirty minutes. Dust with salt and pepper. Bake steaks in the oven fifteen minutes per pound, basting with butter, minced celery and tops, pecans, and a pinch of mace. When done, let steep in white wine. Serve with cinnamon toast. (You may skin this fish.)

BAKED BLACKFISH WITH SPANISH SAUCE

This is the favorite fish recipe of Mabel and Renée Meunier. Use any large baking fish—cobia, channel bass, or sheepshead—but the Meuniers consider the tripletail the best fish for any method or preparation.

Clean and dress a six-pound fish. Leaving the head on adds to the flavor. Remove the gills, and insert chopped onion, parsley, and one or two cloves of garlic in the opening where the fish has been drawn. Place in a baking pan or casserole and add the spicy sauce.

Lay six slices of lemon on top of the fish. Bake for about an hour and a half (depending on the size of the fish) at 350°. Baste often with the sauce. Add two cloves of minced garlic during the last fifteen minutes of cooking. Do not turn the fish during the cooking. Transfer fish carefully from pan to serving platter, using two large spatulas. Garnish with parsley and lemon slices. Serve the sauce from a gravy boat. (Serves six or more.)

Spanish Sauce

Sauté one large onion finely chopped in three tablespoons of fresh bacon drippings until transparent. Add four cans of tomato sauce, one teaspoon of Worcestershire, one teaspoon of chili powder, two tablespoons of cornstarch diluted in one cup of meat stock or water. Stir the sauce while adding the cornstarch liquid. Add some finely chopped parsely, celery, and bell pepper. Add one sprig of thyme and half a bay leaf. Salt and pepper to taste. Simmer over slow fire for thirty minutes.

BLUEFISH

Clean and dress. Rub with olive oil. Place in a greased pan under the broiler for thirty minutes with butter and capers. When done, place over hot water and let steep in white wine until ready to serve. (Serves one or two.)

COBIA FROMAGE À LA CRÈME

Cut fillets thin, wrap an anchovy in each one, and fasten with a toothpick. Make a sauce of four packages of cream cheese and four cups of cream. Add one cup of minced sweet pickles, one cup of melted butter, and a dash of Tabasco. Pour over rolled fillets, and bake in oven fifteen minutes per pound.

COBIA STEAKS
(Lemon Fish)

This is one of the most versatile of all salt-water fish. Prepare the steaks in any manner. The fillets make a wonderful bouillabaisse and are delicious poached with spices and ginger.

CREVALLÉ

Use a small jack. Bleed and clean. Scrub the skin and boil in highly seasoned water and lemon thirty minutes to the pound or until tender. Do not use the dark meat. Flake meat and make into balls with mashed potatoes. Brown in butter.

DOLPHIN

Skin, clean, and cut in fillets. Soak for twenty minutes in lemon juice, then rub with olive oil. Grill with melted butter fifteen minutes to the pound. Serve with Hollandaise sauce (see p. 217).

BLACK DRUM

Clean, scale, and marinate in lemon and oil. Dip in cream, then in rolled corn flakes. Fry fifteen minutes per pound in deep fat.

GROUPER

The flesh of the grouper is considered by many salt-water fish connoisseurs to be unequaled good eating. It is wonderful in a chowder, or broiled, baked, or boiled. Cook fifteen minutes per pound. (This fish may be skinned.)

GRUNT

Clean and skin. Boil fifteen minutes per pound in a cheesecloth sack with herbs and spices, onions, and lemons. Drain and flake. Serve with a sauce of lemon juice, butter, and capers.

POACHED GRUNT

Clean and fillet fish. Poach in a shallow pan with a *bouquet garni* of herbs until fish is tender (fifteen minutes per pound). Sauté mushrooms and shallots in butter and add a sour cream sauce (see p. 224). Add fish and serve hot on French bread.

GULF FISH GLACÉ

Dissolve one envelope of gelatin in one-half cup of cold water. Flake two pounds of boiled fish. Mix with one-half cup of capers, one-fourth cup of minced celery, and one-fourth cup of parsley. Stir one cup of tomato juice and the juice of one lemon in gelatin. Mix liquid with fish and other ingredients. Pour into mold. Place sliced hard-cooked eggs over top of mold.

KINGFISH

Poach mackerel or any other salt-water fish fifteen minutes per pound using *bouquet garni* and lemon slices. Flake fish and mix with new, boiled potatoes and minced parsley. Kingfish is good broiled.

SPANISH MACKEREL

Clean and bone, and cut into fillets. Rub with olive oil, salt, and pepper, and barbecue over coals on wire mesh, cooking fifteen minutes per pound and basting with a sauce of butter, lime juice, anchovy paste, and a dash of vermouth.

POISSON À LA SAUCE MAÎTRE D'HÔTEL

The fish used in this dish may be broiled or prepared as in "Red Fish Laffite." (See p. 133.) After the fish is cooked, make a sauce in a skillet by making a *roux* of butter and two teaspoons of flour. Pour several cups of cream into the brown *roux* and let it thicken. Add salt, white pepper, a dash of minced fennel, a soupçon of garlic, and one-half cup of capers. Let the sauce cool. Add one beaten egg. Cook slowly for a few minutes and pour over the fish. Sprinkle parsley or minced wild leeks over the sauce and serve hot. (Serves four or more.)

BRENNAN'S POMPANO EN PAPILLOTE

Cut pompano into fillets of five ounces each. Parboil for five minutes. For the sauce, mix one tablespoon of melted butter and one tablespoon of flour, and add four chopped green onions, some chopped mushrooms, two truffles, two ounces of white wine, and one pint of fish stock. Simmer for ten minutes. Season to taste. Add eight boiled, cleaned, peeled shrimp to the sauce. Add the same number of oysters and sauté with a dash of white wine and the yolk of one egg. Moisten a heart-shaped parchment bag with butter. Fill the bag with alternating layers of sauce and fish. Fold bag and bake in a hot oven for ten minutes. (Serves one.)

POMPANO

Skin, clean, and remove eyes but leave head on. Place in skillet with a *bouquet garni,* some lemon slices, and a little water. Poach for five minutes or until tender. Make a thick sauce of mushroom soup, truffles, mushrooms, minced shallots, boiled shrimp, and any herbs. Simmer fish in sauce a few minutes. Then put fish and sauce into oiled paper bag or aluminum foil and place in oven in greased pan. Bake in moderate oven for about fifteen minutes. Pompano may be broiled with butter and lime juice, or barbecued. The Creoles believed the pompano had the finest flavor of all Gulf fish. (Serves two.)

RED FISH LAFFITE

Clean and scale fish. Fillet and rub with lemon, salt, and white pepper. Place in a casserole with a little butter and one cup of white wine. Cover and bake fifteen minutes per pound. Remove fish from casserole and add one can of mushroom soup moistened with a little more white wine and a little hot water. Place sauce over fish in platter. Sprinkle with sautéed mushrooms.

CHANNEL BASS (REDFISH)

Scale, clean, and rub with olive oil. Rub inside with butter and lemon juice. Stuff with a mixture of sautéed minced shallots, celery, toast crumbs, and mushrooms. Moisten dressing with sherry or vermouth. Sew fish up and baste with melted butter, cream, and minced hard-cooked eggs. Sprinkle with minced parsley. Bake fifteen minutes to the pound. (Serves four.)

RED SNAPPER

Scale, clean, and rub with olive oil. Boil minced green peppers, parsley, shallots, bay leaves, whole cloves, celery, and a pod of garlic for thirty minutes. Strain and simmer fish in water stock fifteen minutes per pound. Make a sauce of one can of mushroom soup, one can of mushrooms, some boiled shrimp, minced celery, and a little stock. Add raw oysters and simmer sauce until oysters curl. Add one cup of sherry and pour sauce over fish when ready to serve. Serve with mashed potatoes.

SAILFISH

Skin, clean, and cut into fillets. This fish may be barbecued, broiled, or baked as you would cobia, cooking fifteen minutes per pound.

SOUR CREAM SAILFISH

Poach fillets of sailfish with a *bouquet garni* fifteen minutes per pound. Serve with "Sour Cream Sauce" (see p. 224) and dill pickles.

SAKLI

This Indian way of cooking fish is still used in Louisiana. Gut and wash a fish. Leave scales on. Impale on a sassafras limb over coals of hickory. Broil one-half hour or more. When done, skin and eat.

TRIPLETAIL (BLACKFISH)

Clean fish and rub with olive oil. Brush inside with lemon and butter. Stuff cavity with a dressing of boiled rice, pecans, and butter. Sew fish up. Bake in oven fifteen minutes per pound, basting with butter and pecans. Garnish with water cress. (Skin this fish.)

WAHOO À LA HOBBS

Clean and cut two fillets. Sprinkle with salt and pepper and rub with olive oil. Place strips of bacon across fillets and cook under broiler for thirty minutes. Pour one jar of honey into a skillet with the juice of four limes and one-half lemon. Heat until honey melts, then place fish in skillet and steep in sauce for twenty minutes. White wine may be added. (Serves two.)

FRESH-WATER FISH

Away from the Gulf Coast and the sea marshes, the fresh-water streams of Louisiana also offer excitement and variety to the fisherman. Though the state actually can claim no species of trout, any native can tell you where the "green trout"—really the largemouth black bass—are biting.

Even under the name of largemouth black bass, the green trout is masquerading, of course, for it is actually one of the numerous members of the sunfish family. The only true bass found in Louisiana waters are the white and yellow, and the striped variety.

Among the members of the large sunfish family, however, Louisiana anglers find, in addition to the largemouth black bass, the spotted or Kentucky bass, the black crappie (known to Southerners as the "calico bass"), the white crappie (or sac-à-lait, as South Louisiana fishermen call it), the rock bass, and a host of small fry generally referred to as "perch."

In preparing sunfish, scale fish and fry in deep fat or sauté in butter. One or more fish may be fried at the same time, but cold fish should never be placed in the skillet in which hot fish are being fried.

The sweetest sunfish meat is found on fish caught in clear, fast-running water. Those taken from semistagnant streams should be skinned and prepared in a chowder with a dash of filé powder for best flavor results.

BASS À LA MIEL

Clean and scale two fish. Mix two beaten eggs with one jar of honey and two teaspoons of lemon juice. Place fish in this marinade and marinate for several hours in refrigerator. Fry fish twenty minutes in preheated, greased skillet with butter and honey. (Serves two.)

BASS PECAN

Fry four bass fillets or whole small bass in same manner as sunfish. To make sauce, mince pecans and fry in butter. Before serving fish, add a small amount of orange wine and pour over the fried bass. (Serves one.)

BROILED BASS

Marinate the cleaned fish in cream for an hour. Dry and rub with lemon, salt, and pepper. Place in a pan under broiler, cook fifteen minutes per pound, and baste often with butter and lemon juice. When fish is almost done, place sliced cucumbers around the pan and cook until fish is done. Serve with new potatoes. (Serves one or two.)

FALSE RIVER BASS

Clean and scale two fish. Rub with butter, salt, and pepper and chill in refrigerator several hours. Make a stuffing of bread crumbs, egg yolks, and a seasoning of fennel, thyme, and finely minced bay leaves. Mix well and stuff the fish. Sew up and place in a shallow, greased pan. Bake for thirty minutes and baste with sauce of butter and lemon juice. (Serves two.)

LARGEMOUTH BLACK BASS AU GRATIN

Clean and scale two fish. Place in a cheesecloth bag and simmer in water with a *bouquet garni* until tender. Mix together one can of mushroom soup, one cup of cream, one can of mushrooms, and a tablespoon of butter. Flake boiled fish and place in a casserole with the sauce. Put bread crumbs and grated cheese over top. Bake for thirty minutes or until done. When done, sauté a few boiled crawfish tails with minced shallots and sprinkle them over casserole. (Serves two to four.)

REDBONE BASS

Use any fresh-water fish. Clean and scale. Make a *roux*. Add two cups of cream, two teaspoons of dry mustard, two teaspoons of minced dill, a dash of cayenne, and salt. Pour sauce over fish and bake in a casserole. Cook fifteen minutes per pound. (Serves one or two.)

STUFFED WHITE BASS

Prepare the fish as you would "Crappie en Papillote." Stuff with cut-up smoked sausage and bread crumbs softened with sherry.

Sew up fish. Baste with butter, Worcestershire sauce, and lemon. Bake thirty minutes or until done. (Serve one fish per person.)

FRESH-WATER CATFISH: BLUE CHANNEL, FLATHEAD, WHITE, AND OTHERWISE

The Deep Southerner loves his catfish, whether caught on "trot line" or by pole. (Some folk even catch them by hand in underwater holes.) The blue cat is considered superior and is known up North as tenderloin of trout. All fresh-water cats are edible but should always be fried. Cat and corn meal cakes are a stand-by with all river folk. Cook fifteen minutes per pound.

CUTLETS OF BLUE CAT

After the fish is cleaned and skinned, rub with salt and white pepper. Marinate in cream for several hours. Wipe dry and shake fillets in sack of white corn meal, salt, and pepper. Fry in lard in manner recommended for sunfish, turning only once. Drain well on absorbent paper and serve with potatoes au gratin, raw sliced onions, and hush puppies. Cook fifteen minutes per pound.

CHINESE STUFFED FISH

Any type of salt- or fresh-water fish over four pounds in weight may be stuffed in this way: Sauté in butter a small amount of minced shallots, minced celery, and minced almonds. Add a larger amount of minced water chestnuts, bean sprouts, and bamboo shoots. Add a little soy sauce and Bead molasses. Stuff cleaned, scaled fish. Tie fish together with bacon slices secured with toothpicks. Bake fifteen minutes per pound.

CRAPPIE EN PAPILLOTE

Clean and scale fish. Brush inside and out with butter and lemon juice. Sprinkle with salt, pepper, and paprika. Make a sauce of one-half can of mushroom soup, two sprigs of rosemary, four sprigs of mint, and one-fourth stick of butter. Let fish soak in sauce for five minutes. Place in foil or oiled paper bag and pour some of the sauce over the fish. Close envelope and bake about thirty minutes in greased pan. Garnish with fresh mint. (Serve two fish per person.)

DELTA DISH-UP

Scale and clean one large black bass. Place in a pot with one pint of fowl stock and one-half bottle of white wine. Add a few bay leaves and a pinch of thyme. Simmer for thirty minutes until bass is tender. Remove bass from pot and flake. Strain the stock. Make a *roux* and add one-half cup of minced celery, one cup of minced green peppers, and a pinch of mace. Add the stock and simmer a few minutes. Add three cups of minced crawfish and simmer until crawfish are done. Add the fish and one-half teaspoon of saffron. Sprinkle with ground-up shallots. Serve with rice. (Serves two or more.)

FRESH-WATER FISH MARGUERY

Scale and clean a large fish. Place in cheesecloth bag and simmer with spices until tender. Drain, bone, and flake. Cook fifteen minutes per pound. Make a sauce of Hollandaise (see p. 217), truffles, and boiled shrimp. Serve over fish.

PADDLEFISH OR SPOONBILL CATFISH

Clean, skin, and cut into fillets. Dust with pancake flour. Fry in butter fifteen minutes per pound.

POACHED PADDLEFISH

Clean and cut in fillets. Rub with lemon, salt, and pepper. Dust with mace. Poach with a little hot water and butter until tender. Add three teaspoons of dry vermouth and steep. Cook fifteen minutes per pound.

PINE BARK STEW

Fry pieces of salt pork, drain, and put aside. Sauté one-half cup of minced shallots and six peeled, sliced potatoes. Add one quart of hot water, salt, pepper, and, if desired, curry powder. Let simmer a few minutes. Add ten fillets of fresh-water fish and six sliced onions. Simmer for one hour over coals of pine bark and hickory wood. The pine bark gives a slow heat. (Serves six or more.)

SAUTÉ SEC

Use any four-pound fish from salt or fresh waters. Fillet and simmer for forty minutes in a mixture of one bottle of white wine, one pint of hot water, three cut-up lemons, one-half bunch of parsley, one-half cup of bay leaves, salt, and pepper. Remove fish when done and strain the stock. Make a *roux*. Add one cup of minced shallots and one-half cup of minced green peppers. Add several cups of the stock and simmer ten more minutes. Add flaked fish and serve with corn bread. (Serves four.)

SUNFISH AUX HERBES

Scale, clean, and remove head fins. Rub with a little salt and white pepper. Place in an oiled pan under broiler for twenty minutes. Make a sauce of butter, minced shallots, parsley, minced chives, and enough flour to thicken slightly. Baste fish with the sauce until done. These fish require a very short broiling time.

SUNFISH AU BOB SCEARCE

To quote an experienced wielder of the rod and pan, Bob Scearce: "Everybody at sometime or other has caught and fried sunfish. Most people just salt, pepper, and fry in deep fat, but I find that there are certain refinements that will add something extra in flavor satisfaction to this most succulent species of fresh water fish. The sporty little bluegill, stumpknocker, shellcracker, bream, or perch, caught by country urchin and city slicker alike, has the firmest, sweetest meat of all fresh water fish, and, when piled high on the platter in crisp, golden brown profusion, is the rarest of delicacies. Preparation of the frying pan is important. A wide iron skillet or frying pan must be filled to a depth of two to four inches with fresh lard. The fish, of course, should be carefully scaled and cleaned and the head removed. Then take a sharp knife and cut down both sides of the dorsal and ventral fins, lifting these fins out, and leaving only the body of the fish with the back and rib bones. Next score the fish on each side to the bone making the cuts about an inch apart. This will give you from three to five cuts on each side, depending on the size of the fish. These cuts to the backbone will allow the seasoning to penetrate a much greater portion of the fish and will add to the taste. Next prepare your seasoning. Take two brown grocery bags and slip one inside the other. Into these sacks put one cup of white cornmeal, salt and black or red pepper. Shake the contents of sack until blended. Place fish in sack and shake gently. When oil is hot, just before smoking, place enough fish in the skillet to fill, but do not put one fish on top of the other. The fish, while cooking, must be covered with the hot lard without touching the bottom of the pan. Be sure the seasoned meal has penetrated into the cuts in the fish. Hold fish by the tail and shake off any excess meal. Drop fish one at a time into the hot lard. The degree of cooking crispness is left up to the cook, but I recommend that the fish not be cooked too long . . . only until a light golden brown color is achieved. They should be turned, even though floating. When fish are done, remove to a platter with absorbent paper and keep in a warm oven. The fish must be served hot. Halved lemons and catsup may be served with them. Some piscators claim the sunfish and other fresh water small fish should always be frozen before frying." (Serve several fish per person.)

FILET DE TRUITE

Scale and clean two fish. Score sides. Season inside and out with salt, white pepper, and a little lemon juice. Place in a casserole with one cup of stock or hot water, one cup of minced shallots, and three peeled and sliced Irish potatoes. Put strips of salt pork across top and bake forty minutes or until done. (Serves two.)

TROUT MEUNIÈRE

Clean one large striped bass. Then fillet and rub with lemon. Marinate the fillets in cream, seasoned with salt and white pepper, for an hour or so. Dry and dip in flour. Sauté in olive oil for twenty minutes. Drain fillets and add some butter to the skillet. Add minced wild leeks or shallots, capers, and the juice of one lemon. Pour the butter sauce over the fish. Serve very hot. (Serves one or two.)

TRUITE AU BEURRE

Dress and scale one bass. Place in shallow casserole with strips of green pepper and strips of avocado. Place strips of bacon across fish. Bake or broil for thirty minutes, basting often. (Serves one or two.)

TRUITE VERTE (GREEN TROUT)

Scale and clean one bass. Sprinkle with salt, white pepper, celery salt, and lime juice. Grind two bunches of water cress and mix with melted butter. Broil fish for twenty to thirty minutes, basting with "Butter-cress Sauce." (See p. 229.) (Serves one or two.)

WALLEYE

Skin, clean, and stuff a fish with a dressing of bread crumbs, egg yolks, Creole mustard, pickles, salt, and pepper. Baste with a sauce of diluted mushroom soup. This fish may also be barbecued or broiled. Cook fifteen minutes per pound. (Serves two.)

CRUSTACEA

Along the Gulf shores of Louisiana and its neighbor Mississippi one of the favorite springtime and summer sports is "crabbing"—fishing for the blue crab with bits of raw meat tied in the crabbing nets. But the blue crab provides—through the various cycles of its development—year-round eating pleasure to the folk of this region.

Ordinarily thought of as the hard-shelled crab, the blue crab becomes the "soft-shell" during his molting period; and if he is caught between seasons—before he has shed his shell—he is called a "buster," and his shell is removed by hand.

Good crabbers know that they should toss the first crab caught back in for good luck, and that the hard-shelled crabs must be alive when cooked. Before cooking, the crabs should be placed in a tub of cold salt water for about ten minutes, then washed thoroughly with cold water before placing them in a large pot of seasoned cold water. The water should be brought to a boil slowly in order to keep the meat tender.

For seasoning, one may use cut-up lime or lemon, cut-up onion, bay leaves, parsley, mace, cinnamon, cloves, allspice, salt, and pepper; or one may use any number of other herbs and spices or the ready-mix "Crab Boil" available in stores in Louisiana.

The crabs should be allowed to boil gently for about twenty minutes, cooled in the seasoned pot, then drained well and put on ice. After chilling they may be cleaned by removing the eyes, mouth, and stomach in a single operation, pulling back the shell with the hands. The feathery "dead man," found on each half of the body, should be removed at the same time.

In serving crab, provide a nutcracker for the claws. Garnish with a slice of lemon or pickle placed in the claws, and serve with cold beer or ale—and you'll say with the Cajuns, "I eat 'des 'til I bus-me."

CRAB CERES

Use one pound of cooked crab meat. Sauté one cup of minced cooked ham, one minced bell pepper, and two stalks of minced celery with white pepper and salt to taste. Add one cup of bran breakfast food and enough butter to soften. Brown for ten minutes in oven in ramekins until almost ready to serve; then sprinkle a small amount of white wine over top, and finish browning. (Serves six.)

CRAB MEAT A L'AUTRE BORD DU LAC

Use four pounds of lump crab meat, three large cans of tomatoes, four cans of mushrooms, including stems and butter, two medium-sized onions, two cloves of garlic, and one-half cup of olive oil. Sauté onions and garlic in olive oil. Add mushrooms and allow to simmer about ten minutes, then put in tomatoes. Season with thyme, sage, bay leaves, salt, pepper, and a few drops of Tabasco. Let simmer slowly for about two hours, adding crab meat. Serve with boiled rice. (Serves twelve.)

CRAB NEWBURG

Sauté one cup of cooked crab meat in butter. Add juice of one lime, one-half teaspoon each of powdered cloves, paprika, white pepper, and salt. Beat, then stir in one egg yolk and one-half cup of cream. Add to other ingredients and simmer eight minutes. Before serving, add one tablespoon of brandy. Heat and serve on thick pieces of French bread. (Serves two.)

CRAB PIE

Sauté in butter one pound of boiled crab meat with three teaspoons of minced chives, three teaspoons of minced celery, three minced pimientos, and one minced bell pepper. Soak two cups of toast crumbs in white wine. Mix with other ingredients and one cup of cooked rice. Place in a casserole and bake twenty minutes. (Serves six.)

CRAB STUFFED À LA CYPRIÈRE

Mix one pound of cooked crab meat with salt, white pepper, capers, one pimiento, one teaspoon of melted butter, and enough homemade mayonnaise to moisten. Rub six crab shells with garlic and olive oil. Heap mixture in shells and bake in oven for twenty minutes. Top with paprika. Garnish with garlic dill pickles. (Serves six.)

CURRIED CRABS

Sauté three tablespoons of minced parsley and three tablespoons of shallots in butter in a double boiler. Add three tablespoons of flour and three tablespoons of curry powder. Add one cup of cream and one cup of milk. Stir until thick. Add one pound of cooked crab meat and one teaspoon of sugar. Simmer a few minutes. Just before serving, blend in one-fourth cup of sherry. Serve with boiled rice and side dishes of sweet relish, sliced bananas, toasted pecans, and fresh grated coconut. (Serves six.)

HARD CRABS A LA GORENFLO

Boil hard crabs for twenty minutes in the usual manner (see p. 141) with seasoning. Remove shells, and clean crabs, but leave the body intact. Make a sauce of olive oil, vinegar, minced garlic, minced parsley, and dill. Place the crabs in a deep bowl and cover with the sauce. Chill all day, stirring often. Drain and serve as appetizers. (Serve four crab "breasts" to a person.)

LAFAYETTE CRAB CUTLET

Use one pound of boiled crab meat. Mix one bunch of minced shallots, three stalks of minced celery, one-half bunch of minced parsley, and one pinch of dry mustard with one cup of bread crumbs and two beaten eggs. Add enough melted butter and canned milk to soften. Add crab meat and mold into cutlets. Let stand in refrigerator several hours, then roll in cracker crumbs and fry in butter for twenty minutes. (Serves eight.)

PARADISE POINT CRAB COQUILLE

Melt one tablespoon of butter. Add one small onion, minced, and smother, but do not brown, for ten minutes. Add one pound of preboiled crab meat and stir. Next add about three ounces of milk or cream that has been slowly heated. Stir all ingredients together until the mixture has the consistency of heavy cream. Next add two ounces of sauterne, and salt and pepper to taste. Fill six coquilles. Sprinkle grated cheese over each one and bake in a 350° oven until they are brown on top. Serve with toast or crackers. (Serves six.)

NANCY'S STUFFED CRABS

Remove meat from body and claws of eight boiled crabs. Scrape and save shells. Mince one large bell pepper, one large onion, and one clove of garlic. Add two stalks of celery. Sauté in skillet, adding the crab meat. Add one cup of bran breakfast food, one bay leaf, a pinch of thyme, salt, and pepper. Stir all ingredients together with one beaten egg. Stuff shells, which have been rubbed with garlic. After stuffing, squeeze lemon or lime juice on each crab. Bake in oven until golden brown. (Serves eight.)

SOFT-SHELLED CRABS

A soft-shelled crab is the blue crab that has shed his old shell and acquired a new, soft shell. During this period he hides from his enemies—one of them the hard-shelled crab—which feed on him. Often he clings to bankside bushes. Natives catch many soft-shelled crabs in these conveniently placed bushes. In Louisiana the season for soft-shelled crabs usually extends from the first of March to cold weather. But this depends upon the weather—Mme. Soft-Shell must have warm weather in which to change her wardrobe.

Soft-shelled crabs should be washed and cleaned in cold water, never scalding water. Remove "dead man" and dry crabs in a soft towel. Rub with salt and white pepper and soak in milk or cream for twenty minutes. Dry again and dip in egg batter, then in corn meal or rolled corn flakes. Fry for ten minutes in butter. "Old Softie—now he is good—no?" the Cajun remarks, which means he is very good.

BUSTERS

Buster crabs are those caught while they are in the process of molting, and at the stage when the back shell may be cracked free from the apron. In the words of the Cajun crabber, "Me, I don't let hem shed, but peel hem wit my hand."

Wash busters in cold water and clean, removing the dead man. Use only the body. Soak in milk. Sauté in butter, with minced chives and minced parsley for a few minutes, then wrap each crab in bacon and run under broiler for twenty minutes. (Serve two busters per person.)

BARBECUED BUSTERS

Prepare busters as for broiling. Baste with a sauce of melted butter, lime juice, Worcestershire sauce, minced chives, salt, and white pepper until done. If cooked outdoors, the crab may be placed on a piece of wire screen over a pit, or in aluminum foil over coals. Cook for fifteen minutes. (Serve two busters per person.)

SHRIMP

The state of Louisiana produces approximately 70 per cent of this nation's annual shrimp output, distributing it in the form of fresh, breaded, frozen, canned, and dried shrimp and shrimp-bran (a by-product for agricultural use). During the nineteenth century shrimp were brought into New Orleans' French Market by wagon and sold for a penny each. In 1867, the first shrimp were canned at Grand Terre Island, but it was not until 1934 that the first beheaded shrimp were shipped outside the state.

Up until that time, shrimp fishermen obtained their catches in the traditional shrimping grounds in the Gulf of Mexico. In 1937, however, new shrimping grounds were discovered at a depth of ten fathoms. Today, more new grounds and new species are still being found in the fertile waters of the Gulf.

The edible shrimp of Louisiana waters may be divided into two classes—marine and fresh-water shrimp. Among the marine shrimp are the common sea shrimp (also known as the Southern prawn or lake shrimp); the sea bob (or six beards or six barkes); the brown grooved shrimp (sometimes called the red grooved or Brazilian shrimp, or brownies); the pink grooved (or pink spotted) shrimp; and the red shrimp. The fresh-water shrimp include three varieties of river shrimp, running from ordinary to giant size.

APPLE SHRIMP

Peel one pound of raw shrimp. Place in foil with sliced apples, pecans, and butter. Close foil and cook for ten minutes over coals. (Serves two.)

BOILED "SWIMPS"

In the Cajun idiom the word shrimp turns into "swimps," and good Cajuns prefer their "swimps" just plain boiled. All species of shrimp may be cooked in the same manner. To boil, place the washed shrimp (whole or beheaded in their shells) in a large pot of cold, seasoned water. Local shrimp eaters use cut-up lemons, cut-up onions, cloves, cinnamon, nutmegs, thyme, bay leaves, dill, tarragon, rosemary, salt, and hot peppers or a dash of Tabasco sauce for their seasoning. After the water comes to a boil, let the shrimp boil gently for fifteen or twenty minutes. Cool in the pot, or for firmer shrimp drain at once after the cooking is finished. They may be served in their shells or shelled, hot or cold, and with or without sauce. (One pound of boiled shrimp serves approximately two persons.)

CHERAMIE BOILED SHRIMP

Take one pound of shrimp and cut a small slit on top of each so that it can absorb the seasoning and be deveined as they boil. Cool shrimp and peel. Cut-up limes, lemons, and shallots always add to the flavor if dropped in during the boiling. Boil fifteen minutes. (Serves two.)

BROILED SHRIMP

Remove the heads from one pound of raw shrimp and slit down the back of each enough to insert a sliver of garlic. Place under the broiler for ten minutes and baste with parsley butter. Or, peel and vein one pound of raw shrimp, using a sharp knife to cut open the unpeeled shrimp and a pair of scissors to cut the back shell. Make a sauce of one teaspoon of Worcestershire sauce, the juice of one lemon, and one-half stick of butter. Run the shrimp under the broiler, basting often with the sauce. Shrimp may also be cooked in aluminum foil by either of these recipes. (One pound serves four.)

CURRIED SHRIMP

Make a cream sauce with two cups of chicken soup, and add two tablespoons of curry powder. Simmer a few minutes and add one pound of cooked, peeled shrimp. Add one beaten egg yolk and one cup of pure cream. Simmer a few minutes more and serve with boiled rice and side dishes of chutney, fresh coconut, toasted peanuts, and red and green peppers. (Serves four.)

FLAMING SHRIMP EN BROCHETTE

Place one pound of large raw, peeled shrimp on skewers alternately with large mushrooms. Grill over coals for ten minutes. Dip in brandy and serve flaming. (Serves two to four.)

FRIED SHRIMP

Dip one pound of raw, peeled and cleaned shrimp in homemade mayonnaise, then in bread crumbs. Fry in butter for fifteen minutes. Or, sprinkle shrimp with lemon juice and dip first in egg-yolk, then in ready-mix pancake flour, and fry in deep fat for ten minutes. Drain well. (Serves two to four.)

FRIED "SWIMPS" IN WINE

Soak for about thirty minutes peeled, veined shrimp in a mixture of lemon juice, brandy, and pieces of ginger root. Drain and fry for ten minutes in hot oil. Add three cups of Chinese rice wine or orange wine. Steep twenty to thirty minutes. Serve with boiled rice. (Use one pound of shrimp for two persons.)

CANTONESE FRIED SHRIMP

Make a batter of one-half cup of water-chestnut flour, two egg yolks, several ounces of whisky, and salt. Dip large peeled shrimp in batter and fry for fifteen minutes in an iron skillet. (One pound serves two to four.)

GRAND ISLE PILAU

Fry one large piece of salt pork until crisp. Cut into small pieces. Let stay warm in the oven. Mix two cups of hot water with one cup of peeled, uncooked shrimp and one cup of washed, uncooked rice. Stir this well and bring to a boil. Reduce the heat as low as possible immediately and cook on slow fire for about twenty-five minutes. Add the salt pork pieces and a little of the gravy when rice and shrimp are put on to boil. Do not stir the pilau while cooking. Five minutes before it is done sprinkle one cup of fried, minced okra on top. (Serves four.)

ISLE DERNIERE SHRIMP STEW

Fry small pieces of salt meat until crisp. Drain and place in oven to bake until crisp. (These are cracklings.) Sauté one-half cup of minced shallots and one cup of minced bell peppers in grease and a small amount of olive oil. Add one can of tomatoes, one-half cup of chili sauce, and one teaspoon of Worcestershire sauce. Add *bouquet garni*. Add two pounds of raw, peeled shrimp and three teaspoons of chili powder. Boil gently fifteen minutes. Add hot water, if needed. Serve with boiled rice. (Serves eight.)

OLIVE SHRIMP

Boil and peel one pound of shrimp. Make a thick cream sauce. Add shrimp, one cup of cut-up green olives, one cup of minced pimiento, paprika, Tabasco sauce, white pepper, and salt. Serve with boiled rice. (Serves four.)

PONTCHARTRAIN WIGGLE

A "wiggle" may be any conglomeration of shellfish. This one is made of cream, crawfish, shrimp, green peas, and seasoning. Make one cup of thin cream sauce. Add one cup of boiled, peeled crawfish tails, one cup of boiled, peeled shrimp, one-half can of green peas, two teaspoons of Worcestershire sauce, a dash of Tabasco sauce, salt, and white pepper. Simmer a few minutes. Serve on hot toasted pieces of French bread. (Serves two.)

SHRIMP A LA HICKORY CORNERS

Place one pound of washed, unpeeled shrimp in cold seasoned water and boil for fifteen minutes. Remove shrimp from water, peel, and remove vein. While hot, dip in drawn butter, salt, and pepper. (Serves two.)

SHRIMP A L'ITALIENNE

Peel two pounds of shrimp and remove veins. Sauté in butter until pink. Add some fowl stock, one cup of minced black olives, one cup of pimientos. Simmer ten minutes. Add one cup of minced shallots and one cup of minced parsley. Sauté a few minutes. Boil two pounds of spaghetti in salted water for ten minutes. Wash in cold water and drain. Melt butter with a pinch of orégano and pour over hot spaghetti. Top with shrimp and Parmesan cheese. (Serves six.)

SHRIMP À LA KING

Add six tablespoons of flour to three tablespoons of melted butter. Stir in one-half teaspoon of salt, one tablespoon of chopped green pepper, one-fourth teaspoon of paprika, two tablespoons of diced celery, two tablespoons of diced pimientos, and one-fourth teaspoon of parsley. Slowly add three cups of milk and simmer into a creamy sauce. Cook five more minutes. Add one cup of boiled peeled shrimp and two beaten eggs. Cook two minutes more. Serve on buttered toast. (Serves four.)

SHRIMP AU VIN

Peel three pounds of uncooked shrimp. Remove black veins with knife. Chop raw shrimp and sauté in butter until they are pink. Add minced shallots and green peppers. Make a sauce of fowl stock added to "Plain Cream Sauce." (See p. 216.) Pour in skillet with shrimp and simmer for fifteen minutes. Add one cup of white wine and steep. Serve on slices of toasted French bread. (Serves six.)

BRENNAN'S SHRIMP CREOLE

Sauté two large minced Bermuda onions and three chopped green peppers. Add four fresh tomatoes, peeled and chopped, and one pint of game or beef stock. Add one bay leaf, one sprig of thyme, salt, and pepper. Simmer forty-five minutes. Add two pounds of peeled, raw shrimp and simmer an additional twenty minutes or until shrimp are done. Serve with boiled rice. (Serves six.)

SHRIMP HAWAIIAN

Soak one pound of raw, peeled, and cleaned shrimp in lemon and orange juice overnight. Wipe dry. Fry for ten minutes in butter. Serve on pineapple spears sautéed in butter and topped with a mound of grated, fresh coconut and shelled pistachio nuts. Garnish with chutney. (Serves four.)

SHRIMP LOAF

Sauté one and one-half cups of chopped onions, one-half cup of celery, one-half cup of red bell pepper, chopped, and one table-spoon of garlic, chopped, in one-half cup of cooking oil until golden brown. Soak four cups of bread crumbs in warm water for about three minutes, squeeze out excess moisture, and add to sau-téed mixture. Cook for five minutes. Remove from fire and stir in three well-beaten eggs, two tablespoons of chopped parsley, and a pinch of bay leaf. Add two or three pounds of peeled, cleaned shrimp, chopped fine. Cook until the shrimp are a dark pink. Form into a loaf two inches thick, place in a pan, and bake in a moderate oven for twenty minutes. Serve with "Hollandaise Sauce" (see p. 217). Boiled crab meat may be substituted for the shrimp. (Serves eight.)

SHRIMP PIE

Sauté two bell peppers, one-half bunch of shallots, and one clove of garlic. Add one can of tomatoes and a *bouquet garni*. Add one pound of raw, peeled shrimp and cook fifteen minutes. Add hot water if needed. Add one teaspoon of powdered nutmeg. Remove herb sack and add one cup of washed rice for every cup of liquid in pot. Cover tightly and cook fifteen minutes. Remove into a casserole and top with Parmesan cheese. Bake for ten min-utes or until brown. Serve with croutons toasted with garlic butter. (Serves four.)

SHRIMP SAUCE PIQUANT

Sauté for ten minutes twelve peeled tomatoes and one cup of minced green peppers in butter. Add one bunch of minced shal-lots, a pinch of mace, dill, salt, and white pepper. Add two pounds of boiled, peeled shrimp, and serve on lettuce. (Serves four.)

SHRIMP STEW À LA NANCY

Chop two pounds of peeled boiled shrimp. Mince two stalks of celery and one bell pepper. Rub iron pot with garlic and a pinch of marjoram. Boil celery and bell pepper in a small amount of water until tender. Pour one quart of sweet milk into pot with celery and pepper. Add one pinch of thyme, paprika, and the shrimp. Bring to a boil. Then lower heat for five minutes, and, when ready to serve, add one glass of sherry or white wine and salt and white pepper to taste. (Serves eight.)

SHRIMP TUREEN

Use beef or chicken stock and simmer with *bouquet garni* for ten minutes. Sauté one pound of raw, peeled shrimp with one cup of minced celery and tops and one cup of minced shallots. Mix with stock and simmer for fifteen minutes. Before serving, add one-half cup of sherry. Serve with boiled rice. (Serves four.)

SEA MARSH STEW

Sauté for five minutes two cups of boiled, peeled shrimp with one cup of cooked and peeled crawfish tails. Add four cups of cream, a pinch of cayenne, one teaspoon of Worcestershire sauce, a pinch of dry mustard, and salt. Simmer ten minutes. Add one cup of canned green peas, drained, and a dash of fennel and paprika. Cook a few minutes longer and serve on toasted bread or in cooked pastry shells. (Serves four.)

VINOUS SHRIMP

Sauté one pound of peeled cleaned shrimp in olive oil for fifteen minutes. Add one-half cup of French vermouth to the skillet and let the shrimp steep in the vermouth for thirty minutes. Cold, boiled, peeled shrimp may also be marinated in white wine in the refrigerator. (One pound serves two to four.)

CRAWFISH

In the almost continually mild climate of Louisiana it would be difficult to tell when spring arrives each year were it not for the appearance of certain standard signs, such as the blooming of cape jasmine and magnolia—and the appearance of crawfish bisque on restaurant menus and family dining tables from one end of the state to the other. But the popular bisque (see p. 42) by no means exhausts the possibilities of these little denizens of ditch, lagoon, swamp, and waterway. The Cajuns think of them as *écrivisses*— and other Louisianans may refer to them as crawfish, crayfish, or "mud bugs"—but no matter what the name, they're delicious springtime eating.

To catch crawfish, one must rise very early and tempt them with a bit of salt meat on a string. Their color is controlled by the waters in which they live—and well-informed Louisianians know that the largest and tastiest of them all are found in twenty feet of clear water near Houma in Terrebonne Parish.

BAKED CRAWFISH

Boil five pounds of crawfish fifteen minutes, peel, and mash tails. Mix with six cut-up hard-boiled eggs. Sauté one-fourth cup of minced celery stalks and tops in butter. Add eggs and crawfish, then two cups of bread soaked in Louisiana orange wine. Put in one cup of cold boiled rice and a pinch of nutmeg. Mix. Bake in casserole for ten minutes. (Serves six.)

BOILED CRAWFISH

Crawfish must be alive when cooked. They may be purged, washed, and boiled in the same manner as hard crabs. Most swampland epicures prefer crawfish boiled. The tail is peeled and eaten first, then the juice is sucked out of the head.

BROILED CRAWFISH

If you are fortunate enough to get large crawfish, behead them alive. Then insert a thin sliver of garlic and butter in a slit in the back of the tails. Place under the broiler or in aluminum foil over coals for ten minutes. (One pound serves two.)

BAYOU STEW

Sauté one cup of minced shallots in butter a few minutes and add two dozen cooked crawfish, minced fine. Add one can of tomato juice, one teaspoon of Worcestershire sauce, a dash of Tabasco, two bay leaves, a sprig of thyme, salt, and white pepper.

Let simmer a few minutes and add two dozen peeled raw shrimp. Simmer the mixture about fifteen minutes or until shellfish are done. Add one cup of dry white wine and let steep for thirty minutes. Reheat and serve with boiled rice. (Serves four.)

CRAWFISH TAILS IN RUM

Mix one-half of a fifth of rum with four teaspoons of sugar and the juice of one lime. Boil four pounds of crawfish, peel, and remove tails. Clean tails and marinate in the rum, lime juice, and sugar for thirty minutes. Serve chilled or hot. (Serves four.)

LAGOON SCAMPI

Peel the tails of three dozen crawfish, mince, and sauté in olive oil a few minutes. Add several sticks of cinnamon, three whole nutmegs, and a few cloves. Let this steep for half an hour. In another skillet warm some light rum. Remove spices from tails and pour rum over them. Serve over toasted French bread. (Serves four.)

MELISSA'S STEW

Make a *roux*. Add one pod of minced garlic, two bay leaves, a sprig of thyme, and hot water. Place four pounds of cooked crawfish tails and scrapings in pot. Simmer ten minutes. Serve with hot biscuits. (Serves four.)

PIXILATED MUD BUGS

If you feel extravagant and venturesome, purge and wash one pound of crawfish and boil ten minutes in draught beer. Serve with more draught beer. (Serves two.)

MOLLUSKS

CLAMS

Tiny, delicious clams may be found around the outlying coastal islands. They may be dipped in cream and pancake mix and fried in butter. They may also be baked over a fire made in a shallow hole in the beach. Burn the fire down to embers, then place the washed clams on the coals with a moist sack on top and bake until done. Clam chowder may be made by steaming open the washed clams in a kettle and draining out the juice for later use. Next simmer potatoes and juice. Add cut-up clams, a dash of Tabasco, a little allspice, and salt, and pepper. Add cream or milk, bring to a boil, and serve.

MUSSELS

Fresh-water mussels may be made into a chowder in the same way as clams, but since they are much tougher, a longer time is required for steaming and cooking them.

OYSTERS

Louisiana oysters are unexcelled in the quality of the meat and in their flavor, and they should either be eaten raw or cooked as little as possible. Never wash them; simply drain off the juice and save it for sauces and stews.

The tradition that oysters should not be eaten during months with no "R" in the name has a practical rather than a dietary basis: May, June, July, and August are breeding months for them, and they are milky in color and flavorless during this time. They may, however, be eaten safely.

BROILED OYSTERS À L'ABSINTHE

Wrap bacon around raw oysters and fasten with toothpicks. Place in a shallow pan under preheated broiler. Broil until bacon is crisp. A few drops of absinthe may be added. (Serve six per person.)

CREPES AUX HUÎTRES

Make French pancakes as in "Crepes Suzette" (see p. 283). Mince a pint of oysters and sauté in butter for a few minutes. Add a dash of Tabasco to "Hollandaise Sauce" (see p. 217) and pour over the oysters that have been placed on top of the crepes. Or serve with hot mayonnaise and a dash of Tabasco. (Serves two.)

CURLED OYSTERS

Place two tablespoons of catsup, one teaspoon of Worcestershire sauce, one tablespoon of lemon juice, one cup of chili sauce, one teaspoon of celery salt, paprika, white pepper, and one teaspoon of butter in a pan with a small amount of juice. Simmer a few minutes. Drop oysters in and cook until edges turn up. Serve with croutons. (Serve six per person.)

GRILLED OYSTERS

Place rock salt in shallow pan. Open oysters and wipe shells dry. Place oysters back in their shells. Pour melted butter, parsley, and lemon over each oyster. Top with bread crumbs and run under broiler for ten minutes. (Serve one dozen to a person.)

KITCHEN-STEAMED OYSTERS

Place oysters in shells in a deep pan half-filled with water. Cover with wet towels. Steam for twenty minutes on top of stove or until the mouths of the oysters start to open. Open at the table and dip oysters in a sauce of lemon juice and butter.

PARSLEY OYSTERS

Simmer oyster juice in a pan with two teaspoons of butter for a few minutes. Drop oysters in this sauce and simmer until juice is gone. Sprinkle with minced parsley and serve on toast. (Serve six oysters per person.)

OUTDOOR OYSTERS

Place a wash pot over campfire. Put oysters in pot and cover with a wet burlap sack. Steam for about thirty minutes. Open and dunk in butter and lemon. (Serve one dozen per person.)

OR

Dig a shallow hole in beach, make fire in it, and place oysters over coals, covering with wet sack for about thirty minutes; or place them over coals in a pan for thirty minutes with a small amount of water. Open and dip in butter and lemon.

OR

Open raw oysters and wrap with bacon held by toothpicks. Wrap in aluminum foil bag with Worcestershire sauce and butter. Broil fifteen minutes.

BRENNAN'S OYSTERS BIENVILLE

Use the same sauce that is used in the "Brennan's Pompano en Papillote." (See p. 132). Thicken the sauce with six boiled, cleaned shrimp. Allow it to cool. Place a half dozen oysters in a pie pan on top of rock salt. Cover the oysters with the sauce, then sprinkle with grated Parmesan cheese mixed with fine bread crumbs and paprika. Moisten with butter and bake in the oven for twenty minutes. (Serves one.)

OYSTERS ON THE HALF SHELL

Open oysters (a hard job). Serve on shell with a sauce of lemon, horse radish, Tabasco, catsup, and pepper vinegar. Or, better still, eat plain. Each oyster should be dressed separately on the shell with the sauce and not dunked into a sauce bowl.

OYSTER PIE

Make a rich puff pastry and line a casserole with it, saving enough to make a top crust. Measure and roll out top crust and partially bake it and the casserole lining. While crusts are baking, make a cream sauce with one-fourth cup of butter, two tablespoons of flour, one teaspoon of Worcestershire sauce, one cup of sweet milk, a pinch of cayenne pepper, and salt to taste. Pour in one-half cup of oyster liquor and stir. When crusts are partially baked, remove from oven and arrange oysters in the bottom of the casserole with alternate layers of sauce and the slices of four hard-cooked eggs. Just before putting partially cooked top crust in place, sprinkle finely cut shallots and parsley over sauce mixture. Carefully place top crust on casserole and bake in a hot oven until crust is brown (about ten or fifteen minutes). Be sure to slash the top crust so that steam can escape. Boiled shrimp may be used in place of the oysters. (Serves four.)

OYSTERS ROCKEFELLER

Probably the most talked-of oyster dish in all New Orleans' culinary repertoire is "Oysters Rockefeller." But their popularity is by no means restricted to city palates, and several recipes—"extorted" from various cooks in different parts of the state—are given here.

The secret lies in the sauce, since the preparation of the oysters themselves is always the same: arrange raw oysters in their half shells (which have been rubbed with garlic) on a bed of rock salt in a pie pan. Broil until their edges begin to curl, then put some of the sauce on each oyster and broil until the sauce is browned. A few drops of vermouth may be added to any of the sauces given below if you desire. (Serve one dozen oysters per person.)

Shine's Sauce

Grind one cup of fresh spinach with one-half cup of shallots. Add the juice of one lemon, one teaspoon of Worcestershire sauce, and a dash of sherry. Blend into a smooth paste.

Terrebonne Sauce

Grind one cup of Creole lettuce with one-half cup of shallots and one-fourth cup of minced fresh anise. Add a dash each of lime juice, Tabasco sauce, absinthe, and white pepper. Blend into a smooth paste.

Chartres Street Sauce

Grind one cup of fresh spinach with one-half cup of shallots, and one-fourth cup of celery. Add a dash of lemon, a little melted butter, and enough breakfast bran to make a smooth paste. Toss in some flaked crisp bacon before putting on oysters.

Florida Parish Sauce

Grind one cup of lettuce with one-half cup of shallots. Add a dash each of lime juice and Red Devil sauce. Mix with three teaspoons of anchovy paste and top with Parmesan cheese.

OYSTERS ROFFIGNAC

Mince one bunch of shallots fine. Sauté in three ounces of butter, but do not brown. Add two ounces of flour and stir until mixture is smooth. Next add one-half pound of boiled, peeled shrimp, two cloves of garlic, one-fourth cup of mushrooms—all chopped fine—and one pint of oyster juice. Let simmer for twenty minutes, then add one-fourth cup of red wine. Simmer an additional five minutes. Open one dozen oysters and place in pan. Cover with sauce and bake in oven until edges begin to curl. (Serves one.)

SAUTÉ BOURGEOISE

Fry six frog legs and cut off their meat. Sauté frog meat with one cup of boiled crab meat for five minutes. Add one cup of mushrooms and brown. Add one pint of oysters. Season with salt and white pepper. Cook until oysters curl. Add a dash of brandy and let steep for a few minutes. (Serves six.)

AMPHIBIANS
FROGS

Every swamp, marsh, and creek in Louisiana has its full share of frogs, and all are edible except the whistling tree frog. Most popular is the common bullfrog, or Creole frog, which is sold in Northern marts as "African Frog Legs." Another well-liked species is the Southern bullfrog, or lake frog of the fresh-water swamps.

To prepare frog for cooking, sever frog legs as close to the body as possible. Skin and clean. Blanch a few minutes in salted boiling water. Soak the legs in lime or lemon juice and ice cubes (or in milk or cream) for several hours. Dry well and fry.

There are several ways of frying the legs. They may be dipped in thick cream and placed in seasoned flour in a paper bag, or dipped in egg batter and then in pancake flour, then fried, and left to steam for five minutes. Or, they may be dipped in cracker crumbs and fried with mushrooms, a small amount of water with one cup of sherry being added later. If the latter method is used, leave the legs in the pan for half an hour. Other methods of frying use deep fat or butter. Fried legs should be drained immediately when deep-fat method is used.

TURTLES

Many varieties of turtle and tortoise (including the alligator snapping turtle, the common snapping turtle, the green sea turtle, the land gopher, the sea loggerhead turtle, and the famous diamond-back terrapin) are found in Louisiana. Various kinds of cut-up turtle meat may be bought in New Orleans' markets, and oddly enough, the fat female turtle is the most prized.

In preparing a hard-shelled turtle, kill it by cutting off the head. Bleed well, remove the entrails, cut the meat away, and scald the feet. Parboil in water with salt and black pepper and prepare in any way desired.

Soft-shelled turtles should be bled well and scalded in boiling water; and their shell, entrails, and claws should be removed. Wash well inside and out. If all the shell is not easily removed, boil with black pepper and salt until it falls from meat. Prepare in any way desired.

ALLIGATOR SNAPPING TURTLE

This turtle is best when fed on milk several days before killing. Remove meat from shell, cut in pieces, and parboil in salted water for forty minutes with a *bouquet garni*. Remove meat and make a *roux*. Add three quarts of stock, one cup of chopped celery, and one cup of shallots. When ready to serve, add chopped hard-cooked eggs. Simmer one hour or more. Madeira may be added before serving. (Serves six to eight.)

BROILED SEA TURTLE

Soak three pounds of meat in lime juice several hours. Drain and rub meat first in powdered allspice and then in olive oil. Place under broiler or over coals in aluminum foil for forty-five minutes or until tender. (Serves six to eight.)

CAJUN TURTLE STEW

Marinate hunks of turtle meat in salt, pepper, and orange and lime juice for several hours. Drain and boil several hours with one cup of minced shallots, one-half cup of minced green and red peppers, one-half cup of minced celery, a few whole allspice, six Creole tomatoes, a few cloves, four bay leaves, and a pinch of thyme.

DIAMONDBACK TERRAPIN

Skin and clean one terrapin. Cut meat into pieces. Boil in cold water with a *bouquet garni* for one hour or until tender. Remove meat and sauté in butter. Add one cup of sherry and chopped hard-cooked eggs when ready to serve. (Serves four to six.)

GREEN (OR SEA TURTLE) SOUP

Cut four pounds of turtle meat in small pieces. Rub an iron skillet with garlic. Place meat in skillet with a small amount of olive oil. Sauté a few minutes. Add water and boil for several hours with chopped onions, thyme, basil, cut lemon, cloves, and bay leaves. Make a *roux* in a second skillet and slowly add the strained stock. Then add the meat and simmer until meat falls apart. Add chopped hard-cooked eggs and one cup of sherry. Top with nutmeg. Garnish with lime slices. (Serves eight or more.)

Iron work balconies overhang the streets of The Vieux Carre in New Orleans

VII
Entrées

Tomb of "Evangeline" - St. Martinville

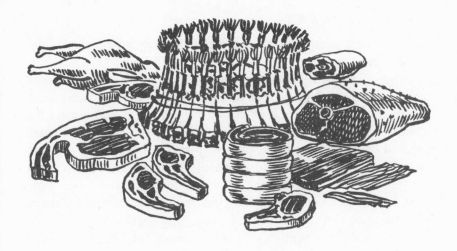

Entrées

Entrées in Louisiana are apt to surprise even the most seasoned epicures—fried pig's feet, calf's head, or curried liver may appear on the table with perfect *savoir-vivre*. The conventional entrées are conspicuously absent, making Louisiana gastronomy an endless wonder and delight.

The *cuisinières* of this Southern section have always had one basic culinary principle—they know they get out of the iron pot only what they put into it in artistry, patience, and skill. But their vocation holds many rewards: the stranger has only to be seated once at their distinguished board to become a lasting friend.

A knowledge of gastronomic lore and culture traditionally has been imparted to Louisiana women from their foreign ancestors. Long ago they learned to present table fare *au morceau*. Last week's turkey carcass could be transformed into gumbo and served with rice and a bottle of claret. Theirs too was a gift of *sang-froid* that could provide a *reveillon* as easily as a midday meal.

These habitants practice two essential rules in the preparation of meat: roasts and other cuts must first be seared in hot fat over a flame or in the oven in order to retain their juices; or, if the meat is to be boiled, it must be placed in already boiling water; and all types of meat must be seasoned with salt *after* it is cooked, since salt toughens it.

Other tricks of meat cookery are familiar to them: sugar, used as a tenderizer, can be rubbed on meat or used in the basting fluid; garlic, in the basting fluid or cut into the meat, is and always has been a stand-by in Louisiana kitchens. There too the French method of marinating meat, especially steaks, in olive oil and vinegar is commonly used, and marinades of wine and brown sugar are mixed both to enhance the flavor and tenderize the meat.

In Louisiana a cut of meat may change its character many times, depending on the wielder of the basting spoon, spice box, and cooking pan. A definite south European influence may be felt in meats prepared by Spanish and Italian chefs, who use flavor combinations of garlic, tomatoes, orégano, and other piquant herbs. Olive oil is, of course, their basic cooking oil.

The French chef, on the other hand, believes that butter is the only proper fat for cooking meat seasoned with sweet herbs, parsley, carrots, and other vegetables; and the Chinese population of Louisiana (yes, there *are* Chinese here!) identify their dishes with peanut oil and ginger, while Louisianians of Russian descent prefer sour cream as the perfect fat for all cooking.

But, *mes amis*, the Cajuns and Creoles are international in their grand cuisine—they use some of all the fats and almost all the herbs in the world.

BEEF

America's favorite and most expensive meat is beef. Connoisseurs of beef will tell you that prime porterhouse does not come from most any steer. In fact, it may have come from a heifer. Beef is usually obtained from steers, bulls, heifers, cows, and stags. Meat from a calf under eight weeks of age is classed as veal. Cattle cuts are divided still further by the United States Department of Agriculture into seven grades, of which the top three are prime, choice, and good.

The most costly cuts are the porterhouse steak, T-bone steak, club steak, pinbone steak, tenderloin steak (filet mignon), tip roast, rib roast, and crown roast. Among the many medium priced cuts

Land's End

are: chuck, brisket, shank, bottom round, eye round, hind shank, boneless rump, flank steak, stew, round steak, heel of round, tip steak, short ribs, blade roast, neck, arm steak and roast, plate, ground meat, rolled roast, and English cut. The beef "odds and ends" include tongue, brains, oxtail, liver, kidneys, sweetbreads, and tripe.

BEEF BRISKET

Tie a four-pound brisket of beef with string, and place in a deep pot with two quarts of boiling water. Season with two sticks of cinnamon, two tablespoons of allspice, a few cloves, three bay leaves, one tablespoon of thyme, one tablespoon of Worcestershire sauce, and one cut-up lemon. Boil gently for one hour or until the meat is tender. In another pot place six peeled turnips, one bunch of peeled carrots, and three sliced onions. Sauté these vegetables in butter for five minutes, then add two cups of white wine and one cup of catsup. Simmer the vegetables an extra twenty minutes or until done. Slice the brisket and serve the vegetables on the side. (Serves ten.)

ROASTED RUMP OF BEEF

Cut two cloves of garlic into slivers and put into a five-pound rump roast by cutting deep holes with a knife. Place the meat in a preheated iron skillet and sear on both sides. Add six cups of water to the meat and place the skillet in a preheated oven. Cook in a hot oven for ten minutes, then turn the heat down low. Roast two to three hours or until the meat is done, basting often. Peeled potatoes, carrots, turnips, and onions may be placed around the roast and cooked with it. The vegetables should be placed in the skillet thirty minutes before the roast has finished cooking. (Serves ten.)

BEEF RAGOUT

Cut three pounds of brisket into chunks and place in a skillet with one pint of beef stock or water, two cloves of garlic, one can of mushrooms, one cup of tomato catsup, and one teaspoon of powdered nutmeg. Simmer for one to two hours or until the meat is done. Add salt and pepper to taste and two cups of red wine. Let this steep for thirty minutes. When ready to serve add two tea-spoons of curry powder and serve with boiled rice. (Serves eight.)

BARBECUED BEEF ON SKEWERS

Cut steaks two inches thick and three to four inches square. Place these alternately on skewers with large pickled onions. Several hours before you are ready to barbecue make a sauce of two sticks of oleo, one bottle of catsup, one-half cup of Worcestershire sauce, the juice of three lemons, one small bottle of olive oil, one cup of brown sugar, and two teaspoons of Tabasco sauce. Simmer this sauce for ten minutes and let blend until ready to barbecue. Place the skewers of meat over a low barbecue fire, basting often with the sauce. When the meat is almost done (about one hour), place sev-eral bunches of dried thyme and bay leaves on the coals so that the meat is smoked by these herbs. (Serve one skewer per person.)

STEAK WITH ANCHOVIES

Cut steaks in long, thin strips. Marinate in olive oil and garlic pods for two hours. Place a fillet of anchovy on top of each steak and roll up, securing with toothpicks. Place the steaks in a roasting pan with one large can of tomato juice, one teaspoon of Tabasco sauce, two teaspoons of lemon, and one cup of olive oil. Roast in a slow oven for thirty minutes or until tender. Season with salt and pepper. (Serve one steak roll to a person.)

ROAST A LA MODE

Marinate for one hour a four-pound beef roast in one cup of red wine, one-half cup of wine vinegar, one cup of olive oil, three bay leaves, a pinch of mace, a pinch of rosemary, and several cloves. Add one clove of garlic to the liquid and pour it over the roast in a roasting pan. Roast for two hours and baste often, sea-soning with salt and pepper when the meat is done. (Serves eight or more.)

BEEF STEW

The success trick of this dish lies in preparing each ingredient separately.

Cut up three pounds of broiled steak and put aside.

Peel and cut crosswise pieces of carrot. Fry these in butter for five minutes and put aside.

Scrape some new potatoes in water and simmer for twenty minutes until they are done. Drain these and put aside.

Sauté two cups of sliced onions for five minutes in butter and put aside.

Sauté one cup of minced celery stalks for five minutes and put aside.

All of the above ingredients should be prepared in the morning. An hour before dinner mix the onions and celery with the meat and meat juice. When ready to serve, add the other vegetables and one cup of chutney. (Serves eight to ten.)

BESSIE'S CHILI

Chop up three large onions, two bell peppers, one small bunch of celery, and five pods of garlic very fine. Sauté in one-half cup of cooking oil for ten minutes. Add five pounds of ground meat and cook until meat is well separated but not brown. Add two cans of Italian tomato paste and one quart of water; cook for fifteen minutes. Add four tablespoons of chili powder, five tablespoons of paprika, one-eighth teaspoon of cayenne pepper, and salt to taste. Cook slowly for one and one-half hours. If chili thickens too much, add more water. When ready to serve, add two cans of Louisiana red kidney beans. Serve with crackers and rice or boiled spaghetti. (Serves ten to fifteen.)

MUSCATROLLI

Sauté ten large onions in one-fourth pound of butter but do not brown. Mix one large can of sliced mushrooms, one large can of pimientos, one can of tomato soup, and one can of tomato sauce or paste with the onions. Fry one pound of ground beef or veal slowly in an iron skillet for thirty minutes or until meat is a light brown. Add to other ingredients.

Boil one sixteen-ounce package of shell macaroni in salted water for ten minutes or until tender. Rinse under cold water and add to the mixture in the iron skillet. Add one pound of shredded, aged American cheese and simmer for ten minutes or until ingredients are well mixed. When ready to serve, this mixture should have the consistency of a good solid dip but not a drip. (Serves twelve.)

MANALE'S MEAT BALLS AND SPAGHETTI

Mix two cups of ground beef with one and a half cups of grated bread, two slices of wet bread, three-fourths cup of Italian cheese, one minced onion, one-half cup of minced parsley, and salt and pepper, to taste. Mix and add six or seven eggs, depending on the moistness of the stuffing. (It must not be too soft.) Roll the mixture into balls, or make into patties if meat is to be served without sauce. Place oil or lard in a frying pan and fry the balls until they are about half done (thirty minutes), then place in the sauce and cook for one hour.

Sauce

Sauté one or two onions in olive oil. Add three cans of tomato paste. Fry a few minutes, then add one can of strained tomatoes and one pod of garlic. Cook half an hour and add the meat balls. Simmer the balls in the sauce for one hour. Serve with grated Italian cheese. This is the famous dish served at Pascal's Manale Restaurant in New Orleans. (Serve two meat balls per person.)

Spaghetti

Italian spaghetti should be used, boiled for ten minutes in hot, salted chicken broth, then rinsed under cold water.

MEXICAN PIE

Fry one pound of ground or chopped meat until it is almost done. Add one cup of minced shallots and four or more teaspoons of chili powder, one teaspoon of salt, a dash of cayenne, and a half teaspoon of black pepper. In a bowl make a mush of three cups of corn meal and enough boiling water to moisten. Place a layer of mush and a layer of meat alternately in a greased baking dish. When the dish is filled, sprinkle the top with grated cheese. Cook about thirty minutes in a medium hot oven. (Serves four.)

SHEPHERD'S PIE

Spread two cups of cooked, chopped meat on the bottom of a baking dish. Grate three large carrots and sprinkle over the meat. Place one cup of grated onions over the carrots. Sprinkle onions with minced parsley. Then make a paste of two cups of boiled potatoes, one teaspoon of flour, salt, pepper, and a little warm cream. Roll the paste out and place over the other ingredients. Punch several small holes in the potato paste. Bake in a slow oven for about an hour. (Serves six.)

YORKSHIRE PUDDING

Marinate a three-inch steak in garlic and olive oil for an hour. Place in an iron skillet and sear both sides in cooking oil. Place three cups of water or beef stock in the skillet. Put in the oven and roast for two hours, basting often. When the steak is done, pour the gravy off and place the steak on a platter to keep warm. Make a pudding of one cup of sifted flour, one teaspoon of pepper, one teaspoon of salt, four beaten eggs, and three cups of warm cream. Blend the batter well and pour into the skillet in which the meat was cooked. Bake the pudding for thirty minutes, and serve in squares with strips of the steak and minced parsley. Place the basting liquid in a gravy boat. (Serves six to eight.)

COLLOPS OF BEEF

Cut round steak in strips one inch wide and three inches long. Rub the strips of meat with lemon juice and black pepper. Sauté a few minutes in butter. Add two cups of meat stock, one cup of tomato catsup, one cup of pecan meats, two bay leaves, and a pinch of rosemary. Let simmer for one-half hour or until the meat is tender, then add one cup of red wine. Serve the meat on strips of toast and sprinkle with minced parsley. (Serve two strips per person.)

VEAL CUTLETS

Sauté cutlets in butter for a few minutes. Add one can of tomato juice and simmer ten minutes. Dry the meat and dip in egg and bread crumbs. Fry for ten minutes or until tender in butter or oleo. When ready to serve make a sauce of two cups of cream, one tablespoon of flour, salt and pepper to taste, and one tablespoon of melted butter. Pour sauce over cutlets and place asparagus, sliced tomatoes, and green peas on the side of the meat. (Serve one cutlet per person.)

VEAL ALCAPARRO

Cut four veal steaks into pieces. Marinate these in two cups of rum and three cups of fruit juice for several hours. Dry and braise for ten minutes in olive oil. Add one cup of pineapple juice, one cup of raisins, and one cup of ripe olives. Cook for one hour or until the meat is tender. Sprinkle minced capers over the meat and serve with boiled rice. (Serves four to six.)

VEAL SCALOPPINE

Cut veal steaks into strips. Marinate in olive oil and garlic for one hour. Dry and dust with flour. Fry for thirty minutes, and when done add several cups of red wine. (Serve one strip of veal per person.)

TÊTE DE VEAU VINAIGRETTE

This recipe has been contributed by Roger Pelletier, who translated it from the French in an old recipe collection of his family. M'sieu Pelletier says this dish was known as "the Gourmet's Delight."

"Use half the head of young calf, halved in its length. Remove bones, brain, and tongue. Scald the head, scrape and rub clean until white and smooth, dipping occasionally in boiling water in the process. Clean the brains in cold water and set aside. Thoroughly clean the tongue and scald. Now cut the half head in four pieces (clipping off the ears). Use a covered pot, and, in a little cold water, stir and blend a teaspoon of flour. Place the four pieces and the tongue in the pot, adding salt, pepper, cloves, and a bunch of seasoning herbs tied together. Now add cold water slowly, stirring to blend the salt, pepper, and flour until all is covered with water. Let come to a boil; then remove to a low fire, and let simmer for three hours. Boil the brains separately in water, the juice of half a lemon, and salt to taste for twenty minutes."

Sauce Vinaigrette

"Use a mixing bowl, and place in it one or two teaspoons of dry mustard, one ounce of olive oil, four ounces of vinegar, salt and pepper. Mince one onion, some shallots, one pickle, two olives, and the yolk of two eggs. Add a few capers, and stir all together with the liquid. Keep warm by placing container in boiling water.

"To serve, use an elongated flat platter. Place the veal in the center lengthwise. Halve the tongue in its length, skin it, and place one piece on each side. Set the brain at one end, a sprig of parsley at the other. The sauce is served in a sauce boat. A bottle of Grave (white wine) will wash it down beautifully."

VEAL PEPPER POT

Boil a knuckle of veal in cold water with a *bouquet garni* and one bottle of red wine for one hour or until tender. When tender, add salt and pepper and place on pieces of toast.

VEAL AU LAIT

Cut veal in two-inch strips and sauté in butter for five minutes. Add three cups of cream, two peppercorns, two tablespoons of grated onion, and one teaspoon of Worcestershire sauce. Roast in a slow oven for forty minutes, basting often. Garnish with minced parsley. (Serve one strip per person.)

SWISS STEAKS OF VEAL

Rub steaks with garlic and pound minced onions and minced stuffed olives into the meat. Dust with flour and fry for thirty minutes over a slow fire. Add one cup of whole stuffed olives and one cup of small pickled onions. Serve with grits. (Serve one steak per person.)

SAUTÉED CALF'S LIVER

Trim the liver and scald. Sauté for five minutes on each side or until tender in a skillet with butter. Sprinkle with minced onions and serve. (One pound of liver serves two.)

WHOLE CALF'S LIVER

Make a dressing of two cups of bread crumbs, one-half stick of butter, one cup of shelled walnuts, one-half cup of shallots, a dash of pepper, and a little minced thyme and basil. Cut the liver and stuff with dressing. Roast for one hour or longer in a slow oven in meat stock and one glass of grape jelly. (Serves ten.)

CURRIED CALF'S LIVER

Trim the liver slices and scald. Cut in small pieces and fry for fifteen minutes or until tender in butter. Add one cup of minced parsley to the liver and one cup of tomato catsup. Sauté a few minutes. Add three cups of cream and simmer five or six minutes. Add three teaspoons of curry powder. Serve with boiled rice. (One pound of liver serves two.)

CALF'S HEAD

Wash and clean head, removing brains. Boil head for two hours in cold water with a *bouquet garni* or until tender. Cut meat from the bone and serve the cooked brains on the side. (Serves six.)

FRIED BRAINS

The brains should be washed and cleaned well in salted water. Leave in cold water for a half hour, then dry and cut in pieces. Dip the pieces into a batter of beaten eggs and a little minced onion and parsley. Dust with flour and fry for ten minutes in cooking oil.

CALF'S HEART

Wash heart in salted water. Make a dressing of one cup of toasted bread crumbs, a little minced parsley, a half cup of grated turnips, and a pinch of sage and pepper. Moisten the ingredients with a little wine. Cut and stuff the heart with the dressing. Roast in a slow oven for two hours or until done. (Serves six to eight.)

KIDNEY STEW

Slice kidneys and place in enough water to cover, with a tablespoon of vinegar, one cup of minced parsley, and a clove of garlic. Stew for a half hour.

SWEETBREADS À LA BOURGEOISE

To prepare sweetbreads, soak in ice water for an hour, then remove membranes. Simmer with water and one tablespoon of wine vinegar for a half hour. Add several cups of dried mushrooms that have been soaked in wine overnight. Serve on toasted French bread. (One pound serves two.)

STEWED TONGUE

Cover tongue with water and stew with a bouquet of spices. Simmer several hours, then add one cup of wine vinegar and two cups of red wine. Let steep in the liquid until ready to slice and serve. (Serves ten.)

ROASTED BEEF HEART

Parboil heart for thirty minutes or until it begins to get tender, then place it in a roasting pan with sliced onions, a pinch of sage, a pinch of tarragon, one cup of brown sugar, and several cups of beef stock. Roast for two hours or until done, basting often. (Serves six.)

PORK

Pork is popular in the South, where city folk prefer the more glamourous cherry-studded boneless hams and stuffed pork chops, and country residents select the "stick to the ribs" cuts of hog jowl, spareribs, and sage-seasoned sausage. Pork is actually the least expensive meat in the market. Smoked hams and shoulder butts are standard rations in many plantation homes. Salt pork bacon, hock, picnic shoulder hams, shoulder butt, and pig's feet are all cuts of

Lafitte's Blacksmith Shop, New Orleans

medium cost. Ham steaks, roasts, and chops are more expensive pork cuts. Pork should be cooked longer than beef or lamb. A low or slow temperature should be used.

BAKED HAM

Place ham in a large pot with enough water to cover. Season with bay leaves, thyme, and any sweet herbs or spices. Simmer for several hours or until ham is tender. Cut the heat off and leave the ham in the pot of water overnight. The next morning trim off the outside fat and skin. Make a paste of brown sugar, dry mustard, and Kijafa, or any other sweet red wine. Score the ham in the shape of diamonds and pat the paste into the ham, covering the outside. Place cloves all over the ham, and brown for twenty minutes in a hot oven, basting with more red wine. Beer may be used to soak the ham and honey used for a glaze.

HOG CHITTERLINGS

Wash and clean the intestines. Scald and place in a pot of cold water with salt, pepper, a dash of cayenne, and bay leaves. Simmer for forty minutes or until tender. The boiled "chittlin's" may be served plain, or rolled in corn meal and fried.

SWEET AND SOUR PORK

Cook ribs or chops for one hour in barbecue sauce. Cut in small pieces. Marinate some ginger root in one glass of bourbon whisky for an hour, then remove. Peel several green peppers by holding them over a flame. Slice the peppers and sauté in butter with pineapple slices. Add the pork pieces and the whisky. Simmer a few minutes.

HOG JOWL

A smoked hog jowl is best used with vegetables. Boil the jowl for several hours. In a separate pot, boil several pounds of black-eyed peas with salt for one or two hours. When ready to serve, place the jowl in the peas, and serve with minced onion. This is the traditional New Year's Day dish in the South.

SALT PORK

Cut slices of lean salt pork and place in a dish with cream. Let this soak overnight. Dry and dip in meal or bread crumbs. Fry for twenty minutes in hot grease until brown.

FRIED PICKLED PIG'S FEET

Dry pig's feet after removing from jar. Dip in well-beaten eggs, then in flour. Fry for ten minutes in butter until brown.

BOILED PIG'S FEET

Boil pig's feet for two hours or until tender. Then add three cups of stock, a pinch of mace, three cups of white wine, two teaspoons of minced parsley, and a *bouquet garni* of spices. Let the feet stew over a slow fire until the liquid has boiled down to about one cup. Add two beaten eggs to thicken and salt and pepper.

SHALLOT PIE

Make a custard with three beaten egg yolks, one-half teaspoon of salt, a pinch of cayenne, one teaspoon of flour, a pinch of white pepper, and one cup of sour cream. Cook in a double boiler for twenty minutes or until thick. Let cool. Sauté in butter one cup of shallots and one-half cup of minced cooked ham and add to custard. Pour into a crust-lined pie pan and bake seven to eight minutes. (Serves approximately six persons.)

ROASTED SHOTE

A shote is a young pig under six weeks old. After the butcher has prepared the pig for cooking, scald it and rub dry. Rub with butter and pepper. Prepare a dressing of bread crumbs, mashed potatoes, chopped onion, chopped celery, minced parsley, sage, butter, and thyme. Add the cooked, sliced pig liver to the dressing. Stuff and sew the pig up. Place in the roasting pan and hold the body in place with skewers. Roast for several hours with water and a *bouquet garni* of herbs. Place a large apple in the pig's mouth when ready to serve. (Serves thirty or more.)

STUFFED PORK CHOPS

Marinate six chops in olive oil, lemon juice, and a pod of garlic. Split the chops lengthwise. Soak one cup of bread crumbs in wine for five minutes and mix with one-fourth cup of minced shallots, one-fourth cup of minced celery stalks and tops, and three table-spoons of minced green peppers. Stuff chops with dressing and hold in place with toothpicks. Place in a roasting pan with three cups of meat stock. Cook for forty minutes in a slow oven. (Serves six.)

LAMB

Lamb is more economical than beef. The cheapest cuts are from the shank, neck, shoulder, and breast. Saratoga chops and the rolled cuts of shoulder are moderately priced, while the most expensive cuts are leg of lamb, steaks of the loin and leg, chops from the loin and rib, English chops, and roasts from the leg. The crown roast is the most decorative and expensive.

LEG OF LAMB

Place leg of lamb on a spit over a low barbecue fire. Make a sauce of one stick of butter, one can of pineapple juice, one cup of brown sugar, one-half cup of Worcestershire sauce, the juice of four lemons, and one-half cup of wine vinegar. Baste leg of lamb as it turns on the spit for at least an hour. As the outside meat browns and cooks, cut it off and place it in a pan of sauce. Continue cutting browned meat off until all the meat is cut from the bone. Garnish with sprigs of mint. (Serves twenty.)

LAMB CURRY

Simmer two pounds of chopped lamb in water with herbs for forty minutes or until it is tender. Place the meat in a skillet with minced shallots and minced green peppers. Add one can of tomato juice and let it simmer ten minutes. Add three cups of cream, three teaspoons of curry powder, and a teaspoon of nutmeg. Simmer a few minutes. Serve with boiled rice and side dishes of raisins, pea-nuts, chutney, and grated coconut. (Serves four to six.)

The Locke Breaux Oak near Hahnville,
"president" of the Live Oak Society because of its size.

LAMB CHOPS

Cut chops several inches thick. Marinate in red wine and garlic overnight. Wipe dry and fry for thirty minutes in butter. Serve on toast with mint jelly.

A HIND OF MUTTON

Parboil the hind quarter in water and spices for an hour. Strain the water and place the meat in a roasting pan with some cloves and one pod of garlic. Baste often with the strained liquid. Cook several hours in a slow oven.

BRUNSWICK STEW

Cut ten pounds of lamb into pieces and place in several gallons of water. Add some herbs and two pounds of peeled potatoes, one quart of butter beans, two quarts of cut corn, three cans of tomatoes, and two pounds of onions. Let this simmer for several hours. Add salt and pepper to taste. This stew should be cooked outdoors over coals. Squirrels and chickens may be substituted for lamb. (Serves twenty or more.)

GERMAN CABBAGE

Parboil a large head of cabbage and drain. Make a dressing of one cup of bread crumbs, two cups of minced lamb, two tablespoons of minced shallots, and a pinch of tarragon and mace. Moisten with a little stock, or water and butter. Stuff each cabbage leaf, but do not loosen the head of the cabbage. After the leaves are stuffed, tie the cabbage with string and place in a casserole. Place bacon strips on the head and cook for forty minutes in a slow oven. (Serves six.)

OPELOUSAS CHICKEN STEW

Clean, wash, and disjoint two hens. Sprinkle with salt and black pepper and marinate in milk for several hours. In a Dutch oven, make a *roux* and add one cup of minced green peppers, one cup of minced parsley, one cup of minced shallots or onions, three bay leaves, one pod of garlic, one pinch of rosemary, and one pinch of thyme. When the *roux* is brown, wipe chicken pieces dry and add to *roux*. Gradually add one pint or more of hot water or chicken stock. Simmer chickens over a slow fire for two hours or until tender. Serve with boiled rice. This recipe will stretch to feed a dozen people.

POULET AU LAIT

Clean, wash, and disjoint two fryers. Rub with a pod of garlic and salt and white pepper. Place in a deep crock and cover with half-milk—half-cream. Keep in the refrigerator overnight. When ready to serve, dry chickens and dip in egg batter and cracker crumbs. Fry for thirty minutes in deep fat until tender. The milk marinade makes the pieces of chicken larger and turns them a lighter color. (Serves four to six.)

JUDGE CHARLES A. O'NIELL'S CHICKEN, SAUCE PIQUANT

Salt, pepper, and flour a disjointed chicken. Sauté in fat until brown, then remove from skillet. Next sauté one small green pepper, sliced; one large Bermuda onion, sliced; one large tomato, sliced; two buds of garlic, minced; and one small bay leaf. Add a dash of Tabasco sauce. Cook until onions are transparent, then return chicken to skillet. Add two cups of stock and simmer mixture slowly for about two and one-half hours. Add one cup of sherry wine and cook about thirty minutes longer. (Serves four.)

CHICKENS AND SALT PORK

Place two young fryers in a roasting pan. Sprinkle with salt, pepper, and a dash of nutmeg. Place thin strips of lean salt pork over the chickens and roast in a medium hot oven for one hour, basting often with three cups of hot water and one cup of white wine. (Serves four.)

CHICKEN AND DUMPLINGS

Clean, wash, and disjoint a hen. Sauté in butter for five minutes. Place chicken in a Dutch oven and cover with two pints or more of water or chicken stock. Add two cups of minced shallots and simmer for an hour. Add one cup of fried, mashed livers and one can of mushrooms. Let simmer for one hour or until chicken is almost done. Drop the dumplings in and cook about ten minutes. (Serves six to eight.)

CHICKEN PUDDING

Clean, wash, and disjoint one fryer. Rub with salt, pepper, and mint leaves. Sauté in butter a few minutes. Simmer for forty minutes with one quart of water and a *bouquet garni*. Make a batter of six beaten eggs, one stick of butter, one tablespoon of flour, and enough cream to thicken. Mix chicken with batter and place in a greased baking dish. Bake in a hot oven for about thirty minutes. (Serves four.)

SUNDAY NIGHT CHICKEN

Clean, wash, and boil one hen with a *bouquet garni* for forty-five minutes or until tender. Remove the chicken and cut up in small pieces. Boil the bones and stock down to one cup. Dissolve one envelope of gelatin in a little cold water and mix the gelatine, chopped chicken, and chicken stock. Add two teaspoons of curry powder. Pour into a mold and top with slices of pimiento and hard-boiled eggs. (Serves eight.)

POULET À LA REINE

Clean, wash, and disjoint two fryers. Place in a bowl with one bottle of orange wine and marinate overnight in the refrigerator. Dry the pieces of chicken and rub with garlic and olive oil. Sprinkle with salt, pepper, and orégano and broil for forty minutes or until tender, basting often with the wine marinade. (Serves six.)

SPANISH CHICKEN

Clean, wash, and disjoint two fryers. Sauté with one pod of minced garlic in butter for a few minutes. Make a basting liquid of two cups of olive oil, one cup of wine vinegar, one cup of minced onions, salt, and cayenne. Place chickens in a roasting pan; bake for forty minutes or until tender, basting often with the liquid. (Serves eight.)

CHICKEN LIVERS WITH SPAGHETTI

Fry two dozen chicken livers in butter for thirty minutes or until done. Boil one package of Italian spaghetti in hot, salted water for ten minutes. Rinse under cold water. Drain and mix with hot chicken livers. Sprinkle with one cup of minced parsley, one tablespoon of paprika, and one package of Parmesan cheese. (Serves eight.)

GUINEA HEN

Clean, wash, and lard a guinea hen. Rub with a pod of garlic and salt and pepper. Make a dressing of three cups of toasted bread crumbs, one-half cup of artichoke hearts, four teaspoons of minced parsley, and one-half cup of canned mushrooms. Moisten with a little fowl stock. Stuff hen and place in a roasting pan, breast down. Roast in a preheated oven for two hours, basting often with fowl stock and minced parsley. Cook until tender. (Serves six.)

CHICKEN GIBLET STEW

Mix one quart of fowl stock with one-half cup of garlic vinegar, one-half cup of red wine, one cup of catsup, three bay leaves, one teaspoon of thyme, one teaspoon of tarragon, and a dash of Tabasco sauce. Place giblets in stock and stew for thirty minutes or until tender. Serve with boiled rice. (Serves four.)

CROUSTADE OF LIVER

Slice the top off a two-day-old loaf of bread. Scoop out the inside leaving only the crust. Fry two dozen chicken livers in butter for thirty minutes or until done. Mix the livers with two tablespoons of minced parsley, and two tablespoons of minced onions. Place these ingredients inside the toasted bread loaf and slice. (Serves four.)

OWEN BRENNAN'S
YOUNG TURKEY A LA PONTALBA

Sauté eight tablespoons of sliced onions, twelve tablespoons of diced, deep-fried potatoes, eight tablespoons of shallots, eight tablespoons of chopped ham, and ten ounces of sliced mushrooms in butter. Add two cups of white wine, then place one young turkey, boned and broiled in butter, on top other ingredients and top with a cream sauce, or "Sauce Bearnaise." (See p. 218.) (Serves four.)

BRENNAN'S TURKEY POMPADOUR

Slice the breast of baked or boiled turkey and put aside. In a saucepan place eight small sausages, three chopped shallots, and three sliced truffles. Cover with one cup of champagne, one-half cup of chicken or turkey broth, salt, and white pepper. Simmer until the sausages are tender. Thicken with the yolks of three eggs and one-half cup of cream. Add a pat of butter during the thickening process. Pour this sauce over slices of turkey, add a dash of lemon, and serve on toast. Garnish with vegetables and slices of lemon. (Serves four.)

TURKEY FOO YUNG

Sauté two cups of leftover, cooked, minced turkey in butter for a few minutes. In another skillet fry two slices of raw ham for thirty minutes. Drain the cooked ham and cut in small pieces. Mix the ham and turkey and add one cup of minced water chestnuts, two teaspoons of soy sauce, six beaten eggs, one cup of minced shallots, and one-half cup of minced bamboo shoots. Blend all the ingredients and drop by spoonfuls into a preheated, greased skillet. Fry for five minutes or until brown on both sides. (Serves six.)

EGGS
CRAB CLAW OMELETTE

Use one-half pound of cooked crab meat. Beat six eggs and one teaspoon of cream. Add one-half cup of minced shallots, one-half cup of minced pimiento, a dash of white pepper, a dash of paprika, salt to taste, and the crab meat. Cook just until firm in a small amount of butter. (Serves six.)

CHILI EGGS

Mince one cup of leftover cooked game with six beaten eggs, one-half cup of black olives, and one teaspoon of chili powder. Fry just until firm. Garnish with pimiento strips and serve with fried duck livers. (Serves six.)

GREEN PEPPER EGGS

Beat six eggs with three teaspoons of minced onions, salt, pepper, and a dash of Tabasco. Cover bottom of casserole with sliced peppers and sliced pimientos. Pour eggs in. Top with peppers and pimientos. Bake slowly for twenty minutes. (Serves six.)

TALLY HO CRAB OMELETTE

Pick meat from one dozen boiled, seasoned crabs. Beat one dozen eggs until light; add six tablespoons of milk, one-half teaspoon of salt, and one-eighth teaspoon of pepper; then put crab meat and two tablespoons of chopped parsley into the well-beaten eggs. Heat four tablespoons each of oil and butter in a frying pan, and add one large onion, finely chopped, and one tablespoon of chopped celery. Cook for ten minutes, then fold in crab meat and well-beaten eggs. Fold from one side to the other, letting uncooked eggs fall at sides. Do not cook too dry. Serve on a hot platter garnished with parsley. Hot rum may be poured over the omelette and set aflame. (Serves ten to twelve.)

ROE

In preparing fish roe, first wash, cut the fibers out, and parboil a few minutes with lemon. Drain well and fry for ten minutes in butter, or bake for thirty minutes in the oven. It may be added to a fish casserole and baked for thirty minutes.

TURTLE EGGS

Any variety of turtle eggs may be boiled for thirty minutes in salted water. The hard yolks should be just popped into one's mouth with a dash of salt and pepper. They may also be floated in turtle stew or soup.

JUDGE HAROLD A. MOISE'S HAM AND EGGS

Use an electric roaster. Put two eggs with a little butter in one pan and a slice of ham in another. Place both pans in the roaster, the one containing the eggs a little later than that with the ham.

BOILED EGG CASSEROLE

Hard-boil twelve eggs for ten minutes. Cut up and mix with
"Lessie's Cream Sauce." (See p. 216.) Bake in oven for thirty minutes. Top with ripe avocado slices. (Serves six.)

TROPICAL EGGS

Fry thick slices of pineapple and banana in butter for five minutes. Mix shaved ginger root in a little white wine and add. Drain
but keep hot. Fry two eggs in butter. Place eggs on plate with
fruit. Sprinkle with fresh coconut. (Serves two.)

SCRAMBLED OYSTERS

Soft-scramble six eggs with a small amount of cream and minced
parsley. When almost done, drop in eight oysters. Cook until
oysters begin to curl. Top with a dash of caviar and serve. (Serves
six.)

OR

Add oysters to an omelette. Pour a small amount of brandy over
omelette and serve aflame.

TURTLE EGGS IN A PUFF

Mash the boiled yolks of turtle or other eggs into a paste. Add
the beaten whites of several hen eggs. Roll into a ball and sprinkle
with flour. Fry in deep fat for five minutes. Serve hot.

CAJUN JAMBALAYA

Arthur Van Pelt, the dean of all Louisiana's outdoor-life writers,
says of the Louisiana jambalaya: "This is not a mixture of boiled
rice and gravy as is frequently served under the name of Jambalaya. Instead it is the completed product of the skillful blending
of many flavors of which none predominates. It should be cooked
in a big iron skillet."

First chop two pounds of Bermuda onions and six celery stalks;
dice one-half pound of sweet-pickled pork, ham, or salt pork. Drain

juice from a hundred fat Louisiana oysters, and save one cup of juice. Heat lard in an iron pot. Fry onions slowly with loving care. Remove them and fry diced meat in the pot. Remove the meat, and place the celery in the same pot, frying a few minutes until tender. Then add the meat, onions, and oysters, and let cook until oysters curl. Add the oysters' juice and two quarts of hot water. Bring the mixture to a boil and season with salt and cayenne pepper. Next add three cups of washed long-grain rice. Simmer and stir the jambalaya until the rice is tender. If it gets too dry, add a little hot water. When the jambalaya is served, place a dot of butter on each serving and sprinkle with minced parsley and paprika. Shrimp, fowl, or game may be substituted for oysters. (Serves a dozen or more.)

POULE D'EAU JAMBALAYA

Skin two coots and remove all fat. Cut up and fry for thirty minutes or until brown. In another skillet brown three chopped onions and one-half bunch of shallots. Combine disjointed coots and onions. Add one-half cup of minced parsley, two tablespoons of tomato paste, salt, and pepper. Simmer for six minutes. Add four cups of uncooked rice and ten cups of hot water. Cook over a low fire until rice is tender (about one hour). (Serves eight to ten.)

RABBIT JAMBALAYA

Dress, wash, and disjoint rabbit. Dust with salt, pepper, and flour. Sear in hot grease, and add minced shallots, green peppers, and enough stock to cover. Simmer for one hour or until almost done. Add two cups of washed, uncooked rice. Cook for thirty minutes or until rice is done. (Serves eight.)

CAMP JAMBALAYA

Use any small birds or game. Dress and disjoint. Sear in grease. Add hot water, any spices or herbs, and onions or tomatoes. Simmer for thirty minutes or until almost done. Add one cup of uncooked rice and cook until rice is done (about twenty minutes). (Serves six.)

OYSTER JAMBALAYA

Fry slices of lean salt pork. Drain. Sauté one cup of minced shallots in butter and mix with pork and pieces of boiled ham. Pour three dozen oysters with juice into skillet. Simmer until oysters curl. Mix three cups or more of boiled rice with oyster mixture. Place in a double boiler until ready to serve. (Serves six to ten.)

MUSKRAT AU CONGRI

Use two cups of cooked muskrat meat. Boil one pound of field peas in water for one hour or until tender. Drain. Mix one cup of boiled rice, peas, and muskrat together. Add a little stock and butter. Cook until dry. (Serves eight.)

CHINESE JAMBALAYA

Boil one cup of rice. Make an omelette and let cool. Slice. Mix one can of minced mushrooms with one and one-half cups of water chestnuts, one-half cup of chopped shallots, and dash of ginger juice that has been marinated with whisky for several hours. Mix these ingredients with omelette and rice for a dish greaseless and as fluffy as a cloud. (Serves eight.)

SCRAPPLE

Make a mush of one cup of corn meal, one cup of hot stock of game or fowl, and salt and pepper. Add pieces of cut-up cooked game or fowl. Let cool. Slice thick and fry in butter or grease. The scrapple may be dipped in eggs before being fried. This is a good and practical camping-out dish. (Serves four.)

JUDGE JOE B. HAMITER'S RED BEANS AND SAUSAGE

Soak one pound of dried red beans overnight. Chop four medium-sized onions and four stalks of celery fine and sauté in one tablespoon of bacon drippings in an iron pot. Add the beans, two bay leaves, two small red peppers, and salt. Cover well with water and boil slowly for one hour. Cut two pounds of smoked, stuffed sausage into one-inch pieces, fry lightly in one tablespoon of bacon drippings, and add to beans. Simmer entire contents for an additional hour. Serve over cooked rice with a side dish of green onions. (Serves six.)

An Acadian homestead in Louisiana

VIII
Side Dishes

Cutting Sugar Cane

Side Dishes

The prolific soil of Louisiana yields almost every type of vegetable and fruit—the famous yams, white rice, fields of shallots, citrus fruits, luscious strawberries—all entremets for her proverbial board.

Pot herbs and vegetables are cooked two ways in Louisiana. The Creole cook first sears the greens in hot butter or grease and then adds hot water and meat for boiling. The North Louisiana chef first boils ham hock or salt meat until it is almost done and then adds the greens. Either manner of cooking makes the dish much more than just a palatable vegetable.

Entremets are kept hot on the Creole stove by leaving them in a *bain-marie* until ready to be served. This early utensil is large and almost square in shape. It is kept filled with hot water so the saucepans containing the side dishes may always be kept hot.

ANISE

Remove tops, wash and cut two pounds of anise in large pieces. Simmer with celery salt, and salt and pepper for ten minutes or until tender. (Serves four.)

FRENCH, GLOBE, OR BURR ARTICHOKES

Boil six artichokes in salted water for twenty minutes or until tender. Drain. Make a dressing of four tablespoons of bread crumbs, a pinch of orégano, one-half cup of minced shallots, one-half cup of minced parsley, three tablespoons of butter, and any cooked game, fowl, or fried bacon. Fill artichoke leaves and place whole, stuffed artichokes in a pan with a little water. Top with Parmesan cheese and bake for thirty minutes. When almost done, pour white wine over artichokes and let steep. (Serves six.)

JERUSALEM ARTICHOKES

Wash and peel or scrape one pound of artichokes. Boil with salt pork for twenty minutes or until done. Serve with butter. (Serves two to four.)

MANALE'S STUFFED ARTICHOKES

Cut off ends and some of stems of burr artichokes. Clean each artichoke well, examining leaves carefully for worms. Place artichokes in a pot of clear water and let soak awhile, then drain. To make the stuffing: mince four slivers of garlic, one and a half cups of grated bread, three-fourths cup of grated cheese, three-fourths cup of anchovies, and salt and pepper. Blend. Stuff each artichoke leaf. Stand artichokes upright in a pot suited in size to the number to be cooked. Fill the pot three-fourths full of water. (Do not bring to top of artichokes.) Pour some imported olive oil into each leaf. Bake for thirty minutes. (Serve one per person.)

ASPARAGUS BUNCH

Wash two pounds of fresh asparagus and tie in bunches. Place upright in pan and boil for thirty minutes. Remove tie. Wrap a pimiento strip around each bunch. Dress with butter or "Hollandaise Sauce." (See p. 217.) (Serve four per person.)

ASPARAGUS AU GRATIN

Place layers of canned asparagus in a casserole with alternating layers of boiled macaroni. Pour "Lessie's Cream Sauce" (see p. 216) over the mixture. Bake in the oven for thirty minutes. Grated cheese and bread crumbs may be used as a topping. String beans and other vegetables may also be cooked this way. (Serves four.)

AVOCADO

Cut avocado in half. Remove seed and scoop out ripe fruit meat. Mix this meat with salt, pepper, and minced pimiento. Stuff shells and bake in hot oven ten minutes. (Serves two.)

COLD CURRIED TUBERS

Boil any tubers—beets, turnips, and others. Arrange on plate with sliced hard-cooked eggs and chutney. Serve with "Buras Citron Sauce" (see p. 216).

BORSCH

Boil two bunches of beets for one hour or until tender and slice thin. Simmer with one cup of fowl stock, a little butter, one teaspoon of lemon juice, salt and pepper, and a little sugar for ten minutes. Dress with sour cream. Borsch is usually thinned and served as a soup. (Serves eight.)

CREOLE STRING BEANS

Pare two pounds beans and cook with salt pork for one hour or until tender. Drain. Sauté for five minutes with butter, one cup of chili sauce, one half cup of minced shallots, and salt and pepper. (Serves six.)

BEAN POT

Cook one package of red beans as for "Red and White." (See p. 207.) Drain off juice. In a deep iron pot place first a layer of beans, then a layer of lean salt pork, next a layer of shallots. Repeat until pot is full. Mix one cup of molasses with a little hot water and pour over all. Rum may be added. Dig a pit and make a fire, letting it burn down to coals. Place covered pot in coals and bank coals all around. Leave overnight. (Serves six.)

DIXIE BROWN BEANS

Wash and prepare one pound of string beans. Place in a pot of water with salt pork. Simmer several hours until the beans have turned brown. Serve with slices of onions. (Serves four.)

BUTTER BEANS

Wash two pounds of beans and place in a pot with water and salt meat. Boil for one hour or until beans are tender. Season with salt and pepper. Add small amount of thick cream. (Serves six.)

BROCCOLI HOLLANDAISE

Remove outer leaves of broccoli and wash and tie in bunches. Steam with a little water for thirty minutes until tender. Serve with "Hollandaise Sauce" (see p. 217) or butter. (One bunch serves two.)

BRUSSELS SPROUTS

Wash and boil two pounds of Brussels sprouts for twenty minutes or until tender. Cook in casserole as you would kohlrabi, adding minced walnuts to casserole and topping with grated cheese. (Serves four.)

CABBAGE

Cabbage must be eaten in some form on New Year's Day to bring money during the New Year. Boil for twenty minutes in a little water.

STUFFED CABBAGE

Hold one head of cabbage under hot running water to wilt. Dry the leaves. Make a dressing of one cup of minced cooked game or fowl, three teaspoons of minced onions, two cups of boiled rice or dry bread crumbs, and salt and pepper. Spread on leaves and roll up. Place in casserole with butter and a little hot water. Cook in oven for forty minutes or steam on top of stove for thirty minutes. Grape leaves may be used for the cabbage. (Serves four to six.)

CHINESE CABBAGE

Wash and shred one head of cabbage. Simmer with salt and butter for twenty minutes or until tender. Dress with sour or sweet cream mixed with soy sauce. Serve with sliced water chestnuts sautéed in butter. (Serves four to six.)

RED CABBAGE

Wash and cut up one head of cabbage. Boil for thirty minutes with ham hock or salt pork until done. Place on casserole with pieces of cooked ham. Pour "Lessie's Cream Sauce" (see p. 216) over this mixture. Cook in oven for ten minutes. Top with almonds. (Serves four to six.)

EMMA'S CANDIED CARROTS

Peel and shoestring one bunch of carrots. Place three cups of sugar in a saucepan with one cup of water. Place carrots in the sauce and simmer for five minutes. Add one-half cup of melted butter. Let the carrots cook in this for a few more minutes. (Serves four.)

CARROTS NUTMEG

Wash, scrape, and cut one bunch of carrots into shoestrings. Soak a few minutes in ice water. Wipe dry and fry in butter five minutes. Sprinkle with ground nutmeg and let steep in covered pan. Whole nutmeg, cinnamon sticks, or curry powder may be used to season. (Serves four.)

CAULIFLOWER

Wash and peel off outer leaves of a head of cauliflower. (Save these for stock.) Place head in water and steam for ten minutes or until almost tender, then transfer to a casserole and pour over it a sauce made of cream, grated cheese, and salt and pepper. Top head with grated cheese and minced parsley. Cook in oven for ten minutes. (Serves four.)

CELERY

Prepare two pounds of celery as you would anise (see p. 196). Add fresh cream and butter before serving. (Serves four.)

ROASTED CORN

Remove outside husks and inside silk of fresh corn; leave inner husk around corn. Place on outdoor broiler at the same time that you are barbecuing something else. Turn corn often for twenty minutes or until done. Serve with melted butter, salt, and pepper. Corn may be roasted in the oven in silks and husks. (Serve one ear per person.)

SUCCOTASH

Mix two pounds of fresh corn cut from the cob with one pound of uncooked lima beans, two teaspoons of butter, and one pint of water. Simmer for one hour. Add one large can of hot tomato juice, and salt and pepper to taste. Cook for thirty minutes or until beans are done. Add a dash of curry powder if desired. (Serves six to eight.)

BRAISED CUCUMBERS

Peel and slice twelve cucumbers. Let soak in vinegar five minutes. Drain. Braise for five minutes in butter and fowl stock. (Serves twelve.)

CUSHAW

Halve cushaw and remove seedy part. Cut in large pieces and boil for thirty minutes or until tender. Sprinkle sugar and cinnamon with a little butter over each piece. Bake in oven. (Serves six.)

BAKED EGGPLANT RADOSTA

Select two large eggplants. Wash, cut in half, and boil until soft. Then scrape insides into a bowl and mix with minced onion, about four slivers of garlic, one cup of wet bread, one-half cup of Italian cheese, one minced green pepper, one-half cup of minced parsley, and salt and pepper. Fry one and a half pounds of peeled shrimp and chop when done. Add shrimp to the eggplant stuffing. A little cooked ham may be added. Beat two eggs and also add to stuffing, and fill the halved or quartered eggplant shells with it. Sprinkle bread crumbs over tops and brown in the oven. (Serves eight.)

LYE HOMINY

Heat a washpot over a low fire. On the side, burn to ashes a fire of cypress and oak. Shell one gallon of corn. Place corn in washpot with one quart of the ashes. Cover with water. Boil several hours over a low fire until corn is tender. Drain and wash the corn in cold water. Wash twice more in successive waters. Peel off remaining husks. (Some will have come off in the boiling.) This hominy may be eaten at once or stored in jars in salt water with a pod of pepper in each jar. Hominy is especially good with any boiled game or fowl. It may also be served as a side dish after being seasoned with a little salt, pepper, and onion; or it may be used in a *roux* with boiled, peeled shrimp and seasoning and served with rice. (The daily breakfast of the old Southern planter consisted of game, fowl, or ham, lye hominy, corn bread, and coffee.)

GRITS

Stir one cup grits into four cups of boiling, salted water. Add a pinch of salt and boil gently for thirty minutes. Cheese, sautéed calf or chicken livers, and butter may be added to cooked grits. Serve hot. (Serves four.)

FRIED GRITS

Cut thick slices of cold cooked grits. Beat several eggs with salt, pepper, and paprika. Dip grits slices in the egg and fry in butter. Serve hot. (Serves two slices per person.)

CHOPPED KALE

Remove roots and wash kale well. Boil with slices of salt pork for twenty-five minutes or until done. Chop and serve with pieces of crisp bacon.

KOHLRABI

Wash, peel, and slice six kohlrabi bulbs. Simmer with salt and pepper for thirty minutes or until done. Serve with butter and capers. (Serves four.)

LETTUCE AND OTHER SALAD GREENS

Lettuce may be broken up and steamed for a few minutes or fried in butter. Romaine, escarole, and water cress also may be cooked either way.

LETTUCE AU CRÊPE

Wilt lettuce leaves and stuff as you would cabbage. Steam only a few minutes. The wilted leaves may also be stuffed with one part pecans and two parts bread crumbs, placed in a casserole with orange wine, and cooked ten minutes in the oven. (Serves two to four.)

MIRLITON (VEGETABLE PEAR)

Steam four vegetable pears for thirty minutes or until tender. Scoop out inside and mix scoopings with minced celery stalks and tops, cooked game or fowl giblets, bread crumbs, and salt and pepper. Stuff pears and bake ten minutes in oven. (Serves four.)

SHRIMP-STUFFED PEARS

Prepare four mirlitons or vegetable pears as above, but use boiled shrimp instead of giblets. Add minced shallots, and salt and pepper. After stuffing pears, top with Parmesan cheese and bake ten minutes in oven. (Serves four.)

DRIED MUSHROOMS

Wash in cold water several ounces of dried mushrooms, which may be bought at any Italian market or store. Let soak in cold water ten minutes, then rinse and drain. Marinate the mushrooms in red wine for several hours before using in sauces, in soups, or in any dish of fish, fowl, or game.

FRESH MUSHROOMS

Always sauté about five minutes in butter until brown before using with any other food. Serve with meat, fish, or fowl.

BOILED OKRA

Wash and boil two pounds of young okra for twenty minutes or until tender. Drain and serve with "Hollandaise Sauce" (see p. 217) or hot mayonnaise. (Serves six.)

ONION GLACE

Peel and slice twelve onions. Scald under hot water. Drain. Simmer in cane syrup and lemon juice for ten minutes. (Serves six.)

PERCY'S STUFFED ONIONS

Remove the skin from six medium-sized onions. Drop into boiling salted water and cook until tender but not too soft. Drain and remove part of the inside layer. Melt two tablespoons of butter in a skillet. Add onion centers, one-half cup of chopped celery, and one cup of bread crumbs. Stir and cook slowly for about ten minutes until celery is tender. Add salt and pepper to taste. Refill the onion shells with this stuffing. Place in a baking dish and cover. Bake in moderate oven ten minutes so that tops of onion will brown. (Serves four.)

CABBAGE PALM SAVANNA

Prepare palm as in "Cabbage Palm Salad." (See p. 59.) Boil in water with salt pork, salt, and pepper for one hour or until tender. Dress with butter. (Serves four to eight.)

PARSNIPS

Wash and scrape one pound of parsnips. Boil for forty minutes or until tender. Mash and mix with cooked sweet peppers and butter. Add raisins and a little cream. Cook in a casserole in the oven for ten minutes. (Serves four.)

PEAS

Shell and wash green peas. If dried peas are used, soak for two hours before cooking. Cook with salt pork, ham hock, or hog jowl for one hour or until tender. Serve with boiled rice and sliced onions. (Field peas must be eaten on New Year's Day for good luck in the coming year.) (Serves six.)

CHICK-PEAS (GARBANZOS)

Soak one pound of peas for one hour. Boil for one hour or until tender with slices of ham or game, chopped green peppers, a pinch of chili powder, cumin seed, salt, and cayenne. Serve with slices of pimiento and boiled rice. (Serves four.)

SAUTÉED PEPPERS

Hold six peppers over fire so that skin may be peeled off. Remove seeds and slice. Dust with salt and white pepper, and sauté in butter for five minutes. Serve with slices of pimiento. (Serves six.)

SAUCE AU SAVANT

Mince one part green peppers and three parts onions. Moisten with a little lemon juice. Salt and pepper. Form into molds.

PEPPERS SOUTH OF THE BORDER

Sauté one can of corn with one-half cup of minced bell peppers, one can of minced pimientos, and three teaspoons of minced onions. Add a few seasoned bread crumbs. Stuff large peppers that have been blanched and peeled. Place in a pan partly filled with hot water and bake for twenty minutes. (Serves four.)

POKEWEED

Boil the tender leaves of the pokeweed in salted water for ten minutes. Serve with melted butter. (Roots and berries of this plant are poisonous.)

BAKED POTATOES

Rub six large Irish potatoes with grease. Bake in a slow oven for forty minutes or until done. Test with a toothpick. When done, scoop out and mash insides. Mix with butter, minced shallots, salt, and white pepper. Top with paprika and reheat for three minutes in hot oven. (Serves six.)

CHIVE NEW POTATOES

Scrape or peel two pounds of new potatoes. Pare into very small rounds. Simmer for twenty minutes or until tender. Place potatoes in skillet with butter and minced chives. Heat. (Serves six.)

PARISIENNE PARSLEY POTATOES

Scrape one pound of small new potatoes and simmer in clear water for twenty minutes or until tender. Mince one cup of parsley and mix it with one cup of melted butter or margarine, salt, and white pepper. Drain potatoes and place in parsley butter. (Serves four.)

POT HERBS AND GARDEN GREENS

Always wash greens and let soak in salted water at least twenty minutes. Dandelions, corn salad, pepper grass, radish tops, beet tops, mustard greens, carrots tops, fennel, spinach, turnip greens, and collards—all may be boiled with ham hock or salt pork together, separately, or in combinations. A few small peppers may be added while cooking. After the greens are cooked for one hour or more, dumplings may be dropped in and cooked ten minutes and served with greens. (Two bunches serves two to four.)

PUMPKIN

Prepare pumpkin by boiling as you would cushaw. Scrape meat from shell and mix it with sugar, lemon juice, honey, and cinnamon. Bake in a casserole for twenty-five minutes, and top with nuts. (Serves six to ten.)

RICE

MARTHA MERCER'S BOILED RICE

Wash one cup of rice in several waters. Drain. Bring one and one-fourth cups of water to a boil. Add rice. Place top on pan and cut fire as low as possible. Cook fifteen minutes without uncovering until every grain stands apart. (Serves four.)

WILD RICE

Wash rice. Soak overnight. Boil in covered pan as for "Martha Mercer's Boiled Rice." Remember that wild rice swells.

SPANISH RICE

Drain washed rice and dry in a cloth. Sauté one cup of rice in butter with a minced garlic pod until garlic is brown. Add one cup of boiling water and a pinch of saffron. Place top on skillet and cook on slow fire fifteen minutes. Hot chili peppers may be added to rice or cooked in it.

MUDDY WATER RICE

Cook rice same way as for "Martha Mercer's Boiled Rice," but substitute meat stock for hot water and add one cup of chopped giblets or minced cooked game. Serve hard-cooked eggs over mound of rice.

CAJUN DIRTY RICE

Cook one cup of rice for fifteen minutes in fowl stock. Add to it cooked, chopped fowl liver or a generous slice of chopped, cooked calf liver. Add four sliced hard-boiled eggs. (Serves four.)

CHILI RICE

Heat three tablespoons of fresh bacon fat in an iron skillet. Brown one cup of uncooked rice in the bacon fat. Add one minced onion, one small minced pepper, and one-fourth cup of minced celery. Sauté until the onion and pepper are soft. Add one teaspoon of chili powder, one No. 2 can of tomatoes, and one cup of hot water. Season to taste with salt, black pepper, and cayenne. Place top on skillet and cook over a very low fire for fifteen minutes or until the rice is done. More water may be added if necessary. (Serves four to six.)

RICE VERT

Place rice in pan and cook as for "Martha Mercer's Rice" adding one-fourth cup of minced shallots, one-fourth cup of minced parsley, and salt and white pepper. (Serves four.)

GARLIC-CHIVE RICE

Sauté in butter for a few minutes three teaspoons of minced onion, one teaspoon of minced garlic, and one-half cup of minced chives. Wash and dry one cup of rice. Place the rice with one and one-fourth cups of hot salted water in a skillet and cook all the ingredients for one minute. Place a tight top on skillet and cook as slowly as possible for fifteen minutes. (Serves four.)

CITRUS RICE

Cook as "Martha Mercer's Rice," using orange juice and a little lemon instead of hot water. Add minced pecans and a little grated grapefruit peel. Rice may also be prepared with orange wine. (Serves four.)

RED AND WHITE (RED BEANS AND RICE)

Soak one pound of red beans overnight. Wash, then boil with salt pork and peppers. Boil three cups of rice as in "Martha Mercer's Rice" and serve it as a meal with red beans. (Serves six to eight.)

FRIED RICE

Cook one cup of rice as "Martha Mercer's Rice," but use game or fowl stock for water. Add one-half cup of minced shallots and a dash of curry powder before rice is boiled. When rice is done, sauté in butter adding a little peanut butter to the mixture. (Serves four to six.)

CALAS TOUS CHAUD

Take one cup of boiled rice. Beat three eggs until thick. Add one-half cup of sugar, one-half teaspoon of salt, one-half teaspoon of nutmeg, and three teaspoons of baking powder. Mix with rice and beat until blended. Drop by teaspoonfuls into deep fat. Fry for ten minutes or until brown. Drain on heavy paper. Sprinkle with powdered sugar. Serve hot. (Serves six.)

RISOTTO

Mix one cup of boiled rice, one-fourth cup of minced shallots, one-fourth cup of minced green peppers, salt, pepper, and one cup of grated cheese. Moisten with fowl stock and cook in oven for twenty minutes. (Serves four to six.)

RICE ORÉGANO

Mix four cups of boiled rice with pieces of cooked game, one can of minced pimiento, and three green peppers. Sauté in butter and add a dash of orégano. Moisten with fowl stock. Place in a casserole and bake in oven for thirty minutes. Sprinkle Parmesan cheese over top. (Serves eight.)

FOWL PILAU

To make pilau (pronounced *purr-loo* in Louisiana), boil any wild fowl with a *bouquet garni* and mace for one hour or until done. Remove herb sack and add some raisins. Add one cup of rice that has been boiled until almost done. Add pinch of saffron, and cook until liquid is reduced. (Serves six.)

OKRA PILAU

Fry several pieces of salt pork. Remove from skillet, and simmer one cup of minced shallots in fat with six peeled tomatoes. Add one cup of game stock and one can of tomato juice. Add young okra and simmer until okra is done (about twenty minutes). Add one cup of preboiled rice and pieces of pork to mixture or serve them on the side. (Serves six.)

HOPPING JOHN

This is a dish from North Louisiana. Boil two pounds of field peas with a ham hock about two hours. Add preboiled rice to peas and liquid, or drain peas and serve rice with ham and peas on the side. (Serves eight.)

JUDGE JOHN B. FOURNET'S TECHE HOLIDAY DRESSING

Wash two and one-half cups of rice and cook in a double boiler with two and one-half cups of water and one teaspoon of salt for forty-five minutes. (Or rice may be boiled and drained.) Chop and clean the giblets of two chickens or one turkey. Add one-half pound of pork, chopped, and place both in a skillet in which two tablespoons of cooking oil have been heated. Stir until browned lightly, then add one large onion, chopped; one small bell pepper, chopped; and one-fourth stalk of celery, chopped. When onions are lightly browned, add the liquor from one pint of oysters; one clove of garlic, chopped; and one-fourth bunch of shallots, chopped. Cover and let simmer until pork is cooked—at least thirty minutes. Add one-fourth cup of water or meat stock if more moisture is needed. When pork is done, add one tablespoon of salt, one-fourth teaspoon of cayenne pepper, and the pint of oysters. Cook slowly until the edges of the oysters curl. Add cooked hot rice and mix gently. Add one-eighth teaspoon of black pepper and one-half cup of chopped pecan meats. Serve piping hot with turkey or chicken and vegetables. (Serves eight.)

RUTABAGAS

Wash and pare two pounds of rutabagas. Cut in quarters or in smaller pieces. Steam in a little water for forty minutes or until tender. Mash with butter and nutmeg. (Serves six to eight.)

SALSIFY (OYSTER PLANT)

Wash and scrape two pounds of oyster plant root. Steam for about thirty minutes or until tender in a little water. Cut in pieces and dress with butter, cream, a dash of Tabasco, and salt and pepper. (Serves six.)

BOILED SCALLIONS

Remove root and wilted tops of two pounds of scallions. Wash and boil for one-half hour in two successive waters. Dress with hot butter and capers or water cress. (Serves six.)

Leeks, onions, wild onions, and garlic may be prepared in this manner.

SKIRRET AND CARROTS

Wash and scrape two bunches of carrots. Boil in salted water for twenty minutes or until tender. Mince fresh skirret or parsley. Add this to sliced carrots with salt, pepper, and butter. (Serves six.)

CREAMED SPINACH

Grind two bunches of spinach and add one cup of ground shallots. Simmer for twenty minutes in cream. Add a pinch of sugar, and salt and white pepper. Serve on toast. (Serves four.)

SAUTÉED SPINACH

Boil one pound of spinach for ten minutes and drain. Sauté for five minutes with butter, minced shallots, and hard-boiled egg slices. Sprinkle with mustard seed. (Serves two.)

SQUASH

Wash one pound of young squash. Remove tough, seedy part, and cut up and boil in salted water for twenty minutes until tender.

Drain. Sauté for five minutes in butter with minced shallots, salt, and pepper until dry. (Serves two to four.)

STUFFED SQUASH

Steam two pounds of squash for twenty minutes or until tender. Scoop out inside fiber and seeds. Reserve part of the inside pulp. Mash this pulp with butter, salt, and pepper. Add one cup of minced pecans and one-fourth cup of seasoned bread crumbs. Fill shells with stuffing and top with strips of bacon. Bake or broil for fifteen minutes. (Serves six.)

AUNT NELLIE'S YAM FLUFF

Cream six boiled or baked sweet potatoes with one teaspoon of butter and one-half cup of brown sugar. Add one cup of shredded pineapple, one cup of nuts, and a small amount of cream. Beat and top with six marshmallows. Bake in a casserole. (Serves six.)

BAKED SWEET 'TATERS

Bake sweet potatoes in their jackets in the oven or over coals in foil with butter for forty minutes. (Serve one per person.)

ORANGE SWEET POTATOES

Boil six sweet potatoes for twenty minutes and slice lengthwise. Let cool for a while. Place in a casserole with one cup of orange juice, one cup of sugar, and one cup of grated coconut. Bake in slow oven for about thirty minutes. Add one-half cup of orange wine and let steep. (Serves six.)

BAKED TOMATOES

Heat skin of six large tomatoes by holding on fork over fire. Peel. Cut off tops and scoop out centers. Mix center pulp with two parts seasoned bread crumbs, one part boiled crab meat, salt, white pepper, and a dash of curry powder. Squeeze a little lemon on each tomato. Cook in the oven in a shallow pan partly filled with hot tomato juice for thirty minutes. (Serves six.)

FRIED GREEN TOMATOES

Slice twelve tomatoes and soak awhile in olive oil and vinegar. Drain, dust with salt and white pepper, sprinkle with mustard seed, and fry in butter for five minutes. (Serves six.)

ENTREMETS SUCRE

Peel one pound of tomatoes by holding over a flame with a fork, letting skin begin to blister, then pulling skin off. Place the tomatoes in a saucepan with two slices of lemon and one cup of sugar. Simmer about ten minutes.

STEWED TOMATOES

Peel and stew twelve tomatoes with one cup of hot water, two teaspoons of cinnamon, one teaspoon of nutmeg, one cup of brown sugar, a small piece of candied ginger, and a slice of lemon. Simmer for ten minutes. Add one small box of graham crackers and bake in oven twenty minutes. (Serves six.)

BOILED COWSLIPS AND WILD OKRA

Wash marsh marigolds and early blue violets. Place in a pot with water and pieces of salt pork. Cook for forty minutes or until these greens are tender.

IX
Sauces and Such

Egrets at Avery Island

Sauces and Such

Experienced Louisiana cooks know that it's often the sauce that makes the dish—the extra something that transforms plain food into earthly delight. And they know too that infinite finesse—the tilt of the pan, the heat of the fire, the final flick of the egg-beater—makes the sauce. Ann Allen's cook, Melissa, in attempting to describe this indefinable something, says, "There ain't nothing to it—you jes' puts the moisture in the mixture." And a Creole *grand dame*, smiling at a failure, has been heard to excuse it graciously with *"Mais c'est un manque savoir vivre Creole* (but that is lack of knowing how to live in the Creole way)." For those who suffer from such a lack the sauces given here need provide no difficulty, however; and it is entirely possible that, with the use of them, any cook can catch a gastronomic glimpse of *la vie Creole*.

SAUCES

ALMOND SAUCE

Sauté one cup of cut almonds and one cup of mushrooms in butter. Add to plain cream sauce.

BURAS CITRON SAUCE

Grate the rind of one Louisiana orange and blend with one-fourth cup of orange juice. Make Hollandaise sauce substituting orange for lemon juice. Sprinkle grated orange rind over top of sauce before serving. Serve over vegetables.

PLAIN CREAM SAUCE

Melt one-half stick of butter in top of double boiler. Gradually add two teaspoons of flour. Blend until smooth, and slowly add one and one-half cups of cream, and salt and white pepper. Cook about twenty minutes, stirring until thick and smooth.

CHEESE CREAM SAUCE

Add one cup of grated Cheddar or other cheese and a dash of paprika to cream sauce.

LESSIE'S CREAM SAUCE

Mix three tablespoons of butter, two and one-fourth cups of milk, three tablespoons of flour, one teaspoon of salt, and one teaspoon of white pepper in a double boiler. Add one cup of grated cheese. Cook for ten minutes. Remove from fire. Add one-half cup of mayonnaise and two teaspoons Worcestershire sauce.

CREOLE SAUCE

Mince shallots and green peppers. Sauté in butter. Add one can of mushrooms, two cans of tomato paste, and one can of bouillon. Simmer at least thirty minutes. Bay leaves, thyme, and other herbs may be added.

GRAPEFRUIT SAUCE

Grate the rinds of one-half grapefruit and one orange. Mix with one-half cup of sour cream. Add a dash of fresh, grated coconut.

HOLLANDAISE

Use a double boiler with the water boiling in the bottom boiler but not touching the top. Place the yolks of two well-beaten eggs in top boiler. Add slowly one-half stick of fresh butter that has been melted. Add more slowly the juice of one large lemon or of two limes. Hold the handle of the top boiler and stir, keeping the pan gently up from the bottom boiler. Work fast, stirring every minute until blended and thickened.

MOJE

Grind one cup of shallots or onions with one-half cup of bell peppers. Add two cups of game stock and simmer for about ten minutes with two teaspoons of cumin seed, a bit of cayenne, and salt and pepper. Strain and serve hot in a gravy boat. Serve with boiled rice.

SABAYON SAUCE AUX PLAQUEMINES

Make a Hollandaise sauce, substituting one cup of hot orange wine for butter and reducing citrus juice by half. Pour hot sauce over any vegetable or fowl.

APRICOT SAUCE

Mash six peeled apricots. Add a dash of nutmeg and one-fourth cup of brandy. Serve cold with game or meat.

GEORGE'S SAUCE FOR BARBECUE

Melt one-half pound of butter in an iron skillet. Add one pod of minced garlic, four minced red onions, two minced white onions, one-half cup of minced shallots, one-half bottle of catsup, three teaspoons of English mustard, four teaspoons or more of Worcestershire sauce, one cup of hot water, and three teaspoons of sugar. Simmer half an hour or more.

WINE BARBECUE SAUCE

Make sauce a day or so before barbecue. Mix one-fourth cup of wine vinegar, six cups of red wine, one cup of olive oil, one-fourth cup of minced onions, one-half clove of garlic, three bay leaves, and a dash each of thyme, rosemary, basil, salt, and black pepper. Keep in refrigerator until ready to use for basting duck or game.

SAUCE BEARNAISE

Mince two pods of garlic and steep in one pint of white wine for an hour. Make a *roux* of two tablespoons of melted butter and one tablespoon of flour in an iron skillet. Add one cup of minced chives and one-half teaspoon of rosemary. Add the wine-and-garlic mixture a cup at a time. Simmer for ten minutes over low heat. Let the liquid cool and add the beaten yolks of three eggs and one cup of minced parsley. One cup of tomato paste may be added if desired.

BERRIES IN GAME

Use whole berries in stuffing of game and place whole berries in drippings from roasted game to use for gravy.

BERRY STEW

Melt one cup of blackberry jelly or jam, add one cup of raisins, and stew about five minutes. Let cool and add one jigger of blackberry cordial. Serve cold for game or cake.

CHEESE-ELDER SAUCE

Mash one package of cream cheese. Add four teaspoons of powdered sugar and one cup of elder flower (or elderberry) wine. Mix well over low heat. Serve cold with cold turkey.

CHINESE SAUCE

Cook three tablespoons of cornstarch with water and whisky for half an hour. Add one-fourth cup of wine vinegar, one-fourth cup of sugar, and one cup of pineapple juice. Simmer a few minutes. Serve over game.

CIDER SAUCE

Peel six apples and cover with cider. Let stand several hours. Simmer a few minutes and serve hot, or drain apples and chill to serve cold. Serve with fowl or desserts.

CITRON SOUR

Mix one cup each of orange and lemon juice. Let stand in a covered crock for one week in a warm place. Add salt and bottle. Keep in refrigerator.

CRANBERRY SAUCE

Melt one can of cranberry sauce. Add one cup Burgundy. Serve hot or cold with pork or game.

CRANBERRY JELL

Wash and simmer one quart of cranberries in one quart of water. Cook until the berries are soft. Strain through a muslin cloth. Mix one cup of sugar with one cup of the juice. Simmer and stir for about seven minutes. Skim and pour into hot, sterilized jelly glasses.

RAW CRANBERRY RELISH

Grind one quart of washed cranberries and one cup of orange peel. Pour sugar over the peel and berries. Add two teaspoons of lime juice and stir. Leave in refrigerator until needed. Serve with fowl or game. Wine vinegar may be used instead of the lime juice (about one-half cup of vinegar to each quart of berries).

CURRANT SAUCE

Melt one jar of currant jelly and simmer with a cinnamon stick and a few cloves for a few minutes. Add one-fourth cup of port wine. Serve hot or cold over game.

SAUCE PIROGUE

Chop six cucumbers with one bunch of water cress. Dust with salt and pepper. Add one cup of sour cream and serve in cucumber boats. Numerous other vegetables may be served cold in sour cream. Serve with meat.

DATE SAUCE

Mince one package of dates and simmer in one cup of wine vinegar or wine. Add one dash of nutmeg. Simmer for five minutes. Serve over game.

GARLIC SAUCE AU PAT CHERAMIE

Mince one pod of garlic and sauté in olive oil until brown. Add juice from broiled venison steak. Add one-fourth cup of minced parsley. Serve over steak.

GARLIC SAUCE FOR ROASTED GAME

Sauté one minced pod of garlic in butter for five minutes. Add six minced shallots, two teaspoons of brown sugar, and drippings from roasted game. Simmer for five minutes and add salt and a dash of Tabasco. Add one cup of red wine and let meat steep in sauce.

GRAPE-ELDER SAUCE

Melt one jar of wild grape jelly; add a small amount of powdered sugar and one cup of elder flower (or elderberry) wine. Mix well over low heat. Serve cold with cold game.

GUAVA SAUCE

Melt one jar of Florida guava jelly. Add the juice of one lime and one cup of sherry. Simmer for five minutes whole guavas in sauce. Serve hot or cold over fowl or desserts.

LAKE HAMILTON SAUCE

Melt one pound of butter. Add one bottle of Worcestershire sauce, the juice of six lemons or limes, salt, and fresh, ground black pepper. Baste often with the sauce using a brush for indoor grill and a cheesecloth swab on a long stick for outdoor grill.

HORSE-RADISH SAUCE

Blend one tablespoon of flour with four teaspoons of butter, and salt and white pepper in double boiler. Simmer. Add one-half cup of prepared horse-radish and a little hot water.

MARASCHINO SAUCE

Pour the juice from two jars of red maraschino cherries into a skillet. Mince the cherries and add. Warm the cherries and liquid. Add one tablespoon of flour. Cook for seven minutes. Stir and add one jigger of maraschino liqueur. Place slices of cooked fowl in this sauce and let steep.

MAY HAW JELLY SAUCE

Melt one jar of May haw jelly. Add one-fourth cup of brandy. Serve hot or cold with game or meat.

MINT SAUCE I

Mince fresh mint and simmer with slices of fresh pineapple for five to ten minutes. Add a teaspoon or more of kirsch liqueur and serve with venison or lamb.

MINT SAUCE II

Mince fresh mint and mash well with powdered sugar. Slowly add one cup of wine vinegar. Chill and serve on game or meat.

MOUTARDE AUX FINES HERBES

Make a paste of one-half can of dry mustard and a little hot water. Add five teaspoons of brown sugar, some salt, and white pepper. Thin with little wine vinegar and olive oil. Serve with cold meat or fowl.

MUSTARD CREAM SAUCE

Add two beaten egg yolks to "Plain Cream Sauce" (see p. 216) in double boiler. Stir five minutes and add two teaspoons of dry mustard and a teaspoon of saffron. Serve on meat or vegetables.

ORANGE SAUCE

Simmer segments of three oranges with four teaspoons of powdered sugar, one cup of grated orange peel, and one-fourth cup of orange juice for about ten minutes. Add one cup of orange wine. Serve hot or cold with game, fowl, or desserts.

BRANDIED PEACH SAUCE

Mash six brandied peaches. Add the juice of one lime and a teaspoon of brown sugar. Serve cold with game.

SAUTÉED PEACHES

Peel and slice one dozen fresh peaches. Sauté five minutes in butter with one cinnamon stick and one whole nutmeg until tender. Drain and serve with game or fowl. Apples may be cooked in the same way.

PECAN SAUCE

Sauté pecan halves in butter and salt, and toast in oven. When toasted, pour one cup of sweet white wine over pecans and keep in oven a few minutes. Serve hot or cold with game or meat.

AZTEC SAUCE

Sauté in butter one cup of minced red and green peppers, one pod of garlic, one cup of shallots, one-half cup of celery, salt, and white pepper. Simmer ten minutes. Serve over meat or fowl.

RUM SAUCE

Brown one-half stick of butter with three tablespoons of flour and two teaspoons of dry mustard. Slowly add one cup or more of hot pineapple juice. Simmer for ten minutes and add one-fourth cup of rum. Serve hot with game or meat.

SAUCE FOR FOWL OR FISH

Melt one pound of butter. Add one bottle of chili sauce, one-half jar of Creole mustard, one bottle of tarragon vinegar, salt and pepper, and a dash of Tabasco. Simmer for ten minutes and use to baste often. Six teaspoons of curry powder may be used in place of Creole mustard. This sauce may be used for basting or may be poured in a stew that is almost done.

STRAWBERRY SAUCE

Stew two cups of strawberries for five minutes with three tea-spoons of powdered sugar. Add one cup of strawberry wine and serve cold with cold fowl.

JUDGE E. HOWARD McCALEB'S ANCHOVY SAUCE

Dissolve one heaping teaspoon of anchovy paste in one heaping teaspoon of Worcestershire sauce; add one heaping tablespoon of tomato catsup, one-third teaspoon of onion juice, one cup of mayonnaise, and salt, paprika, pepper, and mustard to taste.

Judge McCaleb recommends this sauce as particularly good for dunking shrimp.

BEURRE NOIR

Brown butter or margarine five minutes with minced capers and a dash of lime juice. Serve over broiled or fried fish.

BAYOU LAFOURCHE BOOGALEE SAUCE

Purée one pound of boiled crawfish tails with two teaspoons of horse-radish, one teaspoon of onion juice, and one teaspoon of Creole mustard. Add to Hollandaise sauce made with white vine-gar rather than citrus juice. Serve with fish.

CAPER CREAM SAUCE

Add one-half cup of capers and a dash of salt to plain cream sauce. Anchovy paste may be substituted for capers.

CAPER SAUCE FOR FISH, FOWL, OR GAME

To melted butter, add capers and lemon juice.

CREOLE SOUR-CREAM DRESSING

Mince two hard-boiled eggs and mix with three teaspoons of Creole mustard and six minced pickled onions. Add sour cream. Chill.

SHRIMP À LA SOUR CREAM

Mix sour cream and two teaspoons of nutmeg. Add one cup of boiled, cleaned shrimp and a bit of minced parsley.

TO SOUR CREAM

Heat cream slowly until it almost boils. Cut fire off and when cream begins to cool, add a dash of citrus juice or vinegar. Buttermilk may be used in place of soured cream if desired.

ESCABECHE SAUCE

Mix one part olive oil and one part vinegar, mixed with salt, pepper, a soupçon of garlic, and minced dill pickles. This may be served with cold, boiled fish.

SAUCE FUMET DE POISSON

Blend one tablespoon of flour with four teaspoons butter in a double boiler. Add one cup of fish stock. Simmer and add one cup of mushrooms sautéed in butter and then one cup of cream.

NEW ORLEANS MARGUERY SAUCE

To Hollandaise sauce add a small amount of fish stock and a dash of oyster juice or some minced oysters. Serve with fish.

SAUCE NEWBURG

Place four tablespoons of butter in a double boiler. Add one cup of cream and slowly add beaten yolks of two eggs. Cook for ten minutes, stir, and blend well. Remove from fire and whip in pan. Add one-half cup of sherry and whip again. Add a dash of cayenne and salt.

SAUCE SUPREME

Mix the juice of two limes with one cup of mayonnaise and one-half cup of good olive oil, one-half cup of minced parsley, one-half cup of minced capers, four teaspoons of dry mustard, and two teaspoons of prepared horse-radish. Serve hot or cold over fish.

SHRIMP SAUCE

Mix three parts olive oil and one part vinegar. Add three tablespoons of Creole mustard and one-fourth cup each of minced parsley, shallots, and celery hearts. Add salt, white pepper, and paprika. Serve over boiled shrimp. Hard-boiled eggs may be added.

TOMATO SAUCE

Peel twelve red and green Creole tomatoes. Chop up one cup of shallots and one cup of green peppers. Add one cup of tomato juice and a *bouquet garni* of any herbs. Simmer slowly until juice is boiled out. Add six teaspoons of fresh horse-radish and three teaspoons of dry mustard. Chill. Serve hot or cold.

VERMILION SAUCE

Grind one part red and three parts green peppers (removing seed) with equal amount of onions. Mix with twelve peeled, chopped tomatoes and seasoning.

BERRY-FRUIT SAUCE

Stew any combination of berries and fruits (either fresh or dried) with one-half cup of honey. Add one cup of white wine. Serve hot or cold with ice cream, cake, or custard.

BRANDY EGG SAUCE

Beat four eggs and slowly add one-half cup of brandy. Simmer three minutes. Add two teaspoons of sugar and one cup of whipped cream. Pour over cake slices or fresh fruit.

HOT BRANDY SAUCE

Mix two tablespoons of cornstarch in one-half pint of boiling sweet milk. Cook about seven minutes and stir until thick. Add two beaten egg yolks and one cup of powdered sugar. Stir and blend well. Add one-half cup of brandy. Serve hot over custard or cake.

CREPE SUZETTE SAUCE

Spread pancake with sauce made of three teaspoons of grated orange peel, one-half cup of orange juice, one cup of brown sugar, and one-half cup of butter. Simmer until creamy. Dip pancakes in this sauce, then in flame sauce.

FLAME SAUCE

Mix one cup of orange wine with one-half bottle of brandy and one stick of cinnamon. Light. Other liquors or liqueurs may be used. Curaçao is good with brandy or rum. Wild cherry bounce is even better.

FRESH FRUIT SAUCE

Peel and mash six apricots or peaches. Add four teaspoons of brown sugar and one cup of brandy. Mix well and let stay in refrigerator at least several hours. Serve cold with desserts.

HARD SAUCE

Cream one-half cup of butter and two cups of powdered sugar. Add one-half cup of rum. Chill. Serve over cake or custard.

SAUCE AUX MARRONS

Boil chestnuts twenty minutes and roast for ten minutes. Chop up nuts and add to "Hot Brandy Sauce." (See p. 225.)

SHERRY SAUCE

Mix a bar of chocolate with a little sherry. Add cream. Serve hot with desserts or over cold chicken or turkey.

SYRUP LA CUITE

Make a thick syrup of one cup of cane syrup and one cup of brown sugar. When it candies, add one cup or more of minced pecans. Serve with cake or ice cream.

HOT STUFF

WILD CHILIS

Remove seeds from inside of chilis or green peppers by cutting a slit in the side and scooping seeds out. Heat a mixture of half white vinegar, half sugar. Add peppers. Fill hot sterilized jars half way with mixture and add a little dill, garlic, bay leaves, and warm olive oil to finish filling. Seal. Slice these piquant peppers and serve on toasted crackers with a tiny dot of butter. (These are Louisiana's pimientos.)

PEPPER A LA BACCHUS

Use one cup of small peppers. Cover peppers with rum, sherry, or brandy in an open crock and let stand for a week. Remove and bottle.

PEPPER HASH

Grind three parts red peppers and one part green peppers after removing seeds. Grind one part onions and mix with peppers. Add salt. Heat enough vinegar to cover. Simmer about thirty minutes. Sugar may be added for a sweet relish. Seal in bottles. This is a racy complement for game or fowl.

CHIVE VINEGAR

Heat one bottle of white vinegar. Mix with one cup of minced chives, one-half cup of minced onions, salt, and white pepper. Bottle and seal while hot.

CREOLE VINEGAR

Mix one pint of molasses with one gallon of water and two yeast cakes. Let it ferment. Skim and bottle.

SWEET HERB VINEGAR

Mix one bottle of white vinegar with one cup of mint leaves, one teaspoon of rosemary, two bay leaves, one-half teaspoon of mace, and one-half teaspoon of lavender. Heat and bottle.

VINEGAR OF HERBS

Marinate several *fines herbes* in salted vinegar overnight. Stir and strain. Repeat this once a day for four days. Bottle. Mint vinegar may be prepared in the same way.

WILD PEPPER VINEGAR

Wash one dozen wild peppers. Heat one pint of tarragon vinegar with some dill and a pod of garlic. Pour over peppers in a hot, sterilized jar. Seal.

PICKLES

Use two quarts of boiling water and one cup of salt. Mix water and salt. Pour enough to cover cucumbers completely in a crock. Drain off brine every third day. Boil this brine and pour it back over cucumbers. Do this for nine days. Wash cucumbers and slice. Leave slices in one gallon of water and one tablespoon of alum overnight. Wash and place in a crock. Boil vinegar and spices and pour over sliced cucumbers. Pour vinegar off each day for four days, boil it, and pour back over cucumbers each time. Seal jars. Frill your cold-fowl plate with these pickles.

CANDIED GARLIC PICKLES

Buy one large jar of dill pickles. Slice sidewise and place in a bowl with one-half pound of sugar and several pieces of garlic. Mix and seal in jars.

MUSHROOM PICKLES

Use canned, drained, whole mushrooms. Simmer two cups of vinegar with a spice bag for about five minutes. Add a few small hot peppers and pour over mushrooms in hot, sterilized jars. Serve as trappings for game, fish, or fowl.

WATERMELON PICKLES

Since watermelons are so much a part of the Deep South this recipe is a must with game.

Cut watermelon rind crosswise. Remove red meat and green rind, leaving only white part. Cut one pound of rind, wash in cold water, and place in ice water for thirty minutes. Make up a quart bottle of lime water by mixing one tablespoon of slaked lime with cold water. Soak rinds in this water for several hours to make crisp. Wash in cold water, and simmer in ginger and water for an hour. Add five cups of white or brown sugar and the juice of three limes. Simmer until rind is tender. Let stand in syrup for an hour or so. Process in hot, sterilized jars for about thirty minutes with heat at simmering point. (Vinegar, sugar, and whole spices may be used in place of syrup. If this method is used, first soak rind in salt water rather than lime water.)

BUTTERS

These may be used as spreads for bread or canapés, or where butter is called for in recipes.

Let fresh or creamy butter soften and add minced water cress or minced parsley to it.

Boil wild leeks in several waters. After final boiling, strain juice. Mix juice and a pinch of salt with soft butter and white pepper.

Sauté minced garlic in a pan with butter until it browns. Mix with soft butter and a dash of salt and onion juice.

Mix minced anchovies or anchovy paste with a little lime juice. Blend with soft butter.

Mix soft butter with prepared mustard. Marinate chervil, basil, rosemary, chives, balm, and savory in olive oil. Add salt and white pepper to herbs. Add soft butter and blend well.

Mix soft butter with powdered cinnamon and brown sugar or molasses.

Mix soft butter with honey and nutmeg.

Mix soft butter with pecans and syrup.

Mix soft butter with sesame or poppy seeds.

Mix soft butter with a paste of minced, cooked shrimp or crawfish.

Mix soft butter with curry powder.

CHEROKEE ROSES

For this garnish or refreshment use the wild Cherokee rose. White flowers and wild smilax may be used with white candles for the table. Make up mixtures of white, green, and orange cream cheese. Build the roses around olives using a demitasse spoon.

This is a dainty refreshment or garnish for a bride's luncheon.

PRESERVES AND JELLIES

APPLE-PEAR CHUTNEY

Scald and chop four white unions. Mix with six peeled, chopped apples, one cup of chopped pears, one cup of raisins, one cup of candied citrus fruit, one cup of candied ginger, and one cup of grated grapefruit rind. Heat vinegar and pour over mixture. Seal in jars. This is a fine garniture for curry dishes.

SOLAR BERRIES

Mix six quarts of strawberries with two pounds of sugar. Simmer for above five minutes. Place in a flat glass dish with glass top. Expose to hot sun for several hours. Seal in hot, sterilized jars.

WILD BERRY JELLIES

Wash berries and cook until tender. Place in cheesecloth sack and squeeze out all juice. Mix sugar and juice half and half. Cook until cool juice jells on end of spoon.

CANTALOUPE RIND PICKLES

Discard outside rind and the softened part of the meat. Cut rind into small pieces. Soak overnight in enough water to cover and a teaspoon each of alum and salt. Rinse and boil about twenty minutes or until almost tender. Pour water off and add sugar, vinegar, and a bag of spices. Cook until tender. Remove spices and let rind remain in syrup overnight. Seal in jars. Pumpkin and cushaw may be prepared and pickled in the same manner.

CANDIED CHADEE

Use only the peel. Prepare as in "Satsuma Peel."

CUCUMBERS IN WHISKY

Marinate twelve sliced cucumbers in salted water for four days. Mix one part whisky and three parts water. Pour this over cucumbers. Add a few spices. Seal in hot, sterilized jars.

DATES NOUVELLE ORLÉANS

Stuff dates with minced pecans and marshmallows. Place in jars and pour sherry wine over stuffed dates. Seal.

FIG PRESERVES

Wash figs in cold water. Pour boiling soda water over figs. Drain, and wash in cold water. Cook slowly for three hours with sugar and slices of lemon, but no water. Seal in hot, sterilized jars.

PRESERVED BOURBON GINGER

Wash and peel ginger root. Soak overnight in plain water. Slice the ginger and simmer in fresh water for ten minutes or until tender. Drain. Simmer the sliced root in three parts sugar and one part water until it is clear and tender. Add several jiggers of bourbon to the ginger syrup. Place the sliced root in hot, sterilized jars. Pour in enough juice and bourbon to fill the jar.

PRESERVED KUMQUATS

Wash fruit and make a hole in each end. Simmer in water with a spice bag until tender. Remove fruit. Make a syrup of water, sugar, and a little cream of tartar. Cook until syrup thickens. Cook fruit in this syrup about fifteen minutes. Lemons and oranges may be prepared the same way. To make pear or peach conserve, substitute grated rind for cream of tartar. Embellish fowl or game with these fruits.

LOQUAT JELLY

Cover ripe loquats with water and boil gently until tender. Strain hot juice through muslin cloth. Put juice back and bring to a boil. Measure three cups of juice to two cups of sugar and boil rapidly without stirring until jelly is formed. Pour into small jelly glasses. The jelly is pale gold with a bit of moonlight on it. It is subacid, but very delicately flavored.

On the Louisiana plantation muscadine, wild plum, wild grape, and May haw jellies are made by this same proportion and method. In the autumn, there is a plum which ripens before the wild fowl come South. The plums have a faint lavender bloom before they are gathered, but when carried horseback in a sack the bloom rubs off leaving a delicate rose-pink fruit. It is very acid and most delicious with wild game and wild fowl. Jelly is made of these plums by using five cups of juice concentrate to each three cups of sugar.

LOQUAT PRESERVES

Pick loquats when very ripe. Wash and prepare as for fig preserves, but omit the soda bath.

MAY HAW JELLY

Pick stems off ripe, fragrant May haws. Wash thoroughly and cover with water. Boil until the May haws pop their skins. Strain juice through a muslin cloth, not cheesecloth. Use three cups of hot juice to each two cups of sugar. Boil until the jelly sheets off kitchen spoon. (Never stir.) This is the most delicious of all the Louisiana jellies. When properly made, its pink tint has a silver sheen if held to the light. Cook in small quantities for perfect results.

SOUTH LOUISIANA MARMALADE

Wash six oranges, four lemons, and one grapefruit, weigh, and slice evenly. To each pound of fruit add one quart of cold water and let stand in a stone crock for twenty-four hours. The following day, cook slowly for one hour. Drain cooked fruit. Weigh and add an equal amount of water. Add as much sugar as you have fruit and cook until it stiffens when tried in a saucer. Pour into jars and seal.

MINCED PEPPER MELON

Grind six onions with twelve hot peppers (seeds removed). Bring to a boil in one pint of vinegar and a *bouquet garni* of spices. Remove spices and add minced melon preserves. Seal in jars while hot. This is a tasty trifle to serve with game.

PEARS IN PORT

Peel pears and cook in sugar and spices a few minutes. Drain and place pears in a jar. Cover with port wine.

ORANGE PECANS

Make a syrup of one cup of orange juice, one cup of grated orange peel, one cup of sugar, and one teaspoon of salt. Cook until ready to candy. Add two cups of cut pecan halves. Pour out on greased pan. When cool, break nuts.

PRUNES C'EST SI BON

Soak prunes overnight in cold water. Simmer in fresh water with honey and a slice of lemon. Cook gently about thirty minutes or until prunes are almost done. Place in jars and cover with sherry. Seal.

PUMPKIN CHIPS

Prepare pumpkin as you would watermelon rind. After cutting, place in one quart of cold water to which has been added one tablespoon of slaked lime. Soak pumpkin chips overnight. Pour water off and wash well. Boil in clear water for half an hour. Remove to kettle containing two cups of brown sugar, two cups of white vinegar, four cups of water, and a bag of spices. Simmer for one hour. Remove spice bag and seal in hot, sterilized jars.

QUINCE JELLY

Wash fruit and cut in halves. Simmer in water until soft. Strain, and add one cup of sugar to each cup of juice. Boil until a cool drop jells on end of spoon. Bottle.

SATSUMA PEEL

Boil sliced peel of oranges for ten minutes. Drain and mix with a syrup of one part sugar, one part water, one part syrup. Cook until syrup is thick. Drain and roll in sugar. This citron dainty is good with game.

WINE AND WHISKY JELLY

Use one cup of wine or whisky to one and one-half cups of sugar. Heat and add one-fourth bottle of fruit pectin. Seal in jars.

SALAD DRESSINGS

SWEET BOILED SALAD DRESSING

Beat two egg yolks and place in top of double boiler. Add two teaspoons of dry mustard, one-fourth cup of sugar, one-half teaspoon of salt, and one teaspoon of butter. Mix and stir constantly. Add one cup of hot milk or cream. Stir and add very slowly one cup of wine vinegar. Stir for twenty minutes or until well blended and thickened. Add one-half cup of sweet pickles. Serve with cold slaw.

FRENCH DRESSING

In using a French dressing for salad greens, pour the vinegar over the washed, dry greens, toss for about five minutes, then add other ingredients. However, all ingredients may be mixed, kept in refrigerator, and the salad dressed only when ready to serve. Always add dressing to greens a little at a time. Chill a one-pint fruit jar. Pour into jar one part wine, cider, or tarragon vinegar to three parts olive oil. Add salt, pepper, paprika, and celery salt. Shake. Salad herbs that add zest are dill, tarragon, basil, parsley, chives, marjoram, rosemary, and anise and caraway seeds. The dried herbs should be marinated in a little olive oil before being added to dressing. Diced avocado may be added before serving.

MAYONNAISE

Chill mixing bowl, and place in it two egg yolks. Beat with a rotary beater, gradually adding juice of one lemon or lime. Slowly add one-half cup of Wesson oil (mineral oil for reducing diets), white pepper, and a bit of cayenne. Beat until thick. Keep chilled.

CREAMED MAYONNAISE

Add one cup of whipped cream and a teaspoon of lime juice to fresh mayonnaise. Angostura bitters may be used in place of lemon.

CRESS SAUCE

Mix minced water cress, capers, lemon juice, and mayonnaise for cold fish.

JELLIED MAYONNAISE

Dissolve one package of gelatin in a little cold water. Add one cup of mayonnaise and a small amount of spinach or parsley juice for color. Mold. Serve with cold fish or fowl.

LAGNIAPPE FOR MAYONNAISE

Dry mustard, minced chives, minced shallots, Creole mustard, curry powder, powdered spices and herbs, chili powder, capers, chervil, sweet and sour pickles, horse-radish, pimiento, fresh peppers, dill pickles, garlic, Tabasco, Worcestershire sauce, ripe and green olives, mangoes, guavas, nuts, mint, nasturtium and geranium leaves, mushrooms, cucumbers, radishes, all kinds of cheese, sweet condensed milk, whipped cream, chutney, anchovies, and India relish may be used separately or in combinations to add tang to mayonnaise.

THOUSAND ISLAND DRESSING

Add well-drained, peeled tomatoes, celery salt, chopped hard-boiled eggs, and sweet pickles to mayonnaise.

CREOLE MUSTARD

This may be bought in jars or made by mixing one teaspoon of white pepper, one teaspoon of flour, one and one-half teaspoons of prepared mustard, one teaspoon of dry mustard, one teaspoon of fresh or prepared horse-radish, one-half teaspoon of sugar, and dash of celery salt and salt. Add a little hot water and cook until smooth. Herbs may be added if desired.

PAPRIKA DRESSING

Mix one-fourth cup each of minced parsley, chives, celery, and onion, with one cup of half olive oil and half vinegar. Add three teaspoons of paprika, one teaspoon of white pepper, one teaspoon of salt, and three teaspoons of Creole mustard. Make into a smooth dressing and chill.

RED WINE DRESSING

Mix red wine and paprika to dress a green salad.

RENÉE DRESSING

Mix one and one-half cups of olive oil, two teaspoons of tarragon vinegar, two teaspoons of lemon rind, three teaspoons of minced onion, three teaspoons of minced parsley, three teaspoons of sugar, one teaspoon of salt, one teaspoon of mustard seed, one teaspoon of celery seed, one-half teaspoon of dried thyme, and a dash of white pepper. Stir in one cup of thick cream. Mix well in an electric blender and chill at once.

ROQUEFORT SAUCE

Soften one package of Roquefort cheese with a small amount of cream. Add the juice of one-half onion, one-half cup of minced chives, a dash of Tabasco, and a pinch of salt. Add two cups of whipped cream. Blend and freeze.

PAT'S ROQUEFORT SAUCE

Soften one package of Roquefort cheese with a little olive oil, Add two teaspoons of wine vinegar, and a pinch of salt and white pepper. Add enough cream to spread.

WHIPPED CANNED CREAM

Boil a can of evaporated milk five minutes. Chill. Beat in a chilled bowl with two teaspoons or more of lemon juice. Add powdered sugar for a sweeter blend.

AND RELISHES HO'MADE

GROUND ARTICHOKES

Wash and scrape ground artichokes. Soak in ice and water for several hours. Drain and bring to a boil in pot of vinegar and spices. Pour vinegar off and place artichokes in hot jars. Pour hot white vinegar and small peppers over artichokes. Seal jars. Place on water cress to trim a cooked entrée of game, fowl, or fish.

ANN ALLEN'S SHARPIES

Slice green avocado or mirliton (vegetable pear) and place in round, squat jars. Arrange artistically. Pimiento strips may be added for color. Heat white vinegar with a few bead peppers, and salt and pepper. Fill jars. (The vinegar cooks the contents.) Serve as a garnish for game or fish.

SUSY'S GARDEN CURRY

Chop two cups of Creole cabbage. Add two sweet red peppers (without seeds), one cup of minced onion, two teaspoons of salt, and four cups of cooked corn. Add enough cold water to cover and let remain in crock overnight. The next morning place these ingredients in a pan and bring to a boil. Add two tablespoons of curry powder. Stir this constantly and cook until the ingredients are thick and well blended. Seal in hot, sterilized jars.

CUCUMBER SPEARS

Pare three cucumbers lengthwise and scrape out seeds. Sprinkle with one and one-half teaspoons of salt and let stand in a crock overnight. Drain in the morning. Peel and separate two onions into rings. Place onions and cucumbers in hot, sterilized jars. Fill each jar with the following mixture: two cups of white vinegar, three cloves, two peppercorns, one teaspoon of mustard seed, and one teaspoon of sugar. This mixture must have been previously heated, but not boiled.

FRUIT CURRY

Peel, core, and chop ten sour apples. Add one medium-sized sliced onion, two sliced green peppers (without seeds), one sliced red pepper (without seeds), and two cups of white vinegar. Simmer and stir for a half hour. Add one jar of wild plum jelly and one cup of raisins, one teaspoon of powdered ginger, one-fourth teaspoon of cayenne, one teaspoon of salt, and one cup of lime juice. Cook thirty minutes longer. Seal in hot, sterilized jars.

PICKLED PECANS

Soak shelled pecans in salted water overnight. Heat one quart of vinegar with a *bouquet garni*. Drop pecans in. Simmer a few minutes. Let steep for ten minutes. Seal in hot, sterilized jars.

SUSY'S STRING BEAN RELISH

Pare three pounds of string beans. Boil in water until tender. Make a paste of one-half cup of flour, one-half cup of dry mustard, one-half teaspoon of curry powder, one-half teaspoon of turmeric, one teaspoon of salt, and a little water. Add three cups of heated white vinegar. Simmer fifteen minutes and add beans. Cook five minutes and pour into hot, sterilized jars. Pimientos may be added when relish is ready to be packed into jars.

CHILI SAUCE SUPREME

Hold five pounds of not-quite-ripe tomatoes over the flame. Peel off the skins. Mince. Place in a kettle with two cups of white vinegar, two minced onions, two cups of minced celery, two cups of sugar, one-half cup of prepared horse-radish, one teaspoon of salt, one clove of minced garlic, one-fourth teaspoon of cayenne, one teaspoon of paprika, one teaspoon of dry mustard, and a *bouquet garni* of any spices. Cook forty minutes, stirring constantly. Remove herb sack and add two or three small hot peppers (seeds removed). Cook a few minutes and seal in hot, sterilized jars.

GREEN TOMATO CHOWCHOW

Skin one dozen tomatoes by holding over blaze on a fork. Slice. Mince two cups of Creole cabbage, one-fourth cup of celery, one-half cup of green peppers, and one-fourth cup of red peppers (no seeds). Let these stand overnight in a covered crock. Drain in the morning. Mix one-fourth cup of salt, one and one-half cups of white vinegar, one-half cup of water, two cups of sugar, one teaspoon of celery seed, one-fourth teaspoon of cumin seed, one teaspoon of mustard seed, and one-fourth teaspoon of white pepper. Heat this mixture and pour over the drained ingredients. Cook in a saucepan for fifteen minutes. Place in hot, sterilized jars and seal.

MARASCHINO WATERMELON RIND

Cut up four pounds of watermelon rind as for "Watermelon Pickles" (see p. 229 for cutting preparation). Soak this rind overnight in one quart of water with one-fourth cup of salt. In the morning drain and rinse in cold water. Combine ten cups of sugar, two sliced lemons, four cups of water, four cups of white vinegar, three cinnamon sticks, one whole nutmeg, and three teaspoons of powdered allspice. Boil for seven minutes. Add the drained rind and simmer until it is clear and tender. Add one jar of minced maraschino cherries with their juice. Cook for five minutes. Seal in hot, sterilized jars. A teaspoon of maraschino liqueur may be added before sealing, if desired.

A specialty of Magnolia Plantation

X

Crusts and Croutons

The French Market - The Indian Merchants

The Levee at New Orleans

Crusts and Croutons

In the red hills of North Louisiana, the folk like corn pone with their pot herbs and pot likker. Nor do they scorn any other form of corn meal bread, hot biscuits, hot homemade bread, cracklin' bread, johnnycake, and hush puppies.

In the City—New Orleans—the tradition of serving home-baked breads has long disappeared. French and Italian breads—easily obtained in the many fragrant neighborhood bakeries—croutons, and other quick crusts now satisfy the tastes of Orleanians.

But in South Louisiana—*mais oui*—there are many breads, both hot and cold—*pain perdu*, spoon bread, orange bread, oyster bread, cheese biscuits, and French pancakes over which is poured everything from minced rabbit to cranberry cordial.

SWEET BREADS

BANANA BREAD

Sift two cups of flour with two teaspoons of baking powder, one teaspoon of salt and a pinch of soda. Cream one-half cup of shortening into dry ingredients. Add one cup of powdered sugar and two beaten eggs. Add six strained bananas. Bake in a moderate oven for one hour. (Serves six to eight.)

BANNOCK

Mix two cups of flour, one-half teaspoon of salt, two teaspoons of baking powder, and two teaspoons of sugar. Add water or sweet milk and one tablespoon of lard. After mixing, place in an iron skillet coated with fresh bacon drippings. Hold skillet up over low fire or coals until the bread begins to rise, then cook about forty minutes on edges of coals or in the oven with a slow heat. (Serves approximately six to eight.)

CHEESE BREAD

Mix two cups of flour with four teaspoons of baking powder and three teaspoons of salt. Add enough sweet milk to moisten. Add one package of cream cheese and a dash of cayenne pepper. Add one-half cup of liquid cooking oil. Blend and cut into any desired shapes. Sprinkle with paprika and bake for forty minutes in moderate oven. (Serves approximately six to eight.)

HELL-FIRE DOUGH BALLS

This is an old South Louisiana recipe that was used to cure all types of illness. It was also prescribed by witch doctors to bring heat into the heart of the cold one. Grind one cup of shallots with one-half cup of wild chili peppers or a dash of cayenne. Mix with one cup of flour, two teaspoons of baking powder, a pinch of salt, one or two eggs, and enough hot tomato juice to make a batter. Blend well and drop from teaspoon into deep fat. Fry for twenty minutes. Drain well and sprinkle with paprika. (Serves four to six.)

OYSTER BREAD

Mix one cup of sifted flour with one-half teaspoon of salt and one-half teaspoon of white pepper. Add three teaspoons of butter and enough oyster juice to moisten dough. Mix and bake for ten minutes in hot oven. (Serves approximately four.)

PAIN BÂTONS DORÉS

Sift two cups of flour with two teaspoons of baking powder. Sift again. Cut in one cup of butter and add two beaten egg yolks and two teaspoons of lime juice. Blend and add two cups of grated cheese, salt, cayenne, and a dash of Tabasco. Roll out and cut in strips. Sprinkle with paprika and bake for fifteen minutes in hot oven. (Serves approximately four to six.)

PATTIE'S POPOVERS

Sift two cups of flour with one teaspoon of salt and one teaspoon of baking powder. Add two tablespoons of melted butter, three beaten eggs, and one cup of warm milk. Beat and drop in preheated, greased muffin tins. Bake in hot oven for twelve minutes. (Serves approximately four to six.)

RICE MUFFINS

Sift two cups of flour with one teaspoon of salt and two teaspoons of baking powder. Mix one cup of boiled rice with three beaten eggs, one cup of cream or milk, and two teaspoons of melted butter; add to dry ingredients and blend. Bake for fifteen minutes in preheated, greased muffin tins in a hot oven. (Serves approximately four to six.)

SKILLET BREAD

Sift two cups of flour with four teaspoons of baking powder and two teaspoons of salt. Add one or more cups of milk and mix well. Pour batter into greased, preheated deep iron skillet. Cook on moderate fire for fifteen minutes. Turn loaf bottom up and then top with minced crisp pecans. Cook fifteen minutes longer. (Serves approximately four to six.)

SWEET POTATO BREAD

Mix one cup of shortening with one cup of brown sugar. Add the juice of one orange. Beat three eggs and mix with the other ingredients. Beat well and add six baked sweet potatoes. Mix one cup of cream with two teaspoons of butter and warm. Add to the potato mix. Sift two cups of flour with one tablespoon of baking powder and one teaspoon of salt. Add dry ingredients. Mix and pour the potato batter into a greased baking dish. Bake in a preheated oven with a slow heat for about forty minutes. Remove from dish and let cool before cutting. Shelled pecans or fruit may be added if desired. (Serves approximately eight.)

SWEET POTATO DODGERS

Sift two cups of flour with three teaspoons of baking powder, a pinch of salt, and a pinch of nutmeg. Add one-fourth cup of melted butter and one cup of mashed, cooked sweet potatoes. Moisten with one cup of warm milk or cream. Add one-fourth cup of brown sugar. Roll out and cut into any desired shape. Bake in hot oven for thirty minutes. (Serves approximately six.)

BISCUITS

BEATEN BISCUITS

Sift one and one-half cups of flour, one cup of sugar, and one teaspoon of baking powder. Add slowly one-half cup of ice water and one-half cup of chilled milk. Cut in three tablespoons of butter. Knead dough and roll out on a floured board. Beat with a wooden beater until the dough blisters. Cut in desired shapes and bake for thirty minutes in a slow oven. Leave the biscuits in the oven with the door open after baking so that they may dry out and become crisp. (Serves approximately four to six.)

CAREER GIRL CRUSTS

Several quick crusts may be made from the canned oven-ready type of biscuits. Dumplings are made of the biscuits by cutting them in strips and simmering for ten minutes in gravy or stock. Doughnuts may be made by cutting a hole in the center of the biscuits. Game, fowl, or fish pies may be made by placing the biscuits on top of the casserole and baking for twenty minutes in a hot oven. The biscuits also may be eaten plain or sliced to make a shortcake.

AUNT PATTIE'S COUNTRY BISCUITS

Sift two cups of flour and one-half teaspoon of salt with four teaspoons of baking powder. Add two tablespoons of shortening, one-half cup of hot water, and one-half cup of sweet milk. Knead with fingers. Bake in a hot oven for fifteen minutes. (Serves approximately four to six.)

CAMPFIRE BISCUIT

Use dough for "Country Biscuit." Roll into thin narrow strips. Brush with butter. Sprinkle with powdered sugar and wrap around a green stick. Hold stick over fire until bread is done.

DROP BISCUITS

Sift two cups of flour with three teaspoons of baking powder and two teaspoons of salt. Mix with six tablespoons of butter, one cup of milk, and one-half cup of grated American or Parmesan cheese. Knead with finger tips. Mix quickly and drop in greased skillet or muffin pan. Bake for fifteen minutes in hot oven. (Serves approximately six to eight.)

HARDTACK

Mix one cup of flour with one-half teaspoon of salt, one teaspoon of sugar, and water to moisten. Roll paper-thin and bake for ten minutes in a hot oven. This is a perfect flake to eat with outdoor-steamed oysters. (Serves approximately six.)

ROCK BREAD

Use a flat rock (they must be imported in Louisiana). Make a hickory fire on the rock and let burn down to coals. Mix "Country Biscuit" dough and form into a loaf. Brush coals away from rock surface and place loaf on it. Cover the loaf with hot ashes and top with coals. Cook (about forty-five minutes) until you know by testing with a straw that the bread is done.

WAGON WHEELS

Roll out dough as for "Country Biscuits." Place a layer of minced nuts, minced raisins, or candied orange peel and a little butter on top of dough. Make dough into a roll. Slice roll and bake in hot oven for twenty minutes.

CORN BREADS AND CAKES

CORN MEAL CAKES

Make a batter of two cups of buttermilk, one teaspoon of soda, one-half teaspoon of salt, one egg, and enough meal to thicken. Drop into a preheated skillet and fry for ten minutes. (Serves approximately four to six.)

CORN PONE

Mix two cups of corn meal, one teaspoon of salt, three tablespoons of lard, and enough hot water to moisten. Make into pones and fry five minutes on each side in hot lard or butter. (Serves four to six.)

COUNTRY CORN BREAD

Sift one cup of corn meal with three tablespoons of flour. Add one teaspoon of sugar, two teaspoons of baking powder, and one teaspoon of salt. Mix with two beaten eggs, one tablespoon of butter, and one cup of milk. Blend well and pour into a hot, greased pan. Bake in a hot oven about twenty-five minutes. (Serves approximately four.)

COUSH-COUSH CAILLE

Pour clabber over pieces of hot corn bread. This is a favorite Cajun breakfast dish.

CRACKLIN' BREAD

Make cracklings of pork chop fat or salt pork by slicing thin, frying, and then crisping strips in oven. Make batter as for "Cross Lake Hush Puppies" (see p. 249), adding one or two eggs. Add cracklings and bake for thirty minutes in skillet or oven. Break with hand—never cut. One teaspoon of absinthe may be added to the batter.

HUSH PUPPIES

This name originated when fisherfolk threw these savory morsels to their howling dogs around the campfire.

CROSS LAKE HUSH PUPPIES

Mix two cups of flour, one-half cup of meal, two teaspoons of baking powder, one teaspoon of salt, one cup of minced shallots, and enough hot milk to moisten. Make into balls and fry for twenty minutes in deep fat. Serve with raw onions and fried fish. Beer may be used in place of milk. (Serves approximately six.)

HOECAKE HUSH PUPPY

Make as you would "Corn Pone" (see p. 248), but add one-half cup of minced shallots and one beaten egg. Cook as one large cake in a skillet for twenty minutes.

YELLOW MEAL HUSH PUPPIES

Mix one cup of meal, three teaspoons of butter, two teaspoons of baking powder, one-half teaspoon of salt, one cup of minced onions or shallots, and one egg. Add enough hot water to moisten. Make into balls and fry for ten minutes in grease in which fish has been fried. (Serves approximately two.)

PHINEY'S SPOON BREAD

Heat one quart of milk to boiling. Stir in two cups of corn meal with one teaspoon of sugar. Add four beaten eggs, a teaspoon of brandy, and a dash of nutmeg. Beat well. Bake twenty-five minutes in a moderate oven until thick and brown. (Serves approximately six to eight.)

SPIDER BREAD

Sift two cups of corn meal and one cup of flour with one teaspoon of salt, two teaspoons of soda, and a pinch of sugar. Mix with three beaten eggs and one-fourth cup of melted butter. Add enough sour or buttermilk to moisten. Beat and bake in a skillet for forty minutes or in oven. (Serves approximately six.)

RICE BREAD

Mix one cup of corn meal, one cup of cooked rice, two tablespoons of butter, three eggs, salt, and enough sweet milk to thin. Bake thirty minutes in casserole in hot oven. (Serves approximately four.)

SHALLOT POLENTA

Make a corn meal mush with three cups of corn meal, enough hot water to moisten, two tablespoons of butter, a pinch of salt, and two teaspoons of pepper. Let the mush simmer a few minutes. Meanwhile, sauté two cups of minced shallots in butter and mix with two cups of grated cheese. Place a layer of mush and a layer of shallots and cheese in a greased casserole. Bake in a hot oven for a half hour. (Serves six to eight.)

ROLLS OR BREAD
BREAD

Let one pint of sweet milk come to a boil, add one tablespoon of sugar and one heaping tablespoon of lard. When almost cool, add one yeast cake and stir thoroughly. Sift in enough flour to make a stiff batter. Let it rise and then make dough. Add salt and knead dough. Make into rolls or loaves and let rise again. Bake in a moderate oven (fifteen minutes for rolls and forty minutes for loaves) and remove from pan as soon as done. It is best to make up bread at night and place in gallon crock to rise overnight. Knead again early in morning. Let rise and bake at noon. Keep some of the dough in the refrigerator, and when ready to make another batch of bread, let this "starter dough" rise, then add it to new batter. (Serves approximately six to eight.)

BRENNAN'S GARLIC BREAD

Use a loaf of French bread. Rub entire outside crust with garlic. Slice the loaf lengthwise down the middle and cover with melted butter. Sprinkle with grated Parmesan cheese and finely minced parsley. Sprinkle lightly with paprika. Place in the oven until it is hot and crisp.

BETTY MOORE'S CINNAMON TOAST

Cut bread in strips. Mix melted butter, cinnamon, and sugar. Toast one side of bread. Turn and brush with cinnamon butter mixture. Toast.

CROUSTADES

Slice any bread in squares. Fry in parsley butter (see p. 229) or in any other butter.

CROUTONS

Slice any bread very thin. Cut in strips and toast. Serve with soup and other foods.

EDNA GILL'S ROLLS

Dissolve one yeast cake in one-fourth cup of lukewarm water. Mix one-fourth cup of sugar, a scant one-half cup of lard, one and one-half teaspoons of salt, and one egg. Mix well. Add one cup of scalded sweet milk. Let mixture cool and add yeast. Beat in four cups of sifted flour. Place in a well-greased bowl and let rise, then turn into another greased bowl so that top of each batch will not form crust. Pinch off as needed and make into rolls. When rolls rise to twice original size, bake for twenty minutes in a hot oven. (Serves approximately six to eight.)

EMPANADAS

Use dough from recipe for "Edna Gill's Rolls." (See above.) Sprinkle minced game and coriander seeds through the dough. Cut into tiny squares and drop the squares into hot oil to fry for ten minutes. Drain and serve hot.

PAIN PERDU OR LOST BREAD

Cut thick slices of fresh homemade or store-bought bread. Mix two eggs, one-half cup of brandy, one-half cup of sugar, and two teaspoons of orange-flower water. Beat well and let slices of bread soak for five minutes. Fry in butter for five minutes. Sprinkle with powdered sugar. One-day-old bread is better than fresh. Madame Bègué named her lost bread "Poor Knight."

SIPPETS

Cut bread in paper-thin slices; brown in the oven.

TRENCHERS

Split a loaf of French bread lengthwise. Toast or fry in butter. Serve game, fish, or fowl on this gravy-drenched bread.

DUMPLINGS AND NOODLES

COBBLER DUMPLINGS

Mix together two cups of flour, one and one-half teaspoons of baking powder, and a pinch of salt. Add three teaspoons or more of sugar, one beaten egg, and two teaspoons of melted butter. Mix and drop into pot with boiling fruit or fowl. Cook ten minutes. (Serves approximately six.)

CORN MEAL DUMPLINGS

Moisten two cups of corn meal with hot water. Work in one teaspoon of baking powder and a pinch of salt. Make into small balls and drop into boiling cooked greens for ten minutes. (Serves six.)

CREOLE DUMPLINGS

Sift two cups of flour with one-half teaspoon of salt. Add one and one-half tablespoons of shortening and one-half cup of water. Mix and roll out on floured board. Cut into squares and dust with powdered sugar. Drop into pan of hot water and whole spices. Simmer thirty minutes or longer. Remove spices from pan and add one cup of hot orange juice or orange wine. Add one-half cup of sugar and a little grated grapefruit peel. Simmer about ten minutes. Serve with game or fowl. (Serves six.)

PLAIN DUMPLINGS

Mix one cup of flour, one and one-half teaspoons of baking powder, and a pinch of salt. Add to one cup of milk. Beat and drop dumplings into water or pot likker that is boiling for ten minutes. (Serves four.)

KLÖSSE

Cook and cool two cups of riced potatoes. Mix with one-fourth cup of milk and one-half cup of flour. Blend and add one beaten egg yolk and one teaspoon of minced parsley. Beat and drop by spoonfuls into salted boiling water. When dumplings are done, they will rise to the top. (Serves four to six.)

FLIĈKY

Place one and one-half cups of flour in a wooden bowl. Make a hole in the center of the flour and drop in an egg. Add a little water. Stir with a spoon until enough flour is absorbed to turn mixture onto a board. Knead this until it is stiff. Warm the dough with hands before rolling. Roll until the dough is thin-thin. Hang this sheet of dough to dry. Cut in shapes you prefer and scatter them so they do not stick together. Cut cooked game or ham into pieces. Boil the fliĉky (pronounced "fleech-key") in salted water until tender (about twenty minutes). Place the fliĉky, meat, and butter in a casserole and cook in the oven about five minutes, or until the fliĉky are brown on top. Serve with a little green salad.

OLD-FASHIONED NOODLES

Mix one cup of flour and one teaspoon of salt. Add beaten yolks of two eggs. Roll dough out. Let set for two hours. Knead and roll again. Cut in narrow strips. Let set again for thirty minutes before cooking in boiling water for fifteen minutes.

PANCAKES AND WAFFLES
BUCKWHEAT FLAPJACKS

Sift two cups of buckwheat with one-half cup of white flour. Soak one yeast cake in warm water. Heat two cups of water and add to dry ingredients and yeast. Place in a covered crock and let rise overnight. In the morning, add one-half teaspoon of soda, one teaspoon of salt, and one-fourth cup of sugar. Moisten with hot milk. Cook on a greased, preheated griddle for ten minutes. Store a small amount of this dough in the refrigerator to use with new dough. (Serves approximately six to eight.)

GOLLYETTES

The first Acadians made these pancakes without leavening or milk. They used only flour, salt, and water and fried the dough over the coals of the fireplace.

BESSIE'S WAFFLES

As one wanders along the Rue St. Peter in the Vieux Carré, a sign reading "The Coffee Pot" lures one behind the shutters of an ancient cottage into the quaint eating establishment of Bessie Sauveur, who is as famous for her breakfasts as was Madame Bègué so long ago. Here one may enjoy breakfast or brunch in the small front room, where the hospitality is as warm and rosy as the red brick floor, or be served vis-a-vis in the walled patio, where soft breezes carry the aroma of brewing coffee and browning waffles to the sensualist palate.

To make Bessie's waffles, sift three cups of plain flour with one-half teaspoon of salt, one-fourth cup of sugar, and six teaspoons of baking powder. Add one and one-fourth cups of milk and stir into a smooth paste. Break three eggs into paste, beat well, and stir in one-half cup of good cooking oil.

Brush some oil on the top and bottom grids of the waffle iron. When the iron is very hot, pour six ounces of batter into the bottom grid. Do not close until the waffle has cooked for about a minute and begins to bubble up. Do not oil the grids after the first baking. The batter will keep several days in the refrigerator, but it should be raised to room temperature again before it is used.

To clean waffle iron grids when carbon begins to form on them, place a piece of cotton on the bottom grid and hinges and saturate it with household ammonia. Let this stand overnight, then clean with a stiff brush. Repeat if carbon does not loosen with first application.

A street vendor

XI
Gastronomic Gambles

Returning home to Woodland

Gastronomic Gambles

For those favored folk who know the woods and waters, there are few gastronomic gambles. Seafaring people claim that everything that swims in the sea is edible—and an Acadian friend from "down de bayou" asserts that her mother fed the family "anything that ran across the yard."

Undoubtedly this was true in the early days of Louisiana, when life itself was a daily gamble. And today, though most Louisianians have more conservative culinary tastes, the spirit of gastronomic adventure still exists among the folk who make their living in the vast and rich sea marshes of South Louisiana—gathering Spanish moss for mattresses and cushions, palmettoes for fans, vetiver for sachets, wax myrtle for candles, vines and blossoms for the floral market, to say nothing of alligators, crabs, crawfish, frogs, lizards, oysters, shrimp, snakes, and turtles; wild berries, fruits, herbs, and magnolias; and wild honey. They have made their life in the marshes pay—and to them few creatures are strangers, either in the swamp or on the dinner table.

Generally, their tastes are those of their more sophisticated bayou cousins, but as Pierre says, "De luck she cannot be goot all de time, no," and he sometimes turns for sustenance to some of the dishes given here.

SWAMPLAND GAMBLES
ALLIGATOR

The first Louisianians called the alligator the "kro-ko-deel," and it is still called this name by the French. 'Gators are caught first by finding their holes, and then by luring them out after poking a stick down into their underwater dens.

POACHED ALLIGATOR TAIL

A 'gator not over three feet long is the best size to cook. Cut the tail in strips after removing the outer skin. Marinate the meat in lemon juice for several hours. Wipe dry and rub with olive oil. Dust with salt, pepper, and flour, and sear meat in hot butter. Gradually add enough water to cover, then a *bouquet garni*. Simmer until tender.

GRILLED 'GATOR

Prepare the tail as for poaching. Place strips on a grill over coals, and baste with bacon drippings and Worcestershire sauce. Turn often until done.

CROCODILE

When the Cajun speaks of *bête noir* (something feared), he is usually referring to the crocodile. The "croc" has been reported in Louisiana, and since an American species does occur in the Southern section of the United States, it is possible that this reptile has been innocently eaten for alligator. The alligator has a rounded nose, and the crocodile a very pointed one; and the "croc" is capable of raising his body from the ground and running rapidly. Crocodile tail is eaten in some parts of the world, but is said to be much tougher than the alligator's.

ANY SMALL BIRDS

Pluck and dress birds. Place them on a board and roll with a pin to break the breastbone. Melt some butter with minced parsley. Place the birds under the heat and baste often with the parsley butter. Serve on toast.

BLACKBIRDS

There are several types of blackbird in Louisiana, but the best for the pot are the common ricebirds or red-winged blackbirds. Dress birds and brush with a small amount of lime or orange juice, butter, salt, and pepper. Sear in hot butter, then add hot chicken bouillon, raw turnip slices, minced shallots, and minced celery tops. Simmer until tender, then place in a casserole with pie crust around and on top. Bake until browned. The stew may be thickened with flour if desired.

Another old method of cooking these blackbirds was to pluck, dress, and broil them with a sauce of mushrooms and butter. The inside cavity was filled with minced oysters.

CROWS

Dress birds. Brush with lemon juice, salt, and pepper and let stand overnight in refrigerator. Wipe with damp cloth and parboil. Then cook as you would blackbirds.

OWLS

Pick, clean, and marinate in vinegar and oil overnight. Parboil, then dust with flour, and fricassee until done, adding water or marinade.

FRESH WATER EEL

Remove the head, skin and clean the eel, and cut in fillets. Fry in deep fat after dipping in corn meal. Eel must be eaten at once while hot, for the meat has a raw taste when cold. Eel also may be cut crosswise, fried in oil, and steeped in white wine, or boiled with sweet herbs to make a soup.

SNAILS

According to Louisiana biologist Percy Viosca, a basketful of European snails escaped from the French Market one day and strolled across the street where they set up housekeeping in Jackson Square. They are probably enjoying life there still, though some of them—clinging to the leaves of Jackson Square plants—must have been carried to other parts of the state by souvenir-hunting "plant-nappers."

The European snail was once a popular table fancy in New Orleans, but it is seldom seen on menus there today. In the old days, they were imported from Europe by the basketful, cleaned in salt water, soaked in fresh water, and boiled with herbs before being served with a sauce of wine, shallots, garlic, and ham. They may still be purchased on Decatur Street today—but it is snail shells with a canned snail stuffing that today's *escargot* fancier buys.

The Louisiana variety of snail is edible too, but it is not advisable to eat them since they are host to a parasite that does damage to human organs. Of course, if snails are carefully pen-fed the French grapevine way, one has a better chance of enjoying—without dangerous after-effects—the delights of *escargots à la Louisiane.*

SEA-GOING GAMBLES

COWFISH

Remove the outer shell that encases the entire fish body and cut the meat into fillets or steaks. Since the meat of this fish has a delightful fowl-like taste, use one of the recipes given for quail, woodcock, or dove to take best advantage of its natural flavor.

BRETON SOUND CONCH STEW

Gourmets of the outer islands swear that their conches are the same species as those eaten so regularly in the Bahamas and Florida. They prepare them by cleaning and using only the whitest meat. Mince conch meat and marinate in lime juice for twenty minutes. Make a *roux* and add some hot water or oyster juice. Add conch meat and thinly sliced potatoes, some minced shallots, bay leaves, and thyme. Add milk or cream and let simmer until done. White wine may be added when stew is done.

SWEET-WATER GAR

The Indians knew the gars well and called them "nani kallo" (strong fish). Select a small gar; clean and scale. Parboil meat, then run it through a meat grinder with onions or shallots. Add beaten egg yolk and bread crumbs soaked in milk or wine. Make into balls and fry in deep fat. Gar meat is often cut in strips and smoked for a day before it is made into balls. (Do not eat the roe of a gar.)

FRIED OCTOPUS

To clean an octopus, follow same procedure as for cleaning a squid. After washing and cleaning, remove the ink bladder without puncturing. Cut off the head and save. Boil the body and tentacles in a pot large enough to float the tentacles. Place cut-up onion, sliced lemon, bay leaves, dill, salt, and pepper in the pot. Simmer thirty minutes or longer. Drain and cut into pieces. Dip in beaten egg, then in pancake flour, and fry in deep fat.

FRICASSEED OCTOPUS TENTACLES

Prepare octopus for cooking as in "Fried Octopus." Cut the tentacles away from the body and skin them. Cut in slices and braise in hot olive oil for five minutes. Add warm tomato juice, one pod of garlic, a little minced dill, salt, and pepper. Simmer until tender. Serve with boiled rice.

OCTOPUS SALAD

Leftover boiled tentacle meat and boiled head meat may be prepared for a salad in the same manner as Squid Salad.

PORPOISE

To all mariners eating porpoise is "eatin' high on the hog." The meat, they say, is pork-like. This mammal must be bled and butchered like a hog. Cut in any desirable way, and bake, broil, or fry. The steaks are best cut thin and served with fresh pineapple fried in butter.

RAYS

There are several types of ray in the Gulf. Select a ray under ten pounds in weight, and cut off the wings. Parboil these wings in salted water for fifteen minutes. Drain and boil in fresh water with bay leaves, thyme, cut-up lemon, onions, and a little wine vinegar. Cook until wings are tender. Drain and skin. Make a sauce of minced shallots, butter, minced mushrooms, and one-half can of mushroom soup. Simmer for about five minutes. Pour over wings and serve.

FRIED SQUID

Clean squid and remove eyes and ink bladder. Wash well and roll in pancake mix and fry in butter for ten minutes.

SQUID SALAD

Prepare squid as in "Fried Squid." Boil in seasoned water for ten minutes and cut in pieces. Mix with minced lettuce, pickles, and mayonnaise.

Squid salad is popular among the French people of both city and country.

STUFFED SQUID

Prepare squid as in "Fried Squid." Stuff with a mixture of un-cooked squid head meat, boiled rice, minced parsley, and minced cooked shrimp. Stuff body cavity and sew together. Simmer in a gravy of tomato juice, minced green peppers, celery, and shallots.

SAWFISH

Use a fish weighing not over eight pounds. Clean and cut fillets. These fillets may be fried in butter, or broiled with a butter sauce under a broiler.

BLACK TIP (LEAPING LENA) AND OTHER SHARKS

Except for the hammerhead shark, those of the Gulf and inside waters are edible. Although the shark is not eaten along some coasts, it is a nutrient of Louisiana natives who consider the mackerel shark their best eatin' shark. Select a small shark and use only the light meat. Cut the sides into fillets and marinate in lemon juice and olive oil several hours. Dry and poach with a *bouquet garni*, or broil the steaks with butter and shallots. Cut out the dark meat and soak in salt water overnight, then grind the meat and bake in a casserole with shallots, salt, pepper, and a dash of cayenne.

TRIGGER FISH

Although considered an unusual food, this reef-loving fish is actually one of the finest of all our Gulf dishes. This moonfaced fish has a small catch on the dorsal fin, which has given the fish its name. There are three spikes in the fin; by pressing the back spike, the dorsal fin is collapsed. To prepare the fish for cooking, cut a line across the tail and one just behind the head. Next cut through the skin from tail to head at the top and bottom of the fish. Start from the tail and peel the skin off from each side. This leaves two boneless fillets on each side of the backbone. The fillets may be baked, broiled, or poached, and are delicious when barbecued.

Taking care of little Missey

XII
Ambrosia

"The Shadows" on Bayou Teche (1830) - New Iberia

Ambrosia

When Louisiana diners reach the dessert course of their meal—
no matter whether it be the hearty fare of the northern uplands,
the tangy dishes of the languid bayous, or the subtle servings of the
sophisticated city—they look for no more than an ambrosial morsel.
Some exotic trifle or fragment of tradition that will imbue the
diner with nostalgia in the days ahead—and a small *cafe noir*—this
is the proper combination for *le coup de grace de la cuisine Louisianaise.*

AMBROSIA

Ambrosia is the traditional Christmas dessert of the South and
should be served in a cut glass bowl at the table. Cut up oranges,
sugar liberally, and chill. Grate fresh coconut. Mix the oranges and
coconut and chill again.

CIDER APPLES

Soak apple slices in cider. Drain and sprinkle slices with cinnamon sugar. Fry in butter or bake.

BANANAS IN WINE

Cut bananas in halves lengthwise. Place in pyrex dish and cover with four teaspoons of honey, a half bottle of white wine, a teaspoon of lemon juice, and one-half cup of brown sugar. Bake.

FRIED BANANAS

Roll out one small box of corn flakes. Dip banana halves in cream, then in corn flakes. Fry in butter. Pour warmed brandy over bananas and serve aflame.

HABANA BANANA

Sauté banana halves in butter with cooked red beans. Remove beans. Add honey to bananas and simmer with a little more butter. Pour in two gills of banana liquor and cut the heat off. Add beans and steep a half hour. Reheat and serve with powdered sugar.

FRUIT COMPOTES

Apricots may be peeled and marinated in lime juice and kirsch. Pears may be stuffed with nuts and baked or simmered with sweet white wine, or they may be marinated in Cherry Heering. They may also be candied with grated lemon rind and sugar, then dunked in a sweet white wine. Peaches are delightful simmered a few minutes in honey, then served on toasted pound cake. If you have brandied peaches, pour more brandy over them and serve aflame in compotes of pewter. Fresh peach halves may be soaked in peach brandy over night and stuffed with minced nuts and raisins. The distinctive flavor of figs is accentuated by soaking in rum or sherry. Orange segments love to live in sin with curaçao, kirsch, or Cherry Heering.

CAMPFIRE FRUIT

Fruit may be placed on a skewer or on a wire mesh over coals and broiled. Bananas may be broiled in their jackets. Peeled fruit may be basted with honey and butter. Any fruit may be cooked in aluminum foil with butter and honey.

POWDERED FRUIT AND BERRIES

Fresh fruits and berries dipped in powdered sugar or marinated in some form of sweet spirits are ideal after dining on a heavy fare of game.

SPARKLING FRUITS

Marinate fresh pineapple spears, fresh strawberries, fresh pears or peaches, or cherries in brandy for twenty minutes in the refrigerator. Place in a crystal bowl and pour champagne over the fruit.

GRAPEFRUIT AU SHERRY

Cut grapefruit in half and pour some *crème de cacao* in the center. Marinate for several hours. Serve with sherry sauce (see p. 226). The grapefruit may be cut in halves or prepared in segments.

GUAVAS IN RUM SAUCE

Prepare the fresh guavas by slicing, then soaking the fruit in a syrup of thin honey and rum. Serve cold.

HOLIDAY MELON

Marinate segments of orange, strawberries, and sliced peaches in any sweet wine. Fill honeydew melon. Chill and serve.

ISLAND BOMBE

Peel one honeydew melon and cut a slice off the top. Dissolve one package of lemon jello in one-half cup of coconut milk and mix with one cup of coconut meat. Fill the melon cavity with the jello-coconut mix. Then place the top back on. Chill and cut in slices.

MELON AU VIN ROSÉ

For a real summertime taste thrill, cut a plug out of a watermelon. Fill the melon with Almaden Grenache Vin Rosé or any type champagne. Chill the melon for several hours and serve in slices.

PAPAYA

Marinate ripe sliced or mashed papayas in lemon juice. Serve over vanilla ice cream.

PINEAPPLE DISTINGUÉ

Cut the top off a fresh pineapple. Scoop out part of the meat with a grapefruit knife. Mix the chopped pineapple with apples, cherries, and seedless grapes. Marinate the fruit in white wine for an hour. Mix with fresh grated coconut and replace in the pineapple. Place the top on the pineapple and serve at the table.

PLANTAINS

Cut several ripe plantains crosswise. Marinate in honey and lemon juice for ten minutes. Drain and fry in butter.

LA PRUNE

Soak prunes overnight. Simmer in water with two cinnamon sticks and a few cloves for about thirty minutes or until tender. Drain the fruit and cook a few minutes more with one-half bottle of red wine. Chill in wine.

RHUBARB

Remove stalk ends and leaves. Cut in pieces and cook in a double boiler with one cup of brown sugar, one cup of cider, two nutmegs, and one stick of cinnamon for thirty minutes. Mix with one cup of whipped cream or serve plain. Cooked rhubarb may also be mixed with fresh strawberries.

STRAWBERRY CREAM

Mix berries and powdered sugar. Add kirsch and whipped cream. Chill. Berries picked late in the season are most delicious.

BERRIES IN COINTREAU

Mix strawberries with broken mint leaves. Place in orange baskets. Pour cointreau over the fruit and chill.

ICE CREAM AND SHERBETS

The old-time custom of serving a tart ice with a meat or fowl course still prevails in the South, and all forms of ice cream have long been popular dessert courses. Any type of berries, fruit, or melon may be used in making creams or ices; tea, and sometimes milk, ginger ale, or ginger beer can be substituted for water in recipes for ices.

Ice cream may be made in refrigerator trays without cooking these days, but the old-fashioned boiled custard method is still the best. In using either method, however, be sure not to fill the containers to the top, for the liquid will expand as it freezes.

To add a touch of elegance to plain ice cream, try dripping your favorite liqueur or brandy over it, or marinate berries or other fruit in wine for a short while before using as a colorful ice cream topping.

PLAIN ICE CREAM

Mix one cup of cream with one cup of sugar and warm over a slow fire. Add pinch of salt. Let cool and add one teaspoon of vanilla and two cups of whipped or plain cream. Freeze, and add any other flavoring or berries and fruits desired. Honey or syrup may be used in place of sugar. (Serves approximately six.)

BOILED CUSTARD CREAM

Heat two cups of cream and a pinch of salt in a double boiler. Mix two beaten egg yolks with one cup of sugar and slowly add to the cream. Add one teaspoon of cornstarch and cook until thick and smooth. Let the liquid cool and add one teaspoon of vanilla, two cups of whipped cream, and any flavoring desired. Freeze. (Serves approximately four.)

LOUISIANA MOLASSES ICE CREAM

Beat the yolks of four eggs and stir one cup of molasses into the eggs. Place in a double boiler and cook until thick. After the custard has cooled, add two cups of cream and one cup of minced pecans and freeze. The cream may be whipped before adding. (Serves approximately six persons.)

BUTTERMILK CREAM

Mix two cups of buttermilk with a pinch of salt and one cup of grapefruit segments. Dissolve one teaspoon of gelatin in four teaspoons of lime juice. Freeze in hand freezer or refrigerator trays. (Serves two to three.)

BASIC SHERBET RECIPE

Simmer water, fruit, and juices with grated citrus peel and sugar for ten minutes or longer. Strain and add any desired berries, fruit, or melon, tea, ginger ale or ginger beer, or additional fruit juices. With bananas and figs, milk is usually the preferred liquid. Fresh mint simmered a few minutes with several sticks of peppermint candy and water, then mixed with ginger ale and frozen makes a refreshing summer dessert. The beaten whites of eggs may be added to any ice if desired.

Fresh berries, nuts, fruit, and mint make decorative ornaments for ices. A few drops of white or green crème de menthe enhance the flavor of sherbets.

CRANBERRY ICE

Mix one can of cranberry sauce with the juice of a lemon or lime and turn into a refrigerator tray. Freeze and serve with turkey or wild fowl.

ROOSEVELT BAKED ALASKA

Place one brick of ice cream over one slice of sponge cake. Make a meringue of two beaten egg whites mixed with four tablespoons of sugar and one-eighth teaspoon of salt. Place a layer of this stiff meringue over the ice cream and run under the broiler. When browned, sprinkle with rum and burn a few seconds.

BRENNAN'S CHERRIES JUBILEE

For each serving, place eight large pitted Bing cherries drained of juice in a *brûlot* bowl with one teaspoon of sugar and one ounce of brandy. Ignite and burn a few seconds. Pour over vanilla ice cream in a compote.

CORDIAL MÉDOC CREAM

Marinate peeled, seeded grapes in Cordial Médoc for several hours. Drip on top of a compote of ice cream.

ICE CREAM À LA JUBILEE

First place a marshmallow, then a lump of sugar soaked in brandy, atop a serving of plain vanilla ice cream. Light the sugar and serve aflame in a darkened room.

ICE CREAM PRALINE

Place vanilla ice cream in a compote and break pralines over the cream.

THE PRINCESS MADELINE

Mix three tablespoons of rum, three tablespoons of Chilean sauterne, three tablespoons of pineapple cordial, three tablespoons of Mogen David wine, three tablespoons of sugar, and two tablespoons of cherry juice. Add one No. 2 can of drained fruit cocktail and allow the mixture to marinate for six hours. Place several teaspoons of the fruit marinade over custard ice cream in a compote and garnish with a cherry. (Serves eight persons.)

PARADISE POINT PINEAPPLE ICE

Place pineapple sherbet in a compote and drop several teaspoons of white crème de menthe over the sherbet.

BARBARA'S CRÈME GLACÉE

Beat three egg yolks and add one cup of scalded milk. Place in a double boiler and cook until thick. Add one cup of minced macaroons that have been soaked in sherry. Cool and add one teaspoon of vanilla and one pint of whipped cream. Add the beaten whites of three eggs. Ground nuts may be added. Freeze in paper cups. (Serves six to eight.)

DATE PUDDING

Roll out one box of graham crackers and mix crumbs with two ounces of bourbon whisky. Mix one box of dates, chopped; one-half box of marshmallows, chopped; and two cups of pecans, chopped. Add to graham cracker crumb mixture and chill.

FROSTED NOGG

Use either recipe for egg nogg given on p. 330. Freeze.

MRS. MOODY'S FROZEN WHIP

Beat the yolks of three eggs with one-half cup of sugar. Gradually add one-half cup of sherry to the eggs. Add one pint of whipped cream and one cup of minced nuts. Freeze. (Serves approximately six.)

MANGO CREAM

Peel ripe mangoes and mash. Add one cup of apple juice to one cup of mango pulp. Freeze for half hour. Beat and add two cups of whipped cream and fresh ground nutmeg. Freeze again or chill.

MARSHMALLOW CREAM

Mince one small box of marshmallows and heat in one cup of cream and one-half cup of sugar. Let the mixture soak for ten minutes. Add one teaspoon of almond extract, one cup of ground, toasted almonds, and one pint of whipped cream. Freeze. Serve with "Syrup La Cuite." (See p. 227.) (Serves approximately eight.)

AVOCADO MOUSSE

Mash two ripe avocados with three teaspoons of lime juice. Add two cups of whipped cream and chill. Garnish with a green cherry.

MACAROON MOUSSE

In a double boiler make a custard of two egg yolks, three teaspoons of sugar, one teaspoon of vanilla, and one cup of milk. Let thicken and cool. Add two egg whites, beaten, one cup of whipped cream, and one cup of minced macaroons, folding gently into custard mixture. Chill.

SYLLABUB

This is dessert or a refreshment for festive holiday occasions. Whip one quart of cream until stiff. Add four teaspoons of lime juice and two teaspoons of grated lime peel, and four teaspoons of sugar. Gradually pour in one cup of Madeira wine. (Sherry or whisky also may be used.) Sprinkle with nutmeg. (Serves approximately eighteen persons.)

ZABAIONE

Beat two egg yolks and one cup of cream with one-half cup of sugar in a double boiler. Let thicken and slowly pour in one-half cup of white wine. Blend well and chill, or serve warm immediately over cold fruit.

CAKES
BABA A L'ANISETTE

Make a batter by sifting two cups of flour, one-half teaspoon of salt, and two teaspoons of baking powder. Cream two cups of sugar with one-half stick of melted butter. Mix ingredients and add one cup of hot milk. Pour batter into muffin tins and bake in a moderate oven for forty-five minutes. Pour anisette liqueur over each cake when ready to serve. (Serves four to six.)

BRANDY BRIOCHE

Sift two cups of flour with two teaspoons of baking powder and one-half teaspoon of salt. Cream one stick of butter with four eggs, one cup of sugar, and two teaspoons of nutmeg. Mix all ingredients and add two cups of minced pecans and two jiggers of brandy. Place in a greased pan and bake in moderate oven for forty minutes. Keep brioche in a covered container and moisten with brandy every few days. (Serves approximately twelve persons.)

CORN MEAL CRACKNEL

Mix one and one-half cups of meal and one-half cup of flour with one-half cup of brown sugar. Add one-fourth cup of melted butter, two eggs, and one cup of minced nuts. Drop on greased pan and bake ten minutes in hot oven. These sweet biscuits also may be made with two cups of flour and two teaspoons of baking powder, using orange juice to moisten the dough. (Serves six to eight.)

CREOLE COFFEECAKE

Cream one-half stick of butter with one cup of powdered sugar. Add the yolks of three eggs and one-half cup of chicory coffee. Sift two cups of cake flour with two teaspoons of baking powder and one-half teaspoon of salt. Mix all ingredients and bake in layers for thirty minutes in a moderate oven. Place minced nuts between layers and ice with one-half pound of butter creamed with one pound of powdered sugar, using black coffee to mix and adding a little sweet cocoa. Poppy seeds may be added to butter. (Serves approximately twelve persons.)

OLD-FASHIONED GINGERBREAD

Place one-third cup of butter and one cup of molasses in a pan and heat to boiling. Remove from heat at once, add one teaspoon of soda, and beat vigorously. Add one-half cup of sour milk and one beaten egg. Sift together two cups of flour, one-half teaspoon of salt, two teaspoons of powdered ginger, and one-half teaspoon of powdered nutmeg, cinnamon, or cloves. Add to molasses mixture and mix well. Pour into a shallow, buttered pan and bake about twenty-five minutes in a moderate oven or until done and brown.

ESTOMAC MULATRE

Sift two cups of flour with two teaspoons of soda and one-half teaspoon of salt. Cream one-half cup of shortening and one-half cup of brown sugar with three beaten eggs. Add one-half teaspoon of ginger and one teaspoon of nutmeg. Mix all ingredients and add one cup of molasses, a dash of lemon juice, and hot water if needed. Bake in a moderate oven for thirty minutes. (Serves approximately ten persons.)

PAIN PATATE

Sift two cups of flour, two teaspoons of baking powder, a pinch of salt, and one teaspoon of nutmeg. Cream together three egg yolks, one stick of butter, and three cups of brown sugar. Mix all ingredients and add two cups of grated sweet potatoes and three beaten egg whites. Bake in a slow oven for fifty minutes. (Serves six to eight.)

PECAN TORTE

Cream one-half cup of shortening with one cup of sugar. Add two beaten eggs. Add one and one-half cups of sifted flour, one teaspoon of baking powder, and one-half teaspoon of salt. Add enough milk to soften. Pour in greased pan. Whip three egg whites stiff with one-half cup sugar. Add one cup of minced pecans and pour over dough. Bake forty minutes in moderate oven. Cut in desired shapes before baking. (Serves six to eight.)

POUND CAKE

Mix one pound of cake flour, one pound of butter, one pound of sugar, and twelve eggs. Bake for thirty minutes in a moderate oven. (Serves approximately eighteen persons.)

PLUM PUDDING A L'ANGLAISE

Mix together one and one-half pounds of bread crumbs, two ounces of citron, one-half pound of flour, two ounces of chopped almonds, two pounds of suet, chopped fine, two grated nutmegs, two pounds of currants, two ounces of candied lemon peel, two pounds of raisins, the juice and grated rind of one lemon, two pounds of sugar, one teaspoon of salt, sixteen eggs, one wine glass of brandy, and enough milk to make a stiff batter, adding the ingredients in the order given. Let the mixture stand overnight. In the morning, place it in a pudding mold and steam for two hours.

SCONES

Mix four cups of oatmeal with two teaspoons of baking powder and four cups of flour. Add one teaspoon of nutmeg and two teaspoons of cinnamon to four cups of sugar. Mix all ingredients. Add four eggs and one stick of butter. Add a little cream, if needed. Make batter into desired shape and bake in a hot oven for fifteen minutes. (Serves approximately sixteen persons.)

SHORTCAKES

Fruit or berry shortcakes may be made by sugaring fruit or berries, then pouring over pastry cups, pound cake, buttered biscuits, or corn meal muffins.

SKILLET CAKE

Melt one stick of butter in an iron skillet and brown two cups of pecans and two cups of fresh pineapple slices. Add one and one-half cups of brown sugar, glazing nuts and fruit. Make a "Brioche" cake batter (see p. 277). Pour batter into skillet and bake in moderate oven for forty-five minutes. Turn upside down and serve with whipped cream.

SPICE BREAD

Sift two cups of flour, one-half teaspoon of salt, one teaspoon of soda, and two teaspoons of baking powder together. Add two beaten eggs and one-half cup of melted butter. Add one cup of molasses, one cup of brown sugar, and powdered ginger and cinnamon to taste. Mix two teaspoons of lemon juice to one cup of boiling water and mix with other ingredients. Bake in a moderate oven for forty minutes. Cut in squares and serve with whipped cream. (Serves approximately six.)

SPONGE CAKE

Sift the dry ingredients—two teaspoons of baking powder, one teaspoon of salt, and one and one-half cups of flour. Add one cup of sugar. Beat three egg yolks and stir into dry ingredients. Slowly add one-half cup of warm milk. Blend and add one teaspoon of vanilla extract and the beaten whites of eggs. Bake in a shallow pan for forty minutes in a moderate oven.

SWEET BREAD

Sift two cups of flour with two teaspoons of baking powder and one-half teaspoon of salt. Cream together one and one-half cups of butter and two cups of brown sugar. Add dry ingredients. Then add six beaten egg yolks. Mix and add beaten egg whites, one teaspoon of vanilla, and one cup of ground pecans. Place a large bay leaf on the bottom of greased cake pan and pour batter in. Bake in a slow oven for forty minutes.

UPSIDE-DOWN CAKE

Mix a cake batter of one cup of cake flour, one teaspoon of baking powder, one-half teaspoon of salt, four egg yolks, one teaspoon of sugar, and one-half cup of hot milk. Mash four cups of persimmons and brown in butter and brown sugar with minced pecans. Pour cake over nuts and persimmons. Bake for forty-five minutes in a moderate oven and turn upside down. (Serves approximately ten persons.)

COOKIES AND SMALL CAKES
BÂTON D'AMANDE

Cream one stick of butter with one and one-half cups of sugar. Add two cups of sifted flour and one and one-half teaspoons of baking powder, one-half teaspoon of salt, and two teaspoons of almond extract. Add a small amount of cream and roll in strips. Sprinkle dough with minced almonds. Bake strips in a hot oven for twenty minutes. (Serves approximately eight persons.)

JUDGE FRANK W. HAWTHORNE'S BROWN SUGAR SQUARES

Warm one box of brown sugar in the oven in an oven-proof bowl. Add one tablespoon of water and beat. Add four eggs, one at a time, beating thoroughly after each addition. Fold in one and three-fourths cups of flour sifted with one teaspoon of baking powder. Add one teaspoon of almond flavoring and two cups of chopped nuts. Pour into a shallow, oblong baking dish and bake slowly at 250° for forty minutes.

CHUTNEY PUFFS

Pinch off pieces of homemade bread dough. Roll and cut in squares. Place chutney in center. Fold over and fry in deep fat for ten minutes.

MIM FOSTER'S COOKIES

Mix one cup of butter with two cups of sugar. Add one cup of sweet milk, two teaspoons of vanilla, and two teaspoons of baking powder. Add enough sifted flour to make dough soft. Roll out very thin and bake in a hot oven for ten minutes on a greased pan. Caraway seeds may be sprinkled over cakes before baking. Make up batter and leave in refrigerator, using a little at a time as needed. (Serves approximately sixteen persons.)

LES OREILLES DE COCHON

Make a pastry by mixing two cups of sifted flour, one-half teaspoon of baking powder, one-half teaspoon of salt, and one teaspoon of nutmeg. Cream one-half stick of butter with two beaten egg yolks. Mix two teaspoons of lemon juice with one teaspoon of ice water. Mix all ingredients and roll thin on a floured board. Sprinkle dough with powdered sugar. Cut in squares and fry in deep fat for fifteen minutes. Twist edges with fork while frying. Drain and sprinkle with powdered sugar. In the bayou country a split cane fork is used for twisting the dough. (Serves approximately eight persons.)

KATHLEEN BLEDDEN'S SOUR CREAM COOKIES

Cream one cup of butter with two and one-half cups of white sugar. Add three whole eggs. Sift one scant teaspoonful of soda, two teaspoonfuls of baking powder, and from one to two cups of flour. Add alternately to butter-and-egg mixture with one cup of sour cream. Mix well, and add one teaspoonful of orange extract. Keep dough soft. Roll out on a pastryboard dusted with flour (or use less flour and drop cookies from tip of spoon). Roll thin, cut with cookie-cutter in desired shapes, and place on a floured cookie sheet so that cookies do not touch. Sprinkle with granulated sugar. (If drop method is used, sprinkle sugar after cookies are partially baked.) Bake for ten minutes in a hot oven. (Serves approximately twenty persons.)

VOL AU VENT

Mix one stick of butter in two cups of boiling water. Sift two cups of flour and stir into butter-water. Simmer a few minutes and cool. Add five beaten eggs and beat. Roll into desired shapes and bake in a hot oven for thirty minutes. Minced nuts and chutney may be placed in dough. (Serves approximately eight persons.)

CREPES SUZETTE

Beat three eggs with a pinch of salt. Add two tablespoons of sweet milk and two tablespoons of sifted flour. More flour and milk may be added if desired. Make batter very thin and drop on preheated, buttered iron griddle. Fry slowly about three minutes on each side. Serve hot with fresh fruit or a flame sauce. (See p. 226.) Sprinkle cakes with powdered sugar. Heavy cream may be used in place of flame sauce or fruit. (Serves approximately six persons.)

CREPES A LA ORCHARD

Make French pancakes in above manner. Mash fresh peaches and mix with peach brandy. Heat the peach brandy sauce, but do not cook. Place crépes in the sauce for a few minutes. Serve hot.

BRENNAN'S CREPES SUZETTE

To make the batter, beat three eggs, add three ounces of flour, and blend until smooth. Add one-half pint of milk, but keep the batter thin. Just before frying, add one ounce of Kirschwasser. Fry the pancakes paper thin in a small frying pan. Do not lay one on the other.

For the sauce, heat a soufflé pan. Melt three-eighths pound of butter and twelve teaspoons of sugar and blend. Add the minced peel of three oranges and one lemon. Simmer for five minutes. Add slices of the peeled oranges and lemon. Simmer until peel is soft. Remove peels with a fork. Place three thin pancakes in the sauce and allow them to absorb it. Fold cakes in half, then in half again. When twelve cakes are folded in the pan pour evenly three-fourths ounce of Cointreau, then three-fourths ounce of Grand Marnier over the cakes. Pour two ounces of brandy in last. Tilt the pan slightly and move rapidly back and forth over the flame until the brandy ignites. Level the pan and continue the movement until the flame dies. Serve the cakes, three to a person, covered with the sauce.

FLOSSY FLAPJACKS

Cook up a batch of thin corn meal (see p. 248) pancakes or Crepes Suzette. Squeeze a little lemon juice over each flapjack and sprinkle with powdered sugar. Spread with a paste of mashed peaches moistened with brandy. Roll up and serve hot.

DOUGHNUTS AUX HALLES

Sift two cups of flour with two teaspoons of baking powder, one-half cup of sugar, and a pinch of salt. Add one tablespoon of melted butter, one beaten egg, and one cup of warm milk. Blend and drop by small spoonfuls into deep fat. Fry for ten minutes, then drain and sprinkle with powdered sugar. Serve with "Cafe au Lait" (see p. 306). (Serves six.)

These are the familiar and popular "doughnuts" served in New Orleans' French Market coffeehouses.

DESSERT MUFFINS

Mix two cups of sifted flour with one-half teaspoon of soda, one-half teaspoon of salt, and two teaspoons of sugar. Add two beaten eggs, one-half cup of liquid shortening, and one cup of buttermilk. Mix and bake in muffin tins in a hot oven for twenty-five minutes. Serve hot muffins topped with fresh or wine-marinated fruit or berries. Berries and nuts also may be cooked in the muffins. Sweet milk may be substituted for buttermilk; two teaspoons of baking powder for soda, and a large cup of corn meal and one-half cup of flour for two cups of flour. (Serves four to six.)

MAY HAW JELLY ROLL

Place twelve strawberries in one jar of melted May haw jelly for thirty minutes. Blend a sweet roll by mixing one cup of cake flour, one teaspoon of baking powder, one cup of sugar, two beaten eggs, two teaspoons of lime juice, three tablespoons of melted butter, one teaspoon of orange-flower water, and the grated rind of one-half orange. Pour the batter into a pan lined with waxed paper. Bake in a hot oven for twenty minutes. Lift the paper and cake out of the pan and sprinkle with powdered sugar. When the cake is cool, spread with the berries and jelly. Slice and roll up. Place each jelly roll in waxed paper and let chill in refrigerator for an hour or so. (Serves six.)

CUSTARDS AND JELLS

CHOCOLATE BLANCMANGE

Use two tablespoons of cocoa, one cup of sugar, one and one-half tablespoons of flour, one egg, and three cups of milk. Mix cocoa, sugar, and flour until well blended. Add egg and work in until thoroughly mixed. Add milk gradually. Cook over slow flame about twenty minutes or until mixture has a custard consistency, stirring all the time. Put in ice box to chill. Add vanilla to taste. Top with whipped cream. (Serves approximately six persons.)

AUNT SALLIE'S BOILED CUSTARD

Beat thoroughly six egg yolks with four tablespoons of sugar. Warm five cups of cream and slowly mix with the eggs in the top of a double boiler. Stir until thick and add one teaspoon of vanilla. Cook about twenty-five minutes. Cool and pour over lady fingers in a compote. (Serves approximately twelve persons.)

SOUTHERN BREAD CUSTARD

This dish is usually served the day after a picnic when there are lots of sandwich-bread edges left over. Brown the bread crusts and add to two beaten eggs and one-half cup of sugar or any kind of jam or jelly. Add enough cream to moisten and some nuts and raisins. Bake for twenty minutes and serve with fresh cream.

BURNT CUP CUSTARD

Melt brown sugar in pan with a little sugar and nutmeg. Simmer down to almost-burning stage. Pour a little of the sugar sauce into each custard cup. Make a custard of one pint of cream, four egg yolks, two cups of sugar, one teaspoon of flour, and one teaspoon of vanilla. Cook in a double boiler five minutes. Pour into custard cups and bake for forty minutes in pan of water. Turn cups upside down when ready to serve.

YAMMY CUSTARD

Mix six baked yams with one cup of cinnamon sugar, one-half stick of butter, one teaspoon of ground ginger, one-half teaspoon of nutmeg, and two beaten egg yolks. Add one-half cup of cane syrup and enough hot cream to moisten. Top with pecans and bake in a moderate oven for twenty minutes. Serve with fresh cream. (Serves approximately eight persons.)

GERTRUDE'S SHERRY WINE JELLY

This recipe requires two tablespoons (two envelopes) of unflavored gelatin, one-half cup of cold water, two cups of boiling water, one cup of sugar, juice of two lemons, and three-fourths cup of sherry wine. Mix gelatin in one-half cup of cold water. Add two cups of boiling water. Add sugar and lemon juice. Let mixture cool a little and then add the sherry wine. Mold in glass jars. (Yield: two pints.)

KATHLEEN'S PORT JELL

Dissolve two packages of gelatin in little warm water. Add one fifth of port wine and chill. (Serves approximately twelve persons.)

CABINET PUDDING

This ideal Thanksgiving or Christmas dessert requires two tablespoons (two envelopes) of unflavored gelatin, one cup of sherry wine heated to boiling point, one cup of sugar, one cup of cut pecans, one cup of minced crystallized cherries, and eight eggs. Soak gelatin in a little cold water. Beat yolks of eggs thoroughly; add sugar, then hot sherry, gelatin, pecans, and cherries. Stir well. When this is thick and cold, add beaten egg whites. Put in refrigerator to congeal, stirring frequently so that fruit is distributed and does not settle at the bottom. Top with whipped cream. (Serves twelve people.)

PERSIMMON PUDDING

Pick well-ripened persimmons. Wash and mash. For three cups of fruit use one-half stick of butter with a cup of brown sugar and three beaten egg yolks. Add one tablespoon of cornstarch. Mix and add three cups of whipped cream. Place in a buttered casserole in a pan of water and bake in a slow oven for forty-five minutes. This pudding also may be used as a pie filling. (Serves eight or ten persons.)

SWEET TATER PONE

Peel and grate four raw sweet potatoes. Let stand in ice water a few minutes. Drain well and mix with one-half stick of butter, one-half cup of brown sugar, and a dash of powdered allspice and nutmeg. Egg may be added if desired. Add enough milk or water to moisten and bake in moderate oven for forty-five minutes.

Serve cold in compote with "Hard Sauce" (see p. 226), or with fresh cream. (Serves approximately six persons.)

RIZ AU LAIT

Bake for forty minutes two cups of cooked rice in one cup of hot milk or cream, two beaten egg yolks, and two teaspoons of nutmeg. Serve hot or cold with fresh cream. (Serves approximately four persons.)

CHOCTAW SPOON BREAD

The Choctaws influenced the Louisiana pioneers in their daily use of meal, the staple food of the Indians. "Bota Kapusi," or cold corn meal mush, was kept prepared at all times, for the Choctaws had no regular meal hours. They simply kept a corn buffet near the fire.

A dish relished by the first Louisianians was the Indian variety of spoon bread. To make it, heat six cups of hot milk or water to the boiling point. Add enough meal to thicken. Remove from fire and add one cup of molasses and shelled nuts. Powdered spices may be added. Bake for thirty minutes in oven or over coals. Serve with fresh cream. (Serves approximately twelve persons.)

TROPIC TEMPTATION

Simmer a syrup of one cup of water, one cup of coconut milk, and three cups of sugar for five minutes. Add three cups of grated coconut and yolks of two eggs. Remove to a double boiler. Cook until it begins to thicken, then add one cup of white wine. Cook a few minutes. This dessert also may be baked with orange segments. (Serves approximately twelve persons.)

ANGEL'S PIE MERINGUE CRUST

Beat four egg whites until foamy. Add one-eighth teaspoon of cream of tartar and beat stiff. Add one cup of sugar gradually. Add one teaspoon of vanilla and beat until it peaks. Bake in a greased, floured pan or in individual pie shells at 275 degrees for thirty or forty minutes. Cool and fill the shell with fruit.

APPLE CROUSTADE

Peel apples and slice. Simmer with sugar and some white wine. Add a few elderberries or any other wild berries and simmer until berries are done (about one-half hour). Place in individual pie shells and cook for ten minutes.

RED NECK FRIED PIES

Mix two cups of flour, one-half teaspoon of salt, one-half teaspoon of soda, one teaspoon of nutmeg, one teaspoon of powdered cinnamon, and three teaspoons of sugar. Add one-half cup of shortening and enough ice water and lemon juice to thin. Chill pastry for an hour. Roll on a floured board and cut in wide strips. Spread the strips with cooked apples. Fold pastry over apples and pinch the edges with a fork. Chill pies and fry in butter. (Serves approximately eight persons.)

PERCY'S CANTALOUPE CREAM PIE

Sift together one cup of sugar, one-fourth cup of flour, and one-half tablespoon of salt. Gradually stir in one cup of scalded milk and cook in a double boiler until the mixture thickens—about fifteen minutes. Pour some of mixture over two slightly beaten egg yolks, stirring constantly. Return to double boiler and cook two minutes more. Add two tablespoons of butter blended with two cups of cantaloupe. Let mixture cool, then pour into a baked, nine-inch pastry shell. Top with meringue and bake in a 325 degree oven for about fifteen minutes or until meringue is browned.

Meringue

Beat two egg whites to which has been added one-eighth teaspoon of salt. When egg whites are foamy, add four tablespoons of sugar, one tablespoon at a time, beating after each addition until sugar is dissolved. Spread the mixture on cooled pie filling until it touches the crust at all edges.

GARÇONNIÈRE CHEESE PIE

Make a crust of graham crackers moistened with melted butter and a small amount of powdered sugar. Mold into pie pan. Blend four packages of cream cheese with one-half cup of sugar and three teaspoons of lemon juice. Add one cup of fruit if desired. Bake in hot oven for ten minutes. Cool and serve topped with whipped cream. (Serves approximately six persons.)

PERCY'S COTTAGE CHEESE PIE

Press two cups of cottage cheese through a sieve. Combine one-fourth cup of cream and one tablespoon of flour to make a paste. Add to cheese with an additional cup of cream, one-fourth teaspoon of salt, three cups of sugar, one-fourth cup of lemon juice, two teaspoons of grated lemon rind, and four slightly beaten egg yolks. Beat four egg whites until stiff and fold into cheese mixture. Pour filling into a nine-inch pie crust, crimping the edges. Bake in a 450 degree oven for ten minutes, then reduce heat to 350 degrees and bake about forty minutes more (or until a silver knife inserted in the center comes out clean). (Serves four to six.)

Graham Cracker Crust

Roll enough fresh graham crackers to make one and one-half cups of crumbs. Mix with one-half cup of melted butter and two tablespoons of sugar. Knead until crumbs are moistened. Press against sides and bottom of a nine-inch pie pan until the crust is about one-eighth inch thick. Chill for two hours before adding cooled filling. Butter cookies or vanilla wafers may be substituted for graham crackers.

QUEEN'S TART

Bake or buy pastry shells. Make a filling of four egg yolks mixed with one tablespoon of melted butter, three teaspoons of cornstarch, and one cup of cream. Cook in a double boiler. When custard thickens, add one-half cup of segments of Louisiana oranges and one-half cup of minced pecans. Pour custard into the shells and bake for forty minutes in a moderate oven.

PINEAPPLE ROLL

Cut fresh pineapple into large pieces. Sprinkle with cinnamon sugar and wrap in pie crust. Bake in a moderate oven for fifteen minutes.

PRUNE PIE A LA CARAWAY

Prune dishes usually suggest wholesomeness rather than glamour, but this prune pie qualifies on both counts:

Pit two cups of cooked prunes and cut in half. Peel (removing all the inner white peel and seeds) and dice one orange. Combine one-half cup of brown sugar, one-fourth teaspoon of salt, and two tablespoons of cornstarch with one cup of prune juice, and bring to a boil. Stir constantly. Add the prunes and the orange and two tablespoons of butter. Simmer and stir for ten minutes. Pour into a baked nine-inch pastry shell and cover with meringue. Bake in a 300 degree oven for fifteen minutes. (Serves four to six.)

CHES' PUN'KIN PIE

Here in the South, many pies have been called "safe" or "ches'" pies because they were stored in a pie safe or chest—a cupboard usually made of pine and equipped with screen doors. They are still in use in some Louisiana kitchens.

To make the crust, sift two cups of flour with one teaspoon of salt. Cut one cup of cold shortening into flour and salt. Moisten with one-half cup (or less) of ice water. Roll dough thin and place in pie pan.

Fill with two cups of cooked pumpkin, mashed and mixed with one cup of brown sugar, one teaspoon of nutmeg, one-half teaspoon of salt, and one teaspoon of lime juice. Bake in a slow oven for thirty minutes. (Serves four to six.)

This pie crust recipe may be used generally for fruit and custard pies.

FRUIT BALLS

Grind dried figs with raisins and pecans. Add mashed fresh apples. Moisten with port wine. Roll into balls. Then roll in powdered sugar and place in separate waxed papers. Take along on the trail for dessert.

ORANGE ALMOND DROPS

Blanch two cups of almonds and toast in the oven with a bit of oleo. Cut into thin slivers. Cut up one cup of fresh orange petals and sprinkle with three pounds of sugar. Beat whites of six or more eggs until they are stiff and add to nuts and sugared orange petals. Blend and drop on a cookie sheet or greased pan and bake.

ORANGE LIME PECANS

Mix one cup of orange peel and the juice of one lime, one and one-half cups of sugar, and one-half teaspoon of salt. Simmer until mixture candies. Add two cups of shelled pecan halves and drop one pecan at a time on waxed paper.

PRALINES

Pralines or sugared nuts originated in France and were first made of almonds. The Louisiana colonists substituted pecans for almonds because of the abundance of these wild nuts.

ACADIAN PRALINES

Make a syrup of one cup of brown sugar, one teaspoon of butter, and one-half cup of cream. When the syrup spins a thread, add two cups of pecan halves. Drop into the desired size from a spoon onto a buttered plate or waxed paper.

CHAPELETS DE PACANS

String shelled pecans on a piece of thread. Make a syrup of one part water and three parts sugar. Let simmer until thick. Dip nuts into the syrup. Hang the string up so that nuts will harden.

SUGARED NUTS

Beat four egg whites with a little powdered sugar until stiff. Add one teaspoon of orange-flower water or coconut milk. Drop shelled nut halves in the mixture on a buttered pan. Roll in a pan and stick the halves together. Roll in powdered sugar and toast in the oven.

XIII
Come Let Us Warm Ourselves

Picking cotton

Come Let Us Warm Ourselves

Louisiana's spirituous history goes back to the earliest days of the colony, when the LeMoyne brothers—the Sieur d'Iberville and the Sieur de Bienville—founded and developed their first settlements on the Gulf Coast. Like all good Frenchmen, these early colonists brought their wines and brandies with them, and these beverages soon became as essential a part of life in the New World as they had been in the Old.

In 1722, New Orleans was no more than a cypress-walled city of crude cabins and mud-choked lanes, but it still did not lack an atmosphere of European sophistication. In 1728, Sister Marie Hachard, a novice in the convent of the Ursuline nuns, noted that "the Demon possesses here a great empire," and an early journalist recorded that this was a time of wine on every table. Even the ladies of *les bonnes familles* were known to indulge in light liquids as they played *bourré* and *piquet* behind shuttered windows in the Vieux Carré. White wines were sipped at breakfast, and claret was the general luncheon and dinner wine; but as many as five different wines were sometimes served with a plain dinner.

By imposing a revenue tax on all taverns and an impost of $1.00

per barrel on imported brandy, the Spanish were able to reduce some of the Crescent City's air of conviviality. But the laws were never completely enforced, and most New Orleanians still enjoyed their daily toddy of brandy, sugar, and water. The rums of Santo Domingo and tafia rum were also popular "short swallows" of the day.

In 1793, a French refugee from Santo Domingo made spirituous history when he arrived in the city with a secret family formula for a tonic called "bitters." Soon Antoine Amdée Peychaud was serving a mixture of cognac and a dash of bitters in his apothecary shop on Royal Street. For a vessel he used an egg cup, or *coquetier* —a designation which Americans were soon mispronouncing "cocktail" and which they used to refer to the contents as well as the cup itself.

This early cocktail soon became the rage of New Orleans. After the Civil War, whisky—more popular with the American palate— was substituted for the brandy, and other refinements were added. The famous Sazerac cocktail was one of the first of these descendants of Peychaud's concoction. A julep made of rum appeared shortly afterwards too.

Beginning with the days of the Louisiana Purchase, life in New Orleans became colorful, lavish, and exciting. Hostelries became the social centers and meeting places for both Creoles and Americans. In those early days, the Strangers and the Orleans hotels on Chartres Street were favorite rendezvous spots, though their fame was later eclipsed by the St. Charles and the St. Louis hotels. In the old Gem Restaurant a delightful and no-longer-current custom got its start and was soon adopted by other cafés and saloons. Here, on long, high marble tables, the New Orleans *boulevardiers* might help themselves to a hearty free lunch as they enjoyed their toddies, tafias, and cocktails.

In later years, immigration from many European countries has added a further distinctive character to epicurean New Orleans. From Italy in particular have come men whose inherent love of fine food and drink has made them and their descendants some of the most celebrated restaurateurs and mixologists in the city's history.

But the fine food and drink of Louisiana is not confined to the city of New Orleans. Stretching south and west from it and across the Mississippi is a fascinating and varied area whose geography and people have the variety and spice of the gumbo that originated here. This is the land of Evangeline—the home of the Acadians who were driven from Nova Scotia in 1767 and who were given a refuge by the Spanish in Louisiana as they drifted south over a twenty-year period.

The Acadians were simple folk who loved life and the land, and they prospered in Louisiana as they farmed their narrow arpents along the placid waters of the bayous Teche and LaFourche, trapped the muskrat in the cypress swamps, or seined for shrimp and other seafood along the Gulf Coast. Devoutly Catholic, excitably Gallic, and irrepressibly merry, they and their descendants have become famous for their crawfish boils and cockfights, their pirogue races and *fais-dodos*. Every year, the ceremonies marking the blessing of their shrimp fleets or cane fields are nationally reported events; and such dishes as jambalaya, court bouillon, red beans and rice, grits and grillades, *pain perdu*, coush-coush caillé, and gumbo have firmly established them on the culinary map.

Liquid refreshments are always in order at Cajun (a corruption of "Acadian") gatherings, and wakes or *veillées*, which bring together cousins and friends from up and down the bayou, are as enjoyable a part of Cajun social life as the gay charivari. The old custom of serving both solid and liquid refreshments at a wake is still the fashion in South Louisiana—and no disrespect to the departed is ever intended by the mourners who enjoy them.

A "small black" or *café noir* is the universal drink of this happy section and one that is served at all hours of the day. These sips of chicory-and-coffee are often laced with brandy or bourbon, and one of the most enjoyable of the bayou social functions is the *et collation*, or afternoon coffee party. On these occasions, coffee and tall spirituous drinks are served with pastries. In the evenings, the refreshments are served to the accompaniment of a spirited game of *bourré*.

But, though Louisiana was settled by the French and given a distinctive character by them and the Spanish who succeeded them in the southern portion of the state, all Louisiana is not Creole. After the Louisiana Purchase, Americans of Anglo-Saxon background flowed into the state. Some of them settled on the banks of the Mississippi River, where they established a cultural pattern and way of life that has never been equalled for grandeur and opulence. Even today one can see in the crumbling ruins of some of these plantation palaces the evidence of a splendor that is no more. Here on the banks of the great river, guests were entertained for weeks at a time with feasting, dancing, gaming, hunting, and fishing. Private stables were maintained by the planters so that their guests might place wagers on their private races, and the mint julep before breakfast was *de rigeur* before the guest joined the master in riding out over the plantation acres. Strong black coffee, brought to the bedside by a slave and served in an "eye opener set"—a miniature cup and saucer, sugar bowl, cream pitcher, and toast rack—was another regular feature of plantation life.

To be the mistress of such a plantation required a hardy constitution and a good bit of administrative ability. Ante-bellum chatelaines learned from childhood how to make the home remedies and tisanes that were administered to ailing family members and slaves, and the fruit cordials and liqueurs that were served to the visitors who spent entire seasons with the planter's family.

As the decades before the outbreak of the Civil War wore on, more and more of the state was settled. To the rolling hills of the northern portion De Soto had come as early as 1542, and the original land grants in the area were Spanish and French. But the traces of these Latin peoples have been all but erased by a westward movement of Anglo-Saxon and Scotch-Irish settlers who came from the Carolinas to become cotton farmers in the Red River Delta of North Louisiana. At one time, the city of Shreveport was a rip-roaring cotton town, where gaudy steamboats plying the Red River tied up at crude wharves and country gentlemen could be seen taking a swig of whisky or a nip of wine along the levee as they sold their wagonloads of cotton.

Catfish frys and goat barbecues were always occasions for bringing "Red Neck" folk together, and the jug was passed around freely (though never touched by the ladies). Back in the red clay hills, a local product was distilled and bottled. Termed "corn likker," "stump," or "moonshine," it was enjoyed by home folks and strangers alike.

Today, North Louisiana enjoys the same sophisticated sort of tippling as does New Orleans. But the old punches and noggs made with bourbon remain the most popular general refreshments.

Two other areas of the state have contributed a distinctive flavor to its liquid history:

South of New Orleans in the river parish of Plaquemines, the mild winters and rich, alluvial soil have provided the ideal conditions for citrus growing. Louisiana oranges are said to be sweeter than other varieties by those who prefer them, and they serve as the base of a delicious and versatile table wine manufactured in the area.

Slightly to the north and to the east of New Orleans is the center of the nation's principal strawberry producing area. From these strawberry parishes railroad carloads of ripe, crimson fruit are shipped northward daily during the bearing season. Some of the fruit, too ripe for shipment, remains behind, however, and is converted locally into a delicious strawberry wine by the growers.

Different as these many areas are in geography, population, and taste, most Louisianians would agree that they share two characteristics—a fondness for really good food and an inclination to enjoy it in the grand manner. Of all the beverages served throughout the state, perhaps none so epitomizes this combination as *café brûlot*—a delicious, spicy version of the favorite *café noir*, served from a flaming bowl in a darkened room. Only a true culinary artist could conceive so dramatic a presentation of his product; but everyone who knows and loves fine food and drink can appreciate it.

ADVICE AND ACCESSORIES FOR THE BAR

Bar glasses should be kept rim up after washing so that the soap fumes dissipate. Cold drinks should be served in glasses that have been chilled in shaved ice or in the refrigerator; glasses for hot drinks should be preheated in very hot water.

To bring out the bouquet of a spirit the liquid should be poured over the ice first, then the other required ingredients added. Ice should be made with fresh water (mineral water is best). In serving a punch use a large piece of ice in the bowl.

Highballs and other long drinks should be stirred after the ingredients are poured over the ice. Cocktails should be stirred or muddled unless the ingredients are difficult to mix. If a shaker or blender is used, mix quickly to avoid diluting the cocktail.

To frappé a drink pour the ingredients over shaved ice in a cocktail or wineglass.

If wine or other liquids are to be floated on top of a drink, a teaspoon is placed on top of the filled glass, and the "floater" poured slowly over the back of the spoon.

To frost a glass, dampen the rim and press it into powdered sugar just before pouring the drink into the glass.

Liquors, liqueurs, bitters, and bar syrups may be stored upright and left standing for bar use.

Maraschino, vermouth, and other wines should be stored flat on racks, but may be left standing for bar use. Maraschino and vermouth may be uncorked and used again.

Sherry, port, and the other fortified wines should be stored and used standing. After uncorking they may be reopened and used when desired.

The table and sparkling wines should not be recorked after being opened.

Seltzer water must not be re-used unless it is still fizzy.

MEASUREMENTS

Dash – One sixth of a teaspoon
Dram – One eight of a fluid ounce
Gill – One fourth of a pint
Jigger – One to one and one-half ounce
Pony – One ounce
Teaspoon – One eighth of an ounce

Every good domestic bartender will want to check his shelves to be sure he has a collection of the following before attempting to prepare most of the concoctions listed herein:

Absinthe; Abbotts, Amer Picon, Angostura, Bokers, Calisaya, Peychaud, and fruit (orange, lemon, and lime) bitters; cream or milk; eggs; fruits and fruit juices; gomme syrup; grenadine syrup; honey; white, red, and green maraschino cherries; maraschino liqueur or wine; fresh mint; molasses; nuts; olives; pickled onions; orange-flower water; orgeat syrup; raspberry syrup; simple syrup (*l'eau douce*); brown and white sugar; and vanilla.

The fruit juices should, of course, be squeezed just before using. The orange-flower water is imported from France or may be made at home.

BAR SYRUPS AND WATERS MADE AT HOME

Gomme

Mix one part water with one part sugar. Add one or more beaten egg whites. Simmer for five minutes, strain, and bottle.

Grenadine

Mix one part water with one part sugar. Simmer for five minutes. Add pomegranate seeds and simmer one hour or longer. Strain and bottle.

Orange-Flower Water

Mix one part water with one part sugar, and one-half teaspoon of vanilla extract. Simmer five minutes and add separated orange petals. Simmer a half hour or longer. Strain and bottle.

Orgeat Paste

Pound one cup of blanched almonds and blend with one cup of sugar and three teaspoons of orange-flower water. Place in small pots for future use. Orgeat paste may be mixed with rum as a remedial potion.

Orgeat Syrup

Mix one part sugar and one part water. Simmer five minutes and bottle. Add separated orange petals and simmer five minutes. Add one pound of pounded almonds or one teaspoon of almond extract.

Simple Syrup

Mix one part sugar and one part water. Simmer five minutes.

SOME NOTES ON THE SERVICE OF WINES

Among the Louisiana French, the service of wines is considered essential to a full enjoyment of Creole and Cajun cuisine, for they say that wine refreshes the mouth and cuts the grease in the rich and sauce-laden dishes. Like their French cousins, they recommend that wine be sipped in order to enjoy its fragrance, color, and flavor; and they point out that good table wine is bought on the basis of its year of vintage rather than its age.

One need not be a gourmet to select the proper wines to accompany Louisiana cookery. The simple rule of thumb, "Red wines with red meat and white wines with white meat," can serve as an easy guide. Red meat includes red fowl and game; white meat includes white fish, white fowl, and crustaceans. (In Louisiana, three exceptions to the rule are observed: teal duck is served with white wine, dove with red wine, and gumbo with dry red wine.)

Use a dry champagne to start a meal, and a sweet champagne for the dessert course. Sherry and *rosé* are good all-purpose wines, for a dry sherry goes well with all kinds of foods except dessert, when a sweet sherry should be served. Lancer's Crackling Vin Rosé, Almaden Grenache Rosé, and other *rosé* wines also may accompany any course. They should be served slightly chilled.

Vermouth and sherry also may be served as appetizer wines, and sherry is even popular for breakfast. Other light, dry white wines—sauterne, Rhine wine, or chablis—are also popular breakfast wines. This same selection goes well with oysters too.

The heavier type of white wines are favorites with dessert and fruits, especially sauterne. Madeira, muscatel, and angelica are other popular dessert wines. Such red wines as claret, port, burgundy, and Tokay go well with cheese. Claret is the universal wine of the Cajuns of South Louisiana, who say that "a bayou man without his 'red' is *entre nous comme un poisson sur la paille* (between you and me, like a fish out of water)."

In serving wines, never fill the glass to the rim, for it is impossible to sense the bouquet in a full glass. Wine may be served with all courses except the salad.

CHART FOR WINE SERVICE TEMPERATURE

Wine	Temperature	Remarks
Champagne	40°	Ice slowly for several hours. Store flat with cork dampened. These cannot be recorked.
Cherry and current wines (Danish)	70°	Or they may be chilled like other red wines.
Fortified wines—sherry, port, etc.	70°	Store upright. They may be opened and recorked.
Louisiana "dago red"	45°	
Sparkling red wines	40°	Ice slowly for several hours. Store flat with cork dampened. These cannot be recorked.
Other red wines	70°	
White wines (except (fortified dessert wines)	55°	Vermouth should be kept tightly corked because of its fragility.

All wine should be stored in a cool, dark place at a temperature between 50° and 70°.

A FEW LOCAL PREFERENCES IN
AFTER-DINNER LIQUEURS *

Liqueur	*Source*	*Use*
Anisette	Anise seed	After white fowl or crustaceans.
Benedictine	Herbs and sugar	After red meats.
Brandy	Wine	A general after-dinner drink.
Certosa	Fruit or berries	After fowl.
Champagne fine	A superior brandy	After dinner.
Chartreuse (white, green, and yellow)	Herbs and spices	After white fowl or crustaceans.
Cherry Heering	Cherries	After red meats or dark fowl.
Cointreau	Oranges	After fish or fowl.
Cordial Médoc	Bittersweet liqueur	After fowl.
Crème de Cassis	Black currants	After game.
Crème de Cacao	Cacao beans	After red meats, dark fowl, or game.
Crème de Menthe (white or green)	Orange peel and fruit	After white fowl or crustaceans.
Crème Yvette	Violet extract	After fowl.
Curaçao	Orange peel and fruit	After white fowl or crustaceans.
Damiana	A French liqueur	After dinner.
Danziger Goldwasser	A mild liqueur with flecks of gold	After festive dinner.
Drambuie	Scotch whisky	After red meat or dark fowl.
Fiori Alipine	A liqueur bottle with a rock candy tree	After fowl.
Grand Mariner	Oranges	After white fowl or crustaceans.

* All liqueurs should be stored in a standing position.

A FEW LOCAL PREFERENCES IN
AFTER-DINNER LIQUEURS—*Continued*

Liqueur	*Source*	*Use*
Kirschwasser	Cherries	After red meat or game.
Kümmel	Caraway and anise seeds	After red meat or game.
Parfait Amour	A French liqueur	After fish or fowl.
Strega	Oranges	After white fowl or crustaceans.
Sauterne Wine	A full-bodied grape wine	A Louisiana favorite after shellfish and white fowl.
Vanderfly's Dutch Currant Wine	Currants	After dark game or fowl.

HOTEL ROOSEVELT CAFÉ BRÛLOT

Into a bowl place and mix together the finely minced peel of two oranges and one lemon, three sticks of cinnamon that have been well broken up, twelve coriander seeds, one bay leaf, and six cloves.

Have ready about two lumps of sugar per person, three-fourths ounce of brandy per person, and a pot of strong coffee. Place the citrus peel, spices, and herbs in the *brûlot* bowl. At the proper time bring in the bowl. Add the brandy and sugar. Set bowl aflame. Turn off the lights and let the contents of the bowl burn while you ladle the flaming liquid over the sugar, spices, and herbs. Do not let it burn too long as it will result in consuming all the alcohol in the liquor. Pour hot, strong coffee into the bowl, stirring all the while. Turn the lights on and ladle into after-dinner cups.

CAMPFIRE BRÛLOT

Place some brandy in an iron pot and add whole cloves, cinnamon sticks, nutmeg, wild nut meats, and lemon or orange peel. Light and gradually add strong coffee.

FRENCH COFFEE

Use a biggin or French drip coffee pot. Wash the pot with scalding water. Place plenty of coffee, either pure or with chicory, in top of pot. Drip boiling water over the coffee a few spoons at a time. Let stand for a half hour. Serve hot, but never boil it. The Cajuns say, "Ma good fran—des ess what yo' call delish, en facts, de mo' yo' drank de mo' bet' et ess!"

CAFÉ AU LAIT

Prepare French drip coffee. Heat milk to boiling. Mix half hot coffee and half hot milk. Add sugar if desired.

DEV'S CAFÉ BRÛLOT

Pour boiling water into the *brûlot* bowl to heat bowl. Pour water out and place twelve cloves, six lumps of sugar, six slices of lemon peel, and three sticks of cinnamon (broken up) in the *brûlot* bowl. Warm eight ponies of brandy or whisky over a low fire. Mix with the spices in the bowl and light. Add eight cups of hot, black coffee. Stir for one minute. Ladle into demitasse cups. The *brûlot* may be served in orange cups. Always darken the room when mixing. (Serves twelve.)

THE CAFÉ ROYAL

Pour strong black coffee into small cups. Add sugar to taste and one pony of brandy or whisky.

PETIT BRULOT

Serve cup of hot, strong coffee. Place a teaspoon of sugar across top of cup. Drip brandy into spoon and light. Gradually lower spoon into cup while flaming and add more brandy if desired.

SPICED COFFEE

Make a *bouquet garni* of cinnamon, cloves, and nutmeg. Let the bag steep in hot coffee for an hour or so. Remove the bag and add sugar. Serve hot or cold. Brandy, rum, or bourbon whisky may be added when ready to serve.

RUM TEA

Make a tea and let it steep in a pot with whole cinnamon sticks, one nutmeg, and a few cloves. Add one jigger of rum when ready to serve. Serve hot or cold garnished with mint.

COFFEE KIRSCH

Mix one jigger of kirsch, one cup of coffee, one beaten egg white, and dash of sugar. Shake and serve cold. (Serves one.)

PAMPAS BOLO

Use very dry sherry or dry white wine. Mix two jiggers of wine with three teaspoons of lime juice and two teaspoons of sugar. Stir with ice and serve with a twist of lime peel. (Serves two.)

MINT TEA À LA RUSSE

Place mint, tea bags, and sugar in pot. Pour in boiling water and let steep. One jigger of warm rum may be added for each person.

GINGER TEA

Make tea and add candied ginger and slice of lemon. Serve hot or cold. One jigger of rum per person may be added.

COCOA COFFEE

Make French drip coffee. Put several spoons of sweetened chocolate over coffee grounds before dripping.

THE SAZERAC

The sazerac actually took its name from the brandy product Sazerac-de-Forge and made its debut across the bar of the Sazerac Coffee House located on Exchange Alley in New Orleans. The absinthe touch was not added to this brandy drink until 1870 when a barkeeper conceived the idea of adding a bit of this "green goblin" to the famous sazerac. As time passed brandy was replaced by whisky to suit the plebeian taste of the Americans who had infiltrated the Creole city. The location of the imbibing place of sazeracs was later changed to the Sazerac Bar on Gravier Street, and in this hallowed spot ladies were not granted entrance except on the day of Mardi Gras. This old bar has closed its swinging doors, but the Roosevelt Hotel has purchased all rights to the sazerac and the bar name, so now there is an authentic Sazerac Bar in the Roosevelt, one in which ladies are most welcome on any day.

To make a sazerac, muddle together a teaspoon of sugar and a few dashes of Peychaud bitters with a teaspoon of water. Add a dash of Angostura bitters and two jiggers of rye whisky. Rinse the inside of a short, heavy glass with absinthe. Place two ice cubes in this glass and pour the mixed sazerac ingredients over the ice. A small drop of lemon peel squeezing may be added if desired. Some mixers rub the edge of the glass with lemon. (Serves one.)

THE ROFFIGNAC

The roffignac ranks first among the older tall drinks of "La Nouvelle Orléans." In the youthful days of the city the French Market was known as Les Halies, and on Sundays the Creole families gathered there before Mass. The women left their market baskets in the stalls to be filled while they attended Saint Louis Cathedral, and (*on dit*) most of the men sipped roffignac at the round bar inside the market until their wives collected them and the market baskets for the trip home.

The roffignac was named for a former mayor of New Orleans, Count Louis Philippe Joseph de Roffignac. The count added many new improvements to the city during his administration but these virtues have long been forgotten.

To mix a roffignac, use a tall glass in which ice has been placed. Pour in one or more jiggers of whisky. Add a half jigger of Hembarig syrup and fill the glass with Seltzer water. In the country, homemade raspberry syrup was often used in place of the Hembarig. The old sweetin'—Hembarig—is no longer available but old-time tipplers say that a raspberry syrup now on the market resembles the old syrup. (Serves one.)

THE JULEP

The julep should be served in tall silver goblets, which should be chilled in the refrigerator on a small tray so that they may be removed without being touched by hand. Mint leaves should be muddled in a bowl with two teaspoons of sugar for each goblet. Place shaved ice in the goblets, then two layers of muddled mint. Fill the goblet with rum, and stir with a long spoon until frosted and mixed. Sprinkle the top with powdered sugar, and garnish with a fresh sprig of mint.

COUP DE PERIL

Pour two ounces of rye whisky over two ice cubes. Add a piece of rock candy and muddle. (Serves one.)

VIEUX CARRÉ MANHATTAN

Mix two ounces of bourbon whisky with one ounce of Italian vermouth and a dash of simple syrup. Blend well and store in the refrigerator for a day or two. Add a cherry and serve in a cocktail glass. (Serves one.)

SCOTCH FLING

Mix two ounces of Scotch whisky with one teaspoon of lime juice. Pour over ice cubes and fill the glass with ginger ale. (Serves one.)

WHISKY TODDY

Use a short, thick glass. Muddle two lumps of sugar in glass with one teaspoon of Seltzer water (if making a cold toddy) or two teaspoons of boiling water (if making a hot toddy). Add one jigger of whisky and either ice or boiling water and a twist of lemon peel. Brandy, rum, or gin may be substituted for the whisky. (Serves one.)

BOURBON SOUR

Mix two jiggers of bourbon, two jiggers of lemon juice, one jigger of lime juice, and ice. Shake and strain. Frost glass by pressing rim into powdered sugar before filling. (Serves two.)

CREOLE DOWNFALL

Mix one pint of "corn likker" with one pint of ginger ale. Bruise one bunch of mint and remove stems. Place this mixture in a crock in refrigerator for several days or weeks. Serve in a cocktail glass. For a julep use only the "likker" and mint. Use one jigger per person.

THE OLD FASHIONED

Pour two teaspoons of Seltzer in each cocktail glass. Muddle with two lumps of sugar. Add two cubes of ice and fill the glass with bourbon, rye, or Scotch whisky. Add a twist of lemon and muddle with a cinnamon stick. To fancy this up, a dram of Drambuie may replace the sugar.

THE WILD COW

Place one jigger of bourbon or whisky, one teaspoon of sugar, and one and a half cups of milk in a shaker. Add ice and shake. Top with nutmeg. (Serves one.)

ROCK CANDY AND RYE

Pour one jigger of rye whisky over a little ice. Add two pieces of rock candy and stir. This may be served hot, and was once administered as a cure for colds and chills. (Serves one.)

RYE SOUR

Mix one jigger of rye whisky with the juice of one lime and of one-half orange. Chill and serve in a short glass. (Serves one.)

RUM SWIRL

Mix one ounce of rum, two ounces of Cuban banana liqueur, and one teaspoon of lime juice. Pour into a shaker with ice, strain, and serve in a cocktail glass. (Serves one.)

RUM HONEY

Mix one ounce of Demerara rum, one teaspoon of honey, and one teaspoon of lemon juice. Blend with ice in an electric blender and serve in a cocktail glass. (Serves one.)

JUNIOR'S SPECIAL

Mix one part dark rum with one part claret wine. Pour over ice cubes, strain, and serve in a cocktail glass. (Serves one.)

ARTHUR'S DEVIL'S TAIL

Mix one jigger of vodka, one jigger of lemon juice, one-half jigger of apricot brandy, and one jigger of Triple Sec with shaved ice in an electric blender. (Serves one.)

VODKA MARTINI

Mix two parts chilled vodka with one part Dry Sack sherry. Add a dash of orange bitters and pour over ice cubes. Strain and serve in a cocktail glass with a toasted almond. (Serves one.)

BLOODY MARY

Mix one ounce of chilled vodka with two teaspoons of lime juice, a dash of Tabasco sauce, and a pinch of salt. Pour over ice cubes in a tall glass and fill the glass with tomato juice. (Serves one.)

BONNE NUIT

Mix one ounce of chilled vodka with two teaspoons of lime juice and a dash of grenadine. Pour over ice in a shaker. Serve in a cocktail glass. (Serves one.)

DEV'S MARTINI

Mix two parts gin with one part Dry Sack sherry. Pour over ice cubes, strain, and serve in a martini glass with a Spanish olive. (Serves one.)

TROPIC SLING

Mix one ounce of gin with one teaspoon of maraschino liqueur, the juice of one lime, and one teaspoon of sugar. Pour over ice cubes in a tall glass. Fill glass with Seltzer water and garnish with mint. (Serves one.)

COCONUT SLING

Mix one ounce of gin with two dashes of Angostura bitters and two ounces of coconut milk. Pour over ice cubes in a tall glass. Fill glass with Seltzer water. (Serves one.)

ALEXANDER

Mix one ounce of gin, one ounce of crème de cacao, one-half ounce of cream, and one stiffly beaten egg white. Shake with ice and pour into a cocktail glass. (Serves one.)

GOLDEN GLOW

Mix one ounce of Seagram's Golden gin with one-half ounce of French vermouth. Pour over three cubes of ice, strain, and serve in a martini glass. Garnish with a twist of lemon. (Serves one.)

JUDGE CHARLES A. O'NIELL'S ORANGE BLOSSOM

Mix one jigger of gin and one jigger of orange juice. Add a dash of grenadine. Shake with cracked ice and serve frappé. (Serves one.)

THE RAMOS GIN FIZZ

The Ramos gin fizz is a liquid brain child of Henry C. Ramos. It was brought into the light of night in 1888 at the Imperial Cabaret. The Ramos family have guarded the formula for this unusual drink for many years, and duels have been fought over arguments involving its secrets. Even today no one is sure of the science of its blending. Some native fizzers swear that a drop or so of vanilla is necessary, and some say there is a great difference in the drink because of the varying amounts of orange-flower water used. One of its secrets is that it must be shaken, shaken, shaken until it reaches the thick consistency of heavy cream.

The accepted method is to place a few broken cubes of ice in a tall shaker; pour one jigger of gin over the ice; and add one jigger of cream, the beaten white of one egg, one teaspoon of lime juice, one teaspoon of powdered sugar, and several dashes of orange-flower water. Shake until you and the mixture are frothy. A dash of Seltzer water may be added when ready to serve the drink, or may be placed in the shaker. A light colored rum also may be used in place of the gin. (Serves one.)

WHITE-WINGED DOVE

Mix one ounce of gin, one-half ounce of white crème de menthe, and one-half ounce of lemon juice in an electric blender with shaved ice. Serve in a cocktail glass. This drink was created by Peter Trojan especially for LOUISIANA COOKERY. (Serves one.)

GIN AND TONIC

Mix one ounce of gin with one-half teaspoon of lime juice and pour over ice cubes in a tall glass. Fill glass with quinine water that has been separately chilled. (Serves one.)

PAHIT

Rinse a short glass with Peychaud bitters. Pour gin in chilled glass and drink without ice. (Serves one.)

TEQUILA

This Mexican "firewater" is popular in New Orleans. Drink it neat, with a taste of half a lemon and salt before drinking, or mix it with orange juice and a dash of grenadine. It also may be used in place of gin in other drinks.

LOUISIANA FRENCH '75

Mix two ounces of brandy or gin, one teaspoon of lemon juice, and one teaspoon of sugar. Pour over ice cubes in a very tall glass and fill glass with champagne. (Serves one.)

MOONGLOW

Mix one ounce of brandy with one ounce of white crème de menthe. Chill in the refrigerator for several hours and serve in a short glass. (Serves one.)

SKIDMORE TIPPLE

Mix one part Cognac and one part Kümmel. Chill in the refrigerator for several hours and serve in a liqueur glass. (Serves one.)

PASCAL'S BRANDY FLOAT

Pour one jigger of white crème de menthe over a small amount of ice in a liqueur glass. Float one tablespoon of brandy on top. (Serves one.)

OUZO

Pour one ounce of Ouzo over ice and add water or Seltzer water. This brandy also may be drunk straight. (Serves one.)

AQUAVIT

This Scandinavian drink may be served straight or mixed with a few drops of Angostura bitters.

BRANNVIN

Drink this Swedish noggin neat or with Seltzer water in a highball.

BRANDY COCKTAIL

Muddle one teaspoon of sugar with a few drops of Peychaud bitters. Add two ounces of ice and pour one jigger of brandy over the ice. (Serves one.)

SHERRY FLIP

Mix one teaspoon of powdered sugar with one jigger of dry sherry. Pour in beaten white of egg. Shake and garnish with nutmeg. (Serves one.)

WINE COOLERS

Use two gills of any good red or white wine. Pour over ice and fill glass with Seltzer water. Garnish with slice of lime and sprig of mint. Danish Kijafa wine also makes a good cooler.

VIN FRAPPE

Pour one of the dessert wines over shaved ice. Serve with short straw.

THE MASPEROS EXCHANGE AND ARTHUR LAMAZOU

The Masperos Exchange is located at 440 Chartres Street in New Orleans. It has also been known as the Coffee House Exchange, and was originally a slave market and meeting place of the politicians, merchants, and Creole gentlemen of leisure. In Ray Thompson's book, *New Orleans from A to Z*, Thompson says, "always you would find at Masperos either the principals or the details of everything that went on in New Orleans." This was in 1788, and today you will still find excitement and luscious liquids brewing at Masperos. The liquids are the creations of the inimitable bar *maître* and master mixologist Arthur Lamazou. He is one of the few remaining artisans of drink left in "the city that care forgot" but tourists didn't. When you stop by Arthur's to "pass the time of day" you will want to watch his dexterity with the vivid *poussecafé*. . . .

ARTHUR'S POUSSE-CAFÉ

The name of this colorful creation comes from the French word *pouce*, meaning inch. The heaviest syrup (usually a *framboisé*) or liqueur is placed in the bottom of the tall thin liqueur glass. Any number of vivid spirits may be used, but be sure to pour them very slowly and with a steady hand, and float brandy on the top.

Pour in Benedictine first. Next pour in grenadine syrup. The grenadine will go through the Benedictine and settle on the bottom. Next, pour in green crème de menthe. The crème de menthe will go through the Benedictine. Next, pour in *crème de banana*. The *crème de banana* will settle next to the green crème de menthe. Next, pour in *crème de cacao*. The *crème de cacao* will settle under the green crème de menthe. Next, pour in white crème de menthe. The white crème de menthe will settle next to the green crème de menthe. Next, pour in *parfait amour*. The *parfait amour* will settle on top of the *crème de cacao*. Next, pour in Crème Yvette. The Crème Yvette will settle on top of the green crème de menthe. Next, pour in cognac. The cognac will be on top. Now, pour in the chartreuse. The chartreuse will settle below the cognac. The brandy may be burned for a second or so.

THE ABSINTHE DRIP

Although absinthe originated in Switzerland, it soon found a permanent place on the *étagères* of the bars in New Orleans. The old type absinthe was made of wormwood, small absinthe, green anise seed, fennel, star anise, coriander seeds, hyssop, and alcoholic spirits of 190 proof. This liqueur was distilled and colored by mixing with Melissa leaves, mint leaves, citron peel, and liquorice root. The present-day liquid is a synthetic absinthe and is not a narcotic. It should be served in absinthe drip glasses, the bottoms of which resemble large brandy snifters and the top, finger bowls with tiny holes. The ice is placed in the top compartment. Several teaspoons of simple syrup or orgeat water are then dripped over the ice. Then one or two jiggers of absinthe are dripped over the syrup and ice.

THE ABSINTHE SUISSESSE

The suissesse is always made of absinthe or Ojen, but a number of other spirits are used with it in various bars. Place one jigger of absinthe in a shaker with a little ice and the beaten white of one egg. Then add anisette, white crème de menthe or maraschino, and a dash or so of orange-flower water. Shake until frothy and serve in a short glass. A bit of Seltzer water is often used in the shaker. (Serves one.)

THE OJEN

Ojen (pronounced Oh-hen) is another old favorite in New Orleans and South Louisiana. Its name originated in the Spanish word for wormwood, and it is also known as Spanish absinthe. A native

Ojen was formerly made in Louisiana by putting oil of anise or caraway into grain alcohol. This mixture stood in a crock for several days, then as much water as alcohol was added. It was then bottled.

To serve Ojen, chill colored wineglasses. Place two cubes of ice in each glass. Pour the glass almost full of Ojen, and add a few drops of Peychaud bitters. Blue glasses are recommended, making the drink a deep purple. (Serves one.)

ROOSEVELT PINK SQUIRREL

Mix one ounce of white crème de menthe, one ounce of crème de noyau, and one ounce of sweet cream with ice in an electric blender. Serve in a cocktail glass. (Serves one.)

ARTHUR'S SCARLETT O'HARA

Mix one-half brandied peach, the juice of one lime, six maraschino cherries, and one jigger of Southern Comfort with shaved ice in an electric blender. Serve in a cocktail glass. (Serves one.)

ARTHUR'S PEACH WEST INDIES

Mix one-half fresh, peeled peach, a dash of lime juice, one jigger of rum, and a dash of maraschino liqueur, with shaved ice in an electric blender. Serve in a cocktail glass. (Serves one.)

ARTHUR'S BANANA WEST INDIES

Mix one jigger of Argentine banana liqueur with the juice of one lime, a dash of maraschino liqueur, and shaved ice in an electric blender. Serve in a cocktail glass. (Serves one.)

OWEN BRENNAN'S PIRATE'S DREAM

Use a huge glass, capable of holding twenty-six to twenty-eight ounces. Blend the juice of one orange, one-half ounce of grenadine, one ounce of Bacardi rum, one ounce of Myer's rum, the juice of one lemon, two dashes of Angostura bitters, one ounce of Christopher Columbus rum, and one ounce of Ronrico 151-proof rum. Crush some fresh green mint in these ingredients and fill the glass with crushed ice, adding eight to ten cherries at the same time. Decorate the rim with two slices of orange and stick eight to ten straws in the glass. Be careful that the bottom of the glass does not fall out. (Serves one to ten.)

OWEN BRENNAN'S JUNIOR PIRATE'S DREAM

Reduce the ingredients of the Pirate's Dream by one half and serve in a tall glass. (Serves one.)

JUDGE SAM A. LE BLANC'S GRASSHOPPER

A grasshopper is a delicious after-dinner drink which is very easy to prepare. It can add a touch of elegance to an outdoor camping trip too, since none of the ingredients are perishable.

Put equal portions of a good quality of crème de menthe and crème de cacao in an electric blender with canned cream. Blend thoroughly and serve in wine or cocktail glasses with short straws. (Serves one.)

PUNCH PRINCE REGENCE AU VICTOR

This punch of unlimited power was served by Monsieur Victor Béro, at the epicurean institution he established on Bourbon Street in 1830. Alas, the old restaurant is no more, but another famous café—Galatoire's—stands at 209 Bourbon perpetuating the tradition and table fare of the original owner. This punch and the "Punch Romaine" (see p. 321) were favorites in the long ago in Louisiana. Punch is presumed to be the oldest of all blended drinks, dating back over three hundred years. The name comes from the Hindustani word *panch*, meaning five—the accepted number of the ingredients that were used.

Mix eight gallons of curaçao, one quart of brandy, two quarts of white wine, eight gallons of maraschino, one-half gallon of kirschwasser, one-half quart of rum. Add sliced pineapples, sliced oranges, and the peeling of two lemons. Place a large piece of ice in the punch bowl, pour all the ingredients in and add as much

Seltzer water as there is punch-mix. Preserved cherries may be added. (Serves fifty.)

ARRACK PUNCH

Arrack or rack—a drink of the Far East—was often used in old New Orleans as a base for punch. The liquor should be mixed with sugar, and lime or orange juice, then poured over a large piece of ice in a bowl.

A substitute for arrack was recommended in the *Virginia Housewife:* "Dissolve two scruples flowers of Benzoin in one quart of good rum."

MARASCHINO PUNCH

Mix one bottle of Angelica wine with one-half bottle of brandy and one jigger of maraschino. Chill and serve in a punch bowl with a large piece of ice and red and green cherries. (Serves eight.)

MOSELLE PUNCH

Pour one fifth bottle of iced Moselle wine over one-half gallon of frozen citrus sherbet. Serve in clear punch cups. (Serves twelve.)

METTRE A LA VOILE (TO SET SAIL)

Mix one quart of champagne with one quart of applejack. Add several dashes of grenadine. Chill and serve in champagne glasses. (Serves twelve or more.)

RUM AND BRANDY PUNCH

Cut up the rinds of twelve oranges and twelve lemons. Cover with several cups of brandy. Squeeze the juice from three dozen oranges and one dozen lemons and mix with one quart of rum and one pint of brandy. Steep one cup of mixed spices in two quarts of water for half an hour. Add two pounds or less of sugar to the warm water. Mix all the ingredients. Strain and bottle. Champagne, Seltzer water, or cream may be added to this when ready to serve.

A TANGERINE MORNING PUNCH

Slice twelve tangerines and cover with one quart of milk and one quart of cream. Simmer five minutes and strain. Add two pounds of sugar to the warm mixture. Cool and add one quart of brandy. Serve in punch cups garnished with a spoon of whipped cream sprinkled with grated lemon peel.

BRANDY BOWL

Remove the juice of several coconuts by punching the eyes in and draining the juice. Saw the coconuts in half. Chip the meat out and grind. Strain the milk from the ground meat and add to the coconut juice. Place two jiggers of brandy in a blender. Add one jigger of banana liqueur and three jiggers of coconut milk. Add a little ice and blend in the electric blender. To make a container for this drink, sandpaper the outer rim of the coconut halves. Pour the drink into the coconut shells and serve. The coconut cups may be used many times. (Serves two.)

THE AMBROSIA

Pour one pony of brandy over two cubes of ice. Add two jiggers of applejack and a dash of Hembarig or its equivalent. Strain into iced wineglasses and fill each glass with champagne. (Serves six.)

THE SOUTHERN PLANTERS' RUM PUNCH

Pour two drams of rum over shaved ice. Add one teaspoon of brown sugar melted in a little water. Add the juice of one lemon. Swirl and add more shaved ice. Float two gills of sweet red wine over the top. Garnish with a sprig of mint and fresh fruit. Heady dark Jamaican rum is best in this drink. (Serves one.)

THE STIRRUP CUP

Pour one jigger of brandy over a small amount of ice. Add one jigger of cherry bounce (see p. 323), one teaspoon of orgeat syrup, and the juice of half a lemon. Swirl. This country drink was so named because it was the "drink for the road" when visitors departed on horseback or by carriage. (Serves two.)

LEMON-ORANGE PUNCH

Cut up the rind of four lemons and four oranges. Add the juice of twelve oranges and twelve lemons. Pour a pot of hot tea over the fruits and let the mixture steep until it cools. Add one bottle of brandy and either more tea or a bottle of champagne. (A quick punch may be made from the old recipe by using two cans each of the frozen citrus juices.) Serve in a bowl with a large chunk of ice. (Serves twenty-five.)

BOURBON PUNCH

Blend the juice of two lemons and two oranges with one-half cup of sugar. Add one-half cup of grenadine syrup and one quart of whisky. Place in the refrigerator until ready to serve, then add one large bottle of Seltzer water. Serve in a bowl with a large piece of ice. (Serves thirty or more.)

SHORT SHERRY PUNCH

Mix six glasses of sherry with the juice of two limes and one orange. Chill in the refrigerator for several hours and serve frappé. (Serves six.)

ENGLISH BOLO

Pour three jiggers of sherry over two lumps of ice. Add one teaspoon of lemon juice and one teaspoon of sugar. Muddle with a cinnamon stick. (Serves two.)

PUNCH ROMAINE–LE COUP DE MILIEU

In addition to the wines, which—in accordance with French tradition—were served regularly with Creole meals, Louisiana diners of the ante-bellum era usually served a *coup de milieu* in the pause before the entrance of the entrée. The service of this "middle-course cup" grew out of a French custom of serving brandy or other spirituous drinks during the *trou normand*, or brief intermission in the middle of a large dinner. The *punch romaine* was a favorite cup for this period of rest at the table, but other punches, granits, and straight brandy also were served to fortify the diners for the courses to follow. After the *coup de milieu*, the entrée side dishes—the *relevés* and entremets—were brought to the table.

To make the *punch romaine*, mix one ounce of rye whisky, one ounce of dark rum, and the juice of one lemon. Pour over ice and add two teaspoons of simple syrup. Shake, strain, and serve in a punch cup. (Serves one.)

The majority of the following ratafias and cordials are of colonial origin:

SIROP AUX ETAGES

Any fresh berries or fruits in season may be used for this thick cordial. Place the ingredients in layers in a large-mouthed bottle as they come into season. Cover each layer with sugar and whisky. Serve as a liqueur.

DEWBERRY CORDIAL

Mash one quart of berries and mix with one gallon of water, fifteen pounds of sugar, and one yeast cake. Let this ferment in a crock for a month. Strain and bottle.

BLUEBERRY CORDIAL

Boil one quart of berries for half an hour in enough water to cover. Add one pound of sugar and simmer until syrup is thick. Strain the mixture through a cheesecloth sack adding the same amount of whisky as of syrup. Bottle and seal.

ELDERBERRY CORDIAL

Wash one quart of berries and place in a crock. Cover with one pound of sugar and one pint of whisky. Heat the sugar and whisky three times at intervals throughout one week. Strain and bottle. Let stand for several months before using. Peaches may be used in the same manner.

CORDIAL MERISE (CHERRY BOUNCE)

Wash and stem one quart of wild cherries. Place in a crock with one pint of grain alcohol. Stir the open crock frequently for four days. Then cover with cheesecloth and let stand for several months. When ready to serve add a dash of orgeat water to each glass. Whisky may be used in place of the alcohol.

WILD PLUM CORDIAL

Wash one gallon of wild plums and place in a crock with one quart of whisky. Let this stand for several days and then add enough sugar to suit taste. Strain and bottle.

PEAR LIQUEUR

Make a thick syrup of water and sugar. Place peeled pears in the cooled syrup and let stand for two days. Add as much whisky as there is liquid. Bottle.

GRAPE CORDIAL

Peel seedless grapes and place in a jar with sugar and whisky. Seal in bottles.

CAJUN CHERRY BOUNCE

Wash and stem one gallon of wild cherries. Place these in a crock and cover with one quart of boiling water. When the water cools add one quart of brandy or whisky. Let this stand for two weeks, then add one more quart of alcoholic liquid and let stand another week. Add sugar to taste. Strain and bottle. More water may be used to make this a lighter cordial.

MINT CORDIAL

Wash and separate three bunches of fresh mint, but do not bruise. Place in a crock and pour one bottle of brandy over the mint leaves and stalks. Let stand for several days, then duplicate the brandy and mint. Add one pint or more of water, and sugar to taste. Strain and bottle.

ACADIAN MEAD

Dilute three quarts of honey with one pint of hot water. Let this ferment in a crock, then bottle.

BAYOU BEER

Tradition relates that the first beer on the bayou was made of boiled hops, yeast, and the molasses from the early sugar kettles. This mixture was stirred until it fermented, then bottled in old stone jugs.

RUM COCONUT

Select a large, ripe coconut. Punch the eyes in and drain out the milk. Pack the inside with brown sugar. Seal the eyes with paraffin. Place the coconut in a cool, dark place for six months. Remove the paraffin and pour out the rum. Serve as a liqueur with small pieces of the coconut meat.

TOMATO WINE

Peel one gallon of ripe tomatoes after holding each over gas flame on a fork. Mash the tomatoes. Place in a crock with two pounds of sugar. Cover the crock and let contents ferment. Skim everyday. When it has ceased fermenting strain and place in large jugs with loose corks. Let stand without moving for two months. Then bottle in small bottles and seal tight.

BIERE DOUCE

Wash two pineapples, and chop up the pineapple and the rind. Mix with two pounds of sugar and one-half pound of rice. Let stand in crock several months. Strain and bottle. Serve as a liqueur.

THE WILD CREOLE PONY

Place one jigger of rum in a mug with one teaspoon of any fruit syrup. Add a drop of lemon and ice. (Serves one.)

VIN DE CANNE À SUCRE

Mix three parts of molasses with one part of water. Add one yeast cake and let ferment about two weeks. Strain and bottle. Serve as a liqueur.

THE HEART WARMER

Beat the yolk of one egg. Slowly add two jiggers of cognac. Shake with a small amount of shaved ice and a dash of paprika. (Serves two.)

VIN CHAUD

Heat one bottle of good red wine with bouquet of spices in bag (cloves, broken cinnamon sticks, allspice, nutmeg, and a piece of ginger root). Heat to boiling point and remove spice bag. Serve in mugs with hot toasted pecans or as a wassail bowl. (Serves four.)

PRENDRE AU RACCOURCI
(To take a short cut)

Chase two jiggers of bourbon with a glass of ale.

RUM PUNCH

Mix one quart of rich milk, one fifth of rum, and one teaspoon of honey. Shake and serve chilled. (Serves eight or ten.)

BUTTERED RUM

After a long, cold morning in a duck blind, muddle one teaspoon of brown sugar, two jiggers of rum, a few cloves, and one nutmeg. Muddle with a cinnamon stick. Add one teaspoon of butter and fill mug with boiling water. (Serves one.)

CAJUN NOGG

Separate six eggs. Beat the yolks and mix with one-half cup of brown sugar. Slowly add two fifths of whisky and one cup of dark rum. Chill this several hours. Beat the egg whites very stiff and add to the mixture. Pour in glasses and add a big spoon of vanilla ice cream. Top with grated nutmeg. (Makes about four quarts.)

COFFEE RHUM

Place whole nutmegs, cloves, and cinnamon sticks in glögg or *brûlot* bowl. Add a little lemon peel and one teaspoon of sugar for each person. Stir and add one jigger of rum for every cup of coffee. Light and gradually pour in boiling hot coffee. Stir and ladle into cups.

SUSIE'S RUM SHAKE

Mix two jiggers of dark rum, one jigger of absinthe, and one-half cup of fresh pineapple juice. Shake with a small amount of ice.

RUM CUIT

Mix one jigger of rum, juice of one lime, and one-fourth teaspoon of blackstrap molasses. Pour over crushed ice. Serve in a container made by cutting bamboo an inch or two above the joint. The hollow bamboo will make a permanent addition to your bar.

ACADIAN GLÖGG

Pour two quarts of red wine into a pan with two cinnamon sticks, one cup of toasted nut meats, and one cup of raisins, and warm. Pour one-half bottle of brandy and one cup of sugar into another pan. Burn the brandy and add the strained hot wine. Serve in copper bowl with an alcohol lamp or candle to keep hot. Pour into mugs. (Serves twelve.)

BRANDY TIPPLE

Beat two eggs in an electric mixer. Add three teaspoons of sugar and one cup of cognac. Add two cups of strong coffee and chill. Serve in a short glass. (Serves four.)

WILD PERSIMMON BEER

Wash persimmons and simmer with a small amount of sugar in one quart of water for one-half hour. Add one cup of yeast and let ferment for several weeks. Strain and bottle.

KATHLEEN'S BLACKBERRY WINE

When berries are in fruit, mix one gallon of fresh, crushed berries with one gallon of hot water. Let stand in a crock for two days. Strain and for each gallon of juice add three pounds of sugar. Let stand until October. Siphon and strain. Bottle and seal with a cork and sealing wax.

SIROP COGNAC

Boil any fresh fruits or berries. Strain juice off and add cognac.

VIN CRIOLLO

Use one gallon of wild grapes. Wash and place in a crock. Cover with honey and let stand for about a week, then squeeze through cheesecloth. Place one pound of sugar in a crock and pour juice over it. Let juice ferment in crock and when fermentation stops, bottle, cork, and store in a dark, cold place.

ORANGE WINE

Squeeze the juice from five gallons of oranges. Add one cup of minced rind and seven pounds of sugar. Bring mixture to a boil, then let it cool and clear. Strain through cheesecloth and add five gills of fresh juice. Let ferment in a crock, skimming regularly until fermentation stops. Bottle and store.

PETE'S STRAWBERRY WINE

Wash berries and place in a jar with sugar and washed, peeled Irish potatoes cut in two-inch slices. Place top on jar and let stand several months or longer. Do not shake or move. Strain and bottle.

A CORDIAL OF STRAWBERRIES

Simmer for about five minutes one gallon of strawberries with a small amount of water and a few spices. Remove the spices and strain through cheesecloth. Add two cups of sugar and one gallon of fresh berries. Let this stand for several hours. Then mash through cheesecloth. Add one gallon of brandy. Bottle.

APPLE-STRAWBERRY CORDIAL

Simmer one dozen apples in one pint of water for five minutes. Add a little allspice, nutmeg, and mace, and cook ten minutes. Add one gallon of strawberries and one pound of brown sugar. Add about five cups of water and let simmer for five to ten minutes. Cool and strain. Add the same amount of whisky as fruit liquid. Bottle.

STRAWBERRY PUNCH

Wash one gallon of berries and mix with one pound of sugar. Let stand in the refrigerator for two days. Strain and add one bottle of rum. When ready to serve add six cups of tea. Serve in a bowl with a large block of ice. Garnish with fresh strawberries. (Serves twenty.)

SATSUMA CORDIAL

Cup up one dozen Satsuma oranges and place them in two quarts of rich milk. Add a teaspoon of grated lemon rind and boil for five minutes. Cool and add one-half pound of sugar (or less) and one pint of brandy. Strain and bottle.

ORANGE SYLLABUB

Cut a lemon in half and rub both parts with sugar. Cover the lemon with a quart of cream. Add several cups of sugar and one bottle of orange wine. Beat until frothy and serve garnished with nutmeg. Serve in punch cups. (Serves twelve.)

JUJUBE

Make a thick syrup of three parts brown sugar and one part water. Place one quart of the jujube fruit in the cooked syrup for three days. Add the same amount of whisky as syrup. Strain and bottle.

SOUR CITRUS WINE

Remove the rind from six dozen oranges and six dozen lemons. Place the cut-up rind in a crock and pour over this five gallons of boiling water. Place in a *bain-marie* and let it stay warm for several hours. Then add the juice of the two fruits and five pounds of sugar. Add a half pint of yeast. Leave this in the crock to ferment. When the liquid has stopped fermenting, leave it in the crock until it clears. Strain and bottle.

ORANGE CORDIAL

Cut up three dozen navel oranges. Simmer these for twenty minutes in enough water to cover. Add some spices and let steep for half an hour. Add sugar to taste and strain through cheesecloth. Add a pint or more of brandy or one quart of rum. Bottle.

ORANGE WINE SANGAREE

Make a syrup of one cup of brown sugar and two cups of water. After the syrup has simmered a few minutes add spices and let this steep for fifteen minutes. Remove the spices and add one bottle of orange wine. Serve in old cut glasses with a little ice. (Serves ten.)

GRAPEFRUIT BEER

Place six cut-up grapefruit in a crock. Pour three gallons of hot water over them. When cool, add a cup and a half of yeast. Let stand until fermentation has stopped. Bottle at once.

MANDARIN CORDIAL

Mix pieces of mandarin peel with alcohol and let stand for three weeks. Strain and bottle. Add simple syrup to serve.

SAM WATT'S POULET PUNCH

Mix together one fifth bottle of gin, one bottle of orange wine, and one-half bottle of sauterne in a punch bowl with a large block of ice. Lace with Angostura bitters. Serve in martini glasses. (Serves twenty.)

SALTY DOG

Pour one jigger of gin over ice. Fill glass with grapefruit juice. Sprinkle with salt. (Serves one.)

GIN RISQUÉ

Chill gin and pour one and one-half jiggers over ice. Add the juice of two limes or one lemon and a twist of peel. Fill glass with plain water. (Serves one.)

BETTY MOORE'S WHISKY COCKTAIL

Pour two jiggers of bourbon over ice, add a dash of kumquat juice. Add one preserved kumquat and serve. Use a short glass. (Serves one.)

MANDARIN FIZZ

Pour one jigger of gin over some cracked ice. Add the juice of two mandarins and one teaspoon of sugar. Shake and pour into a highball glass. Fill glass with Seltzer water. Garnish with slice of orange. (Serves one.)

AUNT PATTIE'S EGG NOGG

Beat whites of six eggs very stiff. Beat one pint of cream very stiff. Slowly drop one pint or more of bourbon whisky into beaten yolks of six eggs. Add one-quarter cup of sugar and whipped cream. Add egg whites last. Top with grated nutmeg. (Serves four.)

ORANGE POSSET

Grate one teaspoon of white bread. Mix with one cup of water and one teaspoon of grated lemon rind. Simmer a few minutes and add one cup of sugar. Let the mixture cool and add two teaspoons of orgeat paste and one pint of white wine. Add one-half cup of brandy and beat. (An ale posset may be made in the same way.) (Serves four.)

ENGLISH POSSET

Mix three cups of dry sherry with one cup of half-milk–half-cream. Serve with a small amount of ice and top with nutmeg. (Serves four.)

COLONIAL CAUDLE

Mix one cup of thick oatmeal water with the grated rind of one lemon. Simmer a few minutes and strain. Add one cup of sugar, three teaspoons of orange juice, and one pint of dry white wine. (Serves four.)

BRANDY GRUEL

Mix one small cup of barley water with one cup of sugar and several teaspoons of boiling water. Gradually add one cup of brandy. Cool and add the whipped whites of two eggs. (Serves two.)

MULLED APPLEJACK

Mix one quart of applejack with a few spices and six teaspoons of brown sugar. Add three cups of boiling water and serve in mugs. (Serves twelve.)

MILK AU DIABLE

Drop five drops of Tabasco sauce into glass of ice cold milk. Stir.

This drink originates in the section that is the birthplace of Louisiana's "hot stuff" and Tabasco sauce.

The following potions are not in common use today but are included because of their historical value.

TISANE RUM

Steep four cups of green tea and add one cup of sugar. Add the juice of one lemon and two cups of rum. Cool and bottle for future use.

A MILK PUNCH FOR THE ILL

Bring one pint of milk to a boil. Add one cup of sugar and two cups of sherry. Serve hot.

A POTION FOR DYSPEPSIA

Cut up the peel from one orange and mix with one pint of brandy, one teaspoon of rosemary, and one teaspoon of fennel seed.

A POTION FOR ASTHMA

Peel and cut up several roots of Indian potatoes. Place in a crock and cover with whisky.

A POTION FOR DROPSY

Melt two cups of wild honey and warm with one cup of water. Add two cups of Geneva gin. Take in small doses.

EAU SUCREE

In spite of the bounteous fare of the day, Louisiana gourmets of Creole days rarely suffered from overindulgence. They traced their good fortune in avoiding dyspepsia to the service of wines, the *coup de milieu* served between the courses of a large dinner, and the *eau sucrée* that was sipped at the end of a repast. The *eau sucrée*—a mixture of water and sugar combined at the table—was served after the *café noir* and liqueurs. And only after it had been served were cigars enjoyed, for tobacco was believed to decrease palate pleasure if used during a meal.

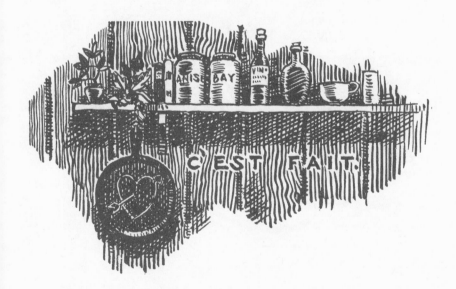

Praline woman

XIV
Appendix

Oak Alley Plantation

Menus

SERVICE DE TABLE

The styles of table service in Louisiana are as complex as the cuisine of the state. Dining hours and the manner in which food is prepared and presented are determined by regional tradition.

A similar difference in table service exists in France—each province has its special form for *le manger et le boire*. Their distinctive table fare is determined by origin of the peoples of Europe who settled in the various regions of France, especially the Germans, English, Spanish, and Italians. In France, as in Louisiana, gastronomy may be separated into two general classes—the rural and the urban.

A visitor in Louisiana is often faced with confusion when invited to dine with a native as dinner may be a large noon meal, a late evening repast, or an elaborate Creole *déjeuner*. The only guides for the guest are the locale of his visit and the nationality of his dinner host.

In South Louisiana the Creoles still cling to the lengthy formal type of table service. As in the days gone by the menu consists of numerous courses. Occasionally a meal is served *ambigu* or in a manner resembling the modern buffet service, but the usual form of Creole service was more formal.

Diner

Hors d'Oeuvres
(relishes)

Soupe
(soup)

Poisson
(fish)

Relevés
(side dishes, usually of starchy foods)

Entrée
(a casserole dish, or dish of fowl, or meat)

Coup de Milieu
(a middle course alcoholic drink, usually a granit, ponche, or frappé)

Plats de Rôt
(dishes of roasted meat, or fowl)

Entremets
(side dishes of vegetables)

Salade
(salad)

Fruits, fromage ou confitures
(fruits, cheese, or confections)

Café Noir

Cognac

Vin Blanc ou Rouge

A typical Creole breakfast, or *déjeuner*, consisted of an hors d'oeuvre, usually oysters; a main course of meat, fish, or fowl, served with side dishes of grits, hominy, or rice cakes; and a compote of fruit, and *café noir* to complete the meal. *Café au lait* was and is always served in the early morning hours.

The French *gouter*, or lunch, was light, often consisting of no more than a soup, an omelet, hot breads, and *café noir*.

A dinner in the provincial section of South Louisiana may be served at noon or at night, depending on the prevailing customs of the town, or region of the state. Boiled crawfish, crabs, or river shrimp nearly always appear on the table as appetizers. Local game, fish, or fowl serves as the principal course. Jambalayas, or court bouillons are favorites as the *pièce de resistance*. Rice and sweet potatoes are the popular side dishes, and small pastries are often served with the *café noir*. The Cajuns of this section say that Mother Nature plans their menus for they enjoy the seasonal foods found in their back yards, fields, and woodlands.

Northern Louisiana prefers noontime for the meal of the day. Soup, followed by garden relishes, begins the meal. The main course consists of meat, fish or fowl—and sometimes all three. A salad or salads and side dishes of potatoes and vegetables are companions of the main course. Cake and ice cream make up the accepted sweet finish for this hearty fare of the country and the cities.

FRIDAY DEJEUNER A LA CAJUN

A Parisian *déjeuner* is a light lunch, but the Cajun variety is more . . . *tres beaucoup* . . .

Absinthe Drip

Crawfish Bisque

Orange Bread   Congo Duck   Dirty Rice

Cucumbers Claiborne

Baba Cake A l'Anisette

Café Noir

Vin Blanc

South Louisiana Catholics, having been given special dispensation by the Church, may eat the fish-eating congo duck (the teal duck) on Fridays.

White wine is always served with teal duck.

The recipes for all the items listed here may be found by consulting the Index.

SUNDAY BREAKDOWN

Custom recommends that at this Anglo-Saxon big lunch you "put the big pot in the little pot and fry the skillet," then "spread yourself." In days gone by, feasts of this kind were eaten at the "all day meetin' and dinner on the ground," which is actually a religious gathering held out-of-doors.

Fresh Orchard Fruit

| Turnip Greens | Fried Turkey Breasts | Yam Fluff |
| Dixie Brown Beans | Hot Buttered Biscuits | Grits |

Poke Salet

Fried Pies

Black Joe
(small black coffee)

The recipes for all of these dishes may be found by consulting the Index.

ALMUERZO
(A Spanish Breakfast)

Ojen Cocktail

Fresh Guavas in Rum Sauce

Roots in Escabeche Sauce   Spanish Rice

Young Turkey à la Pontalba

A Loaf of Spanish Bread

Black Coffee—un Buchito
(Just a swallow)

The recipes for this Spanish-style menu may be found by consulting the Index, except for the bread. It should be bought at a Spanish bakery and served with sweet Spanish coffee.

PATIO BREAKFAST
Peach West Indies

Bessie's Waffles   Turkey Haricot   Entremet Sucre

Café Au Lait

Vin Sauterne

The recipes may be found by consulting the Index.

LA FORTUNE DU POT
(Potluck)

Dev's Martini

Fried Green Tomatoes   Cold Venison Roast   Baked Irish Potatoes

Anise in Oil

Fresh Berries Dipped in Powdered Sugar

Café Noir

Vin Ordinaire

All the recipes for this repast may be found by consulting the Index.

HOLIDAY MENU
Hot Oyster Cocktail

Oignons   Olives

Soupe Aux Crabes Tally-ho

Holiday Game

Calas Tous Chaud

Salade Green Trout

Café Noir   Cabinet Pudding

All recipes for the "Holiday Menu" may be found by consulting the Index

The following menu, created by Eugene Wiolat, *chef de cuisine* of the Roosevelt Hotel in New Orleans, was prepared for a dinner given by the Louisiana Outdoor Writers Association at the annual convention of the Outdoor Writers Association of America at Chattanooga, Tennessee, in 1947.

Shrimp Remoulade

Celery   Mixed Olives

Turtle Soup

———

Fillet of Gulf Trout and Soft-Shelled Crab
Sauté Amandine

———

Parisienne Parsley Potatoes
Broccoli Hollandaise

———

Chapeau Salad

———

Baked Alaska
Café Brûlot

The recipes for the items on this menu may be found in the Index and were provided through the courtesy of Seymour Weiss, managing director of the Roosevelt Hotel, with the co-operation of Mr. Wiolat and Alonzo Bourgeois of the Roosevelt staff. Although it was not included with the original menu the "Roosevelt Pink Squirrel" adds zip as a before- or after-dinner drink.

Solid and Liquid Terminology

À la crème	A solid or liquid prepared with cream.
À la glace	A solid or liquid glazed, candied or iced and frozen.
À la mode	In the fashion of.
À la russe	In the Russian fashion.
Alcaparro	A type of Spanish stew, made with capers.
Amande	Almond.
Ambrosia	Food of the gods. A dessert of oranges, and a drink made with champagne.
Apéritif	A liquid or solid appetizer.
Artichoke	The Jerusalem artichoke is a tuber; the globe artichoke is a plant with a burr-like head.
Au congri	A jambalaya dish of cooked rice, and cowpeas, especially popular on days of fast.
Au morceau	A manner of cooking fragments or leftover foods.
Aux crêpes	With pancakes or crêpes.
Au lait	A liquid or solid prepared with milk.
Aux marrons	A dish prepared with chestnuts.
Au vin	A drink or dish with wine.
À votre santé	A toast to your good health.
Baba	A light cake or "tipsy cake."
Bain-marie	A large open pan shaped like a roasting pan. It was kept half filled with near boiling water in which a set of saucepans were kept hot for vegetable and other dishes.

Bannock	A type of bread, usually baked over coals.
Barbecue	To grill or broil with a highly seasoned sauce.
Baste	To moisten with a liquid while cooking.
Bâton d'amande	Almond stick. A type of bread or cake.
Beat	To whip with a fast motion.
Bécassine	The snipe.
Bec scie	Saw beak. The merganser duck.
Beignet	A fritter or doughnut.
Beurre	Butter.
Beurre noir	Black butter.
Bière douce	Sweet beer. An Acadian drink.
Bisque	A thick soup, or stew.
Blanch	To scald by plunging into boiling water.
Blancmange	A sweet custard.
Blanquette	A stew of meat or fowl with herbs.
Bleeding	Eggplant and cucumbers may be "bled" by slicing off the ends, and rubbing these slices for a few minutes against the ends of the reduced vegetables. (Some Southern perfectionists will not eat these vegetables until they are thus "purified.")
Bœuf	Bison or beef.
Bolo	An English wine cup.
Bombe	Ice cream or pudding shaped in a mound, or a melon or fruit served as a dessert.
Bonne femme	Housewife, housekeeper, or female servant.
Bon vivant	One who lives in high style.
Bordelaise	A meat sauce made with wine or garlic.
Borsch	The Ukrainian dish of beets or soup of beets.
Bouchées	Little savories or mouthfuls.
Bouillabaisse	French chowder, said to have been first prepared in Marseille, where it was made of fish of the Mediterranean Sea.
Bouilli	The *bouilli*, or beef brisket, was brought to Louisiana by the French colonists. In the mother country it was served only for family meals. In Louisiana the versatile Creoles served it in soup and as an entrée. The same *bouilli* that was used to flavor potage was used again in hash for breakfast. It is still a popular dish in the French restaurants of Louisiana.
Bouillon	A clear broth made of fowl or meat.
Bouquet garni	A bouquet of herbs or spices. The herbs and spices may be tied together or placed in a cheesecloth sack and tied or sewed together. This seasoning bouquet is removed from the food after it is cooked.
Bourgeois	In a plain or simple manner.
Bourré	A food that is stuffed.
Bourse	A coffeehouse or exchange.
Brace	A pair, or two of a kind.

Braise	To sear, then simmer or smother with a small amount of water.
Branchu	The wood duck.
Bread	To dredge in flour, meal, or bread crumbs before cooking.
Brioche	A French pastry or bread served for breakfast.
Brochette	A skewer. *En brochette*, cooked on a skewer.
Broth	A thin soup.
Burgoo	An American stew of meat or fowl.
Cachet	A distinct character.
Café au lait	Coffee with milk.
Café brûlot	Spices and other ingredients burned with brandy or other spirits to which hot coffee is added.
Café noir	Black coffee.
Caille aux raisins	Quail with grapes.
Calas tous chaud	Fried rice cakes.
Canard cheval	Horse duck. The canvasback.
Canard français	French duck. The mallard.
Canard gris	Grey duck. The gadwall.
Canard noir	Black duck.
Carte du jour	Menu of the day.
Caudle	A gruel, or hot drink of spirits, eggs, and spices.
Ceres	Goddess of grain and plants.
C'est si bon	It's so good.
C'est la cuisine Creole	It is Creole cooking.
Champagne fine	A superior type of brandy.
Chanteclair	Food marinated in wine before cooking.
Chapeau	A wreath, or hat; a wreath of salad greens.
Chapon	A crust of bread rubbed with garlic for salads.
Chaud	Warm or hot.
Chef de cuisine	Master cook or chef.
Chicory	A plant of the dandelion family. The leaves are used for salads, and the root is roasted and mixed with coffee.
Chitlin's	Chitterlings. The cleaned and cooked intestines of a pig or calf.
Chowder	A heavy, thick soup, usually of fish.
Cobbler	A Southern dessert made with sweet dumplings; also a wine drink.
Collation	A coffee or tea party.
Colle	A paste.
Collops	Sautéed meat.
Collins	There are three boys in the Collins family—John, made of whisky; Tom, of gin; and Charley, of rum. Each is mixed with a bit of sugar, lemon juice, ice, and Seltzer water.
Composée	A composite of herbs or flowers.

Compote	A dish of fruit in syrup.
Consommé	A mild soup.
Cooler	A tall drink of wine or other spirits mixed with lemon juice and water or Seltzer water.
Côte joyeux	Joyful coast.
Coquemar	A skillet.
Coquille	A shell, or food served in a shell.
Cordon bleu	A first class chef. Originally it was a blue cord which was conferred on a chef by King Louis XV.
Couple de perdrix	A brace of quail or partridges.
Court bouillon	A thick soup or stew of fish.
Coush-coush caillé	Corn bread and clabber.
Cracknels	Fancy biscuits, or strips of bread.
Cream	To blend by mashing or beating.
Crêpe suzette	Thin French pancake served with a flaming sauce.
Croustade	Fried bread; a dish cooked with bread crusts.
Croustille	Little crust.
Croûte	Small slice of bread; food that is crusted.
Crouton	Toasted or fried bread strip.
Cuisinier	One who cooks food.
Cuite	A thick liquid or boiled syrup.
Cup	A small punch of a pint or less.
Cutlet	A cut of meat or fish; a croquette of that shape.
Dash	A pinch or more.
Daube glacée	A highly seasoned, jellied meat.
De bonnes choses à manger	Good things to eat.
Déjeuner	Late breakfast or lunch.
Délicieux	Delicious.
Devil	To make peppery.
Diable	The devil; food prepared with hot seasonings.
Dirty rice	A Cajun dish of rice cooked with bits of liver.
Dos gris	Grey back. The scaup duck.
Doucement	Food cooked gently in a covered pot.
Draw	To remove the intestines.
Dress	To garnish; to anoint; to remove outer covering and internal organs of any animal, fish, or fowl.
Dust	To sprinkle.
Dutch oven	A round iron pot with a cover.
Eau douce	Sweet or simple syrup.
Écrevisse	Crawfish.
Elixir	Rejuvenating spirit.
Empanada	A Spanish pastry or patty.
Enfants de la mer	Babies of the sea. Small shrimp.
Entrée	A dish that follows the fish course; a side dish, or a main course viand.
Entremet sucré	A sweet side dish.

Escabeche	A Spanish sauce.
Escargot	Snail.
Estomac mulâtre	Mulatto stomach. A type of cake brown in color.
Étage	Layer.
Faisandé	A high, gamy flavor, used to describe fowl that has hung until "ripe."
Filé	A powder, originated by the Choctaw Indians, made from the pounded leaves of the sassafras tree.
Filet or fillet	A cut of meat; a lengthwise cut of fish.
Fines herbes	A mixture of herbs.
Fin gourmet	A lover of fine food.
Fizz	A drink of spirits, cream, egg whites, sugar, orange-flower water, citrus juice, and ice.
Flake	To break apart.
Flambé	To serve aflame.
Flićky	A Bohemian noodle dish.
Flip	An English drink of eggs, sugar, and spirits, served hot or cold.
Florentine	A food prepared or garnished with spinach.
Fold	To blend with a gentle motion.
Fooyung	A Chinese egg dish.
Framboise	Raspberry flavor.
Frappé	A liquid prepared with shaved ice, or half frozen.
Fricassee	To simmer in a seasoned liquid.
Fritter	A fried batter or croquette.
Fromage à la crème	Cream cheese.
Fry	To cook in hot fat.
Fumet de poisson	A broth or stew of fish.
Garniture	An ornament.
Gastronomy	The art of enjoying food.
Gelatin	A congealed dish.
Glacé	Coated with a syrup, or glazed.
Glace de viande	Glazed or compressed meat.
Glögg	A stout beaker of hot rum, aquavit, or brandy, mixed with raisins and hot wine and served in a Glögg bowl.
Gollyettes	An Acadian type of bread.
Gotdam	The ruddy duck.
Goût	The sense of flavor or taste.
Granit	A half-frozen drink.
Grill	To broil under or over the heat.
Grillade	Meat seasoned with hot peppers.
Grits	A gruel popular in the South.
Grogg	An Anglo-Saxon bumper made of diluted rum and spices.
Guacamole	A Spanish avocado salad or paste for appetizers.
Gumbo or gombo	A rich soup originally made of okra, and probably

	brought to Louisiana from the West Indies. The Creoles changed this okra soup to "gumbo filé," as they learned to like the sassafras filé powder sold to them by the Choctaws. The evolution of gumbo was gradual as various fowl, fish, and meats were tried and relished in the Creole gumbo.
Gumbo Zhèbes	A thick soup made with a *roux* and six or seven greens or herbs. It is served on Holy Thursday for good luck.
Haricot	A kind of bean; a type of hash.
Hassenpfeffer	A German rabbit stew.
Haute cuisine	Superior cookery.
Haut ton	High taste.
Huître	Oyster.
Huîtres en coquille à la Rockefeller	Oysters dressed with a sauce made of eighteen ingredients and so named because of its richness.
Italienne	In the Italian manner.
Jambalaya	The principle ingredient of this Spanish-Creole dish is rice. Like Gumbo, there are dozens of different kinds of jambalaya.
Jerked meat	The Indians prepared their charque, or jerked meat by placing it over a low fire. Meat may be jerked by the sun or by the smoking method.
Julep	The customary plantation drink made of spirits, sugar, mint, and crushed ice and served in a tall glass with mint.
Junket	A feast.
Kebobs	Food that is breaded and cooked on a skewer.
Klösse	A German dough, or dumplings.
Knead	To work with the hands.
Lace	To add alcoholic spirits to food or drink.
Macaroon	Small almond flavored cakes.
Maître d'hôtel	The master steward, and a sauce named for him.
Marguery	The name given a famous French dish; a sauce of cream, wine, oysters, and shrimp.
Marinade	A liquid in which food is soaked before cooking.
Marinate	To soak food in a liquid.
Marionnette	Puppet. The bufflehead duck.
Marron	Chestnut.
Mead	A fermented liquor.
Mell	To mix.
Mélange	A mixture, or to mix.
Melt	To change from solid to liquid.
Merise	Wild cherry.

Meunière	Cooked in a plain or rural manner.
Miel	Honey.
Mince	To cut in small pieces.
Minestrone	An Italian soup of beans.
Modicum	Small amount.
Mole	A Spanish dish, usually of fowl.
Mousse	A frothy dessert, or other whipped foods.
Moutarde	Mustard.
Moje	A Spanish sauce or dish of onions and peppers.
Muscatrole	A Spanish dish.
Mystères de goût	Mystery of flavor.
Newberg	A thick sauce of egg yolks, butter, cream, wine, and spices.
Noix	Walnuts.
Oiseau	Bird.
Oiseau confit	Pickled fowl.
Oreille de cochon	Pig's ears. A Creole pastry with curled edges.
Pain bâton doré	Golden bread stick.
Pain patate	Sweet potato cake.
Pain perdu	Lost bread, or French toast.
Paille-en-queue	A tropic bird. The pintail duck.
Pare	To peel.
Parboil	To partly cook by boiling.
Pâte	A paste.
Pâté	A pastry or pie.
Peel	To remove the outer layer of anything with a knife.
Pemmican	A mixture of berries, suet, and meat, usually made with dried meat.
Perdreau	Partridge, or quail.
Perdrix	An older partridge.
Pièce de résistance	Principal dish of a meal.
Pilaf, or pilau	A rice dish.
Pimiento or Pimento	A hot seasoning fruit or berry made into pepper.
Pinch	Half a teaspoon or less.
Piquante	A pungent type of sauce made of garlic, herbs, peppers, butter, shallots, and other ingredients. It is used extensively in Louisiana for all kinds of foods.
Piquer	The deer.
Pitcher cream	Fresh cow's cream.
Polenta	An Italian mush or pudding.
Poach	To simmer gently.
Pompadour	A rich dish or sauce named for the Marquise de Pompadour.
Ponche	A Spanish punch.
Papillote	Oiled paper for cooking. *En papillote,* a method of

cooking pompano and other foods in a paper bag, invented by the mother of Jules Alciatore in honor of Alberto Santos-Dumont, the famous balloonist of Brazil. The fish fillets are placed in the paper bag with a rich sauce of wine and shrimp, sealed, then cooked. This balloon-bag recipe was created in 1900 at Antoine's restaurant in New Orleans.

Pot-au-feu	Pot of the fire. A soup.
Potion	A drink; or a liquid or solid measurement.
Posset	An English drink made of milk and wine, usually brewed in a posset pot and served hot.
Pot likker or plantation soup	The juice or stock from greens.
Poulet	Fowl.
Poule d'eau	Fowl of the water. The coot.
Pound	To tenderize by mashing with a downward motion.
Praline	A type of confection made in Louisiana of a sugar paste and nut meats.
Printanière	Spring-like. The blue-winged teal duck.
Provençale	A type of cookery formerly applied to viands of the south of France.
Punch	The oldest of our mixed drinks, usually made of five ingredients.
Purée	A thin soup; food that has been put through a sieve.
Purge	To clean the intestinal tract of crabs by submersing in cold water and table salt.
Ragout	A seasoned stew of meat or fowl.
Ratafia	A type of cordial or liqueur made of berries, fruits, and other basic essences with brandy or liquor added.
Red	The name applied to red wine in Louisiana.
Relevé	Side dish usually served with or after an entrée.
Rémoulade	A French sauce for salads.
Réveillon	A midnight repast.
Rickey	A sour drink made with spirits, citrus juice, Seltzer water, and ice.
Rissole	Meat or fowl cooked in a pastry; a meat and rice dish.
Risotto	An Italian rice stew.
Riz au lait	A dish of rice with milk.
Rouleau or *roulade*	Food prepared in a roll; to roll.
Roux	A basic brown sauce.
Roll	To press out flat.
Sabayon	A rich sauce made with wine and eggs. See also Zabaione.
Sachet	A bouquet or faggot of herbs or spices.
Sago	A starch essence taken from the Sago or Jerusalem palm.

Sakli	The Indian word for trout.
Salata	An Italian salad.
Salet greens	Salet greens or herbs are usually the wild greens that are native to Louisiana.
Salmi	Game or fowl roasted or prepared in a hash.
Sangaree	A spicy refreshment of sugar, hot spiced water, and wine or rum.
Sauce de pain	A bread sauce.
Sauté	To fry a short time in light fat.
Sauté belle	A fine stew.
Sauté sec	A plain stew.
Scald	To bring to a boil; to dip in boiling water, or soak in boiling water for a short time.
Scalopini	An Italian meat dish.
Scone	A type of coffee cake that originated in Scotland.
Sear	To seal the surface by heat.
Scrapple	A type of meat cake, made of herbs and other ingredients, that is usually fried.
Simmer	To cook a liquid below the boiling point.
Sippet	A thin piece of toast, or a slice of fried bread.
Sirop aux étages	Syrup and fruit or berries in layers.
Skewer	To place food on a metal pin or stick to cook, or serve.
Sling	A long drink of spirits, sugar, and spices.
Soak	To cover with a liquid.
Soignée	Sharp, or racy.
Soirée	A Creole evening gathering at which festive refreshments are served.
Sole	The flounder was named "sole" by the Creoles as its meat resembled the flesh of the "sole" they had known from the waters of the Mediterranean Sea.
Sour	A short cocktail of citrus juices and rum or whisky.
Soupçon	A hint of something, as a "soupçon" of garlic in a stew.
Soupe-en-famille	A family soup, or plain soup.
Soy	A dark sauce obtained from soy beans.
Spécialité de la maison	The specialty of the house.
Spirits	Alcoholic liquids.
Spoonbill	The shoveler duck.
Steam	To cook by moisture.
Steep	To marinate in a liquid, usually after cooking.
Stock	A cooking liquid.
Stew	A mixture of foods cooked in a sauce; also a short, hot drink of butter, sugar, and spirits.
Stew	To cook below the boiling point.
Stir	To blend, or mix with a rotary motion.
Stirrup Cup	A short tipple of whisky or other spirits, sugar, and lemon peel.

Sweetbreads	The pancreas or thymus glands of an animal, especially a young calf.
Swimps	A colloquial name for shrimp.
Swizzle	A West Indian drink made of rum, honey, and ice, and served with a swizzle stick.
Syllabub	A frothy dessert, or drink.
Tafia	A type, or brand of rum.
Timbale	Food prepared in a mound; a pie.
Tisane	A tea, or light drink.
Toddy	A short drink of spirits, sugar, and hot water or ice.
Torte	A small pastry.
Truite au beurre	Trout in butter.
Truffle	The edible ascus fruit.
Truite verte	Green trout (the black bass).
Truss	To retain the original shape by tying or sewing.
Velouté de poisson	A smooth dish made of fish.
Viande de haut goût	Food of superior flavor.
Vinaigrette	A salad sauce.
Vin	Wine.
Vin blanc	White wine.
Vin de cannaie	Fermented cane juice.
Vin rouge	Red wine.
Vin rosé	A pink wine.
Vinous	Pertaining to wine.
Violon	Violin. The redhead duck.
Vol-au-vent	A pastry, or puff paste.
Vrai régal	A true feast.
Wassail	A festive punch which was served at Christmas or special occasions. The punch is made of spirits blended with fruit juices.
Whip	To beat with a fast movement.
Zabaione	An Italian drink or frothy wine dessert.
Zin-zin	The baldpate duck.

General Glossary

Arlatex	A section in Louisiana adjoining Arkansas and Texas.
Attaque de nerfs	An attack of nerves.
Banquette	An early type of sidewalk.
Bateau	A type of bayou or river boat.
Bateau plat	A type of flat river boat.
Batture	Alluvial plains.
Bayou	A stream or canal.
Belle chasse	Good hunting.
Big house	The main dwelling on a plantation.
Bistineau	A lake in Louisiana.
Bogue Falaya	A stream in Louisiana, "long river."
Bonne nuit	Good night.
Bocage	A grove.
Boogalee	A Cajun.
Bourré	Stuffed; a French card game.
Bourgeoisie	First citizens.
Bousillage	An early type of architecture in Louisiana.
Brackish	Salty or saline.
Brake	A wooded swamp.
Calcasieu	A parish in Louisiana meaning "crying eagle."
Cajun	A Louisianian of Acadian descent, whose ancestors were expelled from Nova Scotia in 1760 and settled in the bayou section of the state.
Chacun à son goût	Everyone to his own taste.

Charivari	A surprise serenade for a wedding.
Chatelaine	The mistress of a home.
Chemin-à-haut	High road.
Chêne	Oak.
Chênière	A coastal ridge covered with oaks.
Chèvrette	Small goat.
Chicot	The name of a lake in Louisiana which translated means "stump."
Chuka-chaha	The Indian word meaning "night cabin."
Conquérant	Conqueror.
Coup de main	A helping hand.
Côte joyeux	The happy coast.
Creole	The descendants of the French and Spanish *emigrés* in Louisiana during the colonial period, 1699-1803.
Chrétien Point	The Lessley Gardiner plantation home built in 1831.
Criollo	The Spanish word from which Creole is derived. The meaning is native to a certain locality.
Cyprière	A cypress grove, or forest.
Des Allemands	Of the Germans.
El camino real	The royal road. This historic road was once known as the San Antonio Trace. The road ran from Mexico City to Natchitoches, Louisiana. Louis de Saint Denis used this route, as did David Crockett and the other Americans who assisted Texas in her fight for freedom.
Étagère	A set of shelves, or a whatnot.
Fais-dodo	"Go to sleep." A dance of the Acadian country.
Florida parishes	The parishes in Louisiana that once were a part of Florida.
Garçonnière	Separate quarters for the bachelor members of a family.
Grand côte	Big hill.
Hé, bien soit	Well, be it so.
Îlet	Island, or sections of old New Orleans that were surrounded by water.
Isle Dernière	An island and once fashionable resort off the coast of Louisiana. In the storm of 1856 over two hundred persons perished there.
Joie de vivre	Joy in living.
Kisatchie	A group of hills near Natchitoches, Louisiana.

La Fourche	A bayou in South Louisiana known as "the longest street in the world" as there have been homes along the bayou banks for two hundred years.
Lagniappe	Something thrown in for good measure.
Les Halles	The original name of the French market.
L'autre bord du lac	"Across the lake." An expression used by people of New Orleans for all places located across Lake Pontchartrain.
Mais oui	But yes.
Ménage	Household or home.
Mettre à la voile	To set sail.
Mon pays	A person's birthplace, or home.
Mouchoir de l'ourse	"Handkerchief of a she-bear." The name of a bayou in Louisiana.
On dit	It is said.
Osengo	The name of a plantation that was once owned by the Land family.
Petit caillou	Little pebble.
Petit Paris	The little Paris. The name given the town of Saint Martinville, Louisiana, because so many royal refugees settled there during the French Revolution.
Picayune	A small coin, or a trifle.
Piquet	A French card game.
Pirogue	A type of canoe used in Louisiana. It was originally made of one log.
Plaquemines	A parish in Louisiana meaning "persimmons."
Pointe à la Hache	A town in south Louisiana meaning "point of an axe."
Quien sabe?	Who knows?
Radeau	A type of boat.
Raquette	An Indian game played with a ball and racket.
Red bone	A person of Indian and Negro descent.
Red neck	A name given to the natives of North Louisiana because of the sunburned necks of these farmer folk.
Rue	A street.
Rustique	Rural, rustic.
Safe	A type of kitchen cabinet known also as a ches' or chest, and used as a place of storage for pies and breads.
Salina	A meadow in the marsh.
Salle à manger	Dining room.
Sang-froid	Poise, or presence of mind.
Sans souci	Without worry.
Savanna	Grassy flat, or marsh.

Savant	A person of learning.
Savoir-vivre	Good manners, or breeding.
Teche	A bayou in South Louisiana, the "snake."
Terrebonne	"Good land." A parish in Louisiana.
Tickfaw	"Pine rest." A town in Louisiana.
Tout à fait	Entirely, or a complete combination.
Veillée	A wake, or funeral.
Veilleuse	A night light used in Louisiana to heat teas.
Vermilion	A parish in Louisiana, meaning "red."
Vieux Carré	The original section of New Orleans, the "old square."
Wold	An upland plain.

Index

crab, 42
    quick, 43
    St. Landry, 43
    shrimp, 42
Blackberry wine, 327
Blackbirds, 261
Black drum, 131
Black jewfish, 129-30
Bloody Mary, 311
Blue cat, cutlets of, 137
Bluefish, 130
Blue runner, 126
Bobwhite (*see* Quail)
Bonito salad, 66
Bonne Nuit, 311
Borsch, 197
Bouchees, Bayou, 30
Bouillabaisse
    and court bouillon, 44
    Gulf, 144
    Golden Meadow, 44-45
Bourbon
    balls, 33
    punch, 321
    sour, 309
Brains, fried, 175
Brandy
    bowl, 320
    brioche, 277-78
    cocktail, 314
    egg sauce, 225
    gruel, 331
    tipple, 326
Brannvin, 314
Breads, 250
    banana, 243
    bannock, 244
    cheese, 244
    cinnamon toast, Betty Moore's, 251
    corn, country, 248
    corn pone, 248
    coush-coush caille, 248
    cracklin', 248-49
    croustades, 251
    croutons, 251
    dough balls, hell-fire, 244
    empanadas, 251
    garlic, Brennan's, 251
    gollyettes, 254
    hardtack, 247
    oyster, 244
    pain bâton dorés, 245
    pain perdu, 252

popovers, Pattie's, 245
    rice, 250
    rock, 247
    shallot polenta, 250
    sippets, 252
    skillet, 245
    spider, 250
    spoon
        Choctaw, 288
        Phiney's, 249
    sweet potato, 245-46
    trenchers, 252
    wagon wheels, 248
Broccoli Hollandaise, 198
Brussels sprouts, 198
Bucolic bits, 27
Burgoo, small game, 87
Busters, barbecued, 145
Butter beans, 198
Buttermilk cream, 274
Butters, 229-30

Cabbage
    Chinese, 199
    German, 182
    palm salad, 59
    palm savanna, 203
    red, 199
    stuffed, 198-99
Caesar salad, 58
Café au lait, 306
Cailles aux raisins, 108
Cakes
    baba l'Anisette, 277
    Brandy brioche, 277-78
    coffee, Creole, 278
    gingerbread, old-fashioned, 278
    estomac mulâtre, 278-79
    pain patate, 279
    pecan torte, 279
    pound, 279
    scones, 280
    short, 280
    skillet, 280
    spice bread, 280
    sponge, 281
    sweet bread, 281
    upside-down, 281
Calas tous chaud, 208
Calf's
    brains, fried, 175
    head, 175
    heart, 175-76

Mixed
  Absinthe Suissesse, 316
  Acadian Glögg, 326
  Aquavit, 314
  Arrack Punch, 319
  Aunt Pattie's Egg Nogg, 330
  Bloody Mary, 311
  Bourbon Punch, 321
  Brandy Bowl, 320
  Brandy Tipple, 326
  Brannvin, 314
  Brennan's Pirates' Dream, 317-18
  Buttered Rum, 325
  Cajun Nogg, 325
  Coconut Sling, 312
  Coup de Milieu, 321-22
  Creole Downfall, 310
  English Bolo, 321
  Gin and Tonic, 313
  Gin Risqué, 330
  Heart Warmer, 325
  Judge O'Neill's Orange Blossom,
    312
  Julep, 308-309
  Lemon-Orange Punch, 321
  Louisiana French '75, 313
  Mandarin Fizz, 330
  Maraschino Punch, 319
  Mettre à la Voile, 319
  Moselle Punch, 319
  Mulled Apple Jack, 331
  Orange Syllabub, 328
  Orange Wine Sangaree, 329
  Ouzo, 314
  Pahit, 313
  Pampas Bolo, 307
  Punche Romaine, 321-22
  Prendre Au Raccourci, 325
  Punch Prince Regence Au Victor,
    318-19
  Ramos Gin Fizz, 312-13
  Rock Candy and Rye, 310
  Roffignac, 308
  Rum and Brandy Punch, 319
  Rum Cuit, 326
  Rum Punch, 325
  Salty Dog, 330
  Sam Watt's Poulet Punch, 329
  Scotch Fling, 309
  Sherry Flip, 314
  Short Sherry Punch, 321
  Southern Planter's Punch, 320
  Strawberry Punch, 328
  Stirrup Cup, 320
  Susie's Rum Shake, 326
  Syllabub, 277
  Tequila, 313
  Tropic Sling, 312
  Wild Cow, 310
  Wild Creole Pony, 324
Possets and Potions
  Colonial Caudle, 331
  Brandy Gruel, 331
  Eau Sucree, 332
  English Posset, 331
  Milk Punch, 332
  Orange Posset, 330
  Potion for Asthma, 332
  Potion for Dropsy, 332
  Potion for Dyspepsia, 332
  Tisane Tea, 331
Duck
  à la nude, 100
  baked
    canvasback, 99
    French duck, 99
    mallard, 99
  broiled, 100
  congo, 100
  chutney, 34
  gumbo, hunters' camp, 40
  mandarin, 100-101
  mud-baked, 101
  on the coals, 100
  pintail, braised, 99-100
  preparation of, 96-97
  roasted, with berries, 101
  sippets, 34
  sauce with tortillas, 102
  spaghetti with, 102
  species of, 95-96
  teal
    chênière, 101
    with cherries, 101
  timbales, 34
Dumplings
  cobbler, 252
  corn meal, 252
  Creole, 252-53
  flicky, 253
  klösse, 253
  plain, 253

Eau sucree, 332
Eel, 261
Egg nogg, Aunt Pattie's, 330

Sauces—*Continued*
  marguery, New Orleans, 224
  may haw jelly, 221
  minced pepper melon, 233
  mint sauce I, 221
  mint sauce II, 221
  moje, 217
  moutarde aux fines herbes, 221
  mustard cream, 221
  Newburg, 225
  orange, 222
  peach
    brandied, 222
    sautéed, 222
  pecan, 222
  pirogue, 219-20
  rum, 222
  Sabayon sauce aux Plaquemines, 217
  Sherry, 226
  shrimp, 225
    à la sour cream, 224
  Spanish, 129-30
  strawberry, 223
  supreme, 225
  syrup la cuite, 227
  tomato, 225
  vermilion, 225
Sausages, à la Wold, 85
Sauté bourgeoise, 159
Sawfish, 264
Scallions, boiled, 210
Scampi, lagoon, 154
Scones, 280
Scrapple, 190
Sea trout, silver, 126
Shallot
  pie, 179
  polenta, 250
  porridge, 52
Shark, 264-65
Sharpies, Ann Allen's, 237
Sheepshead, 128
Shepherd's pie, 172
Sherbet, basic recipe, 274
  cranberry, 274
  pineapple ice, 275
Sherry
  flip, 314
  muskrat, 89
  sauce, 226
Shoat, roasted, 179
Shortcakes, 280
Shrimp

à la Hickory Corner, 149
à la king, 150
à la sour cream, 224
à l'Italienne, 149
apple, 146
au vin, 150
boiled
  "swimp," 146-47
  Cheramie, 147
broiled, 147
canape, 28
Creole, Brennan's, 150
curried, 147
en brochette, flaming, 147
enfants de la mer, 29-30
fried
  Cantonese, 148
  jumbo, 148
  in wine, 148
Hawaiian, 150
in sour cream, 68
loaf, 151
Neptune, 67
olive, 149
paste, cold, 28
pie, 151
Pontchartrain wiggle, 149
puffs, 30
rémoulade, 67-68
salad
  bowl, 68
  Shine's, 67
sauce, 225
  piquant, 151
sherried, 27
stew
  à la Nancy, 151-52
  Isle Derniere, 148-49
  Sea Marsh, 152
-stuffed pears, 202
tureen, 152
vinous, 152
whets, 28
Silversides, 126
Sippets, 252
Skidmore Tipple, 314
Skirret, and carrots, 210
Slaw, peasant, 61
Snails, 261-62
Snipe
  barbecued, 117
  bécassine paprika, 117
  broiled, 117